Home Handicrafts

An exciting new range of designs for the home and family

edited by Mary Harding

octopus

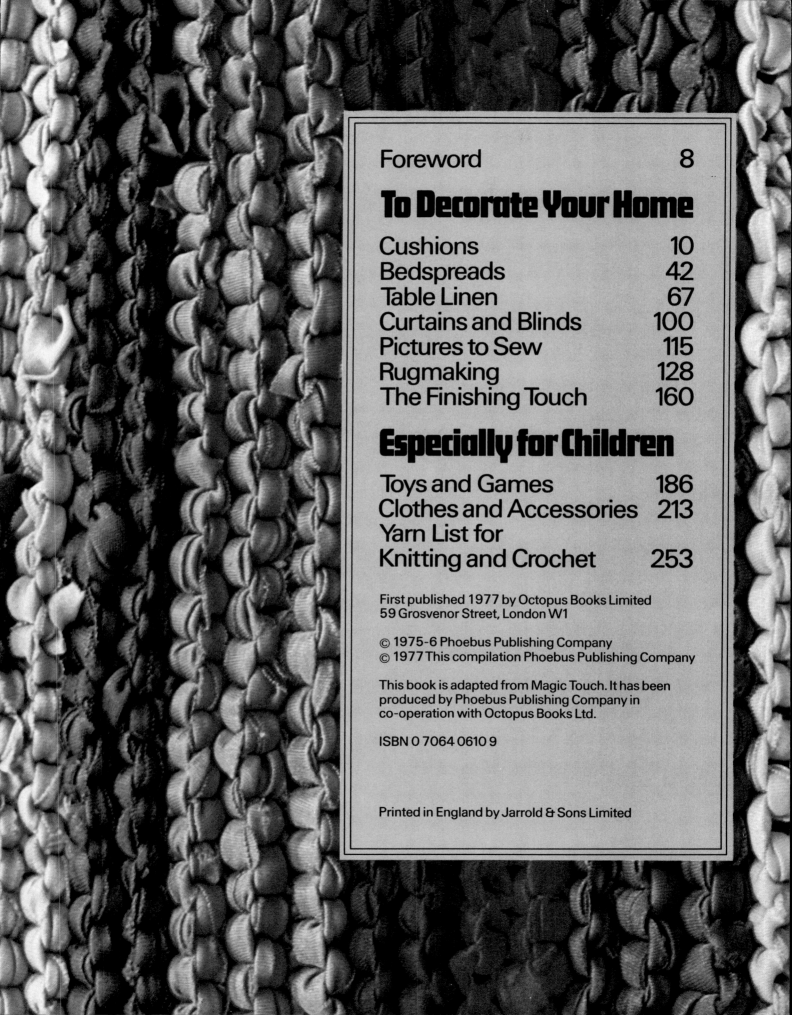

First published 1977 by Octopus Books Limited
59 Grosvenor Street, London W1

© 1975-6 Phoebus Publishing Company
© 1977 This compilation Phoebus Publishing Company

This book is adapted from Magic Touch. It has been
produced by Phoebus Publishing Company in
co-operation with Octopus Books Ltd.

ISBN 0 7064 0610 9

Printed in England by Jarrold & Sons Limited

Foreword

Home Handicrafts is a different kind of crafts book. *Home Handicrafts* is a modern-looking book all about home-making, providing ideas, schemes, patterns and know-how for making wonderful things for your home and family. No matter how inexperienced at needlecrafts and crafts you are, there is something in these pages for you. Crochet, knitting, sewing, patchwork, appliqué, embroidery, needlepoint, rugmaking—all these techniques are included with up-to-date designs and clear, easy-to-understand instructions, plus pictures showing how every stage is to be attempted. And if you feel that you would like to start with something very simple, there are some easy-as-pie crafts to try too—braiding with sisal, for instance, to make a circular rug, knitting on a spool knitter to make braids, or china painting.

Sixteen special features have been selected to help you choose from over two hundred colourful and exciting designs in the book. Each one is labelled **Feature** for easy recognition.

Here are just a few of the riches in store: the chapter on cushions has 46 different designs for you to try—brilliant needlepoint patterns worked on canvas, bargello, appliqué, patchwork—even knitted cushions in thick, creamy yarn. You are also shown how to work drop-in seat covers and fit them to your chairs. There is a bright new idea for making alternative furniture for your home using big cushions.

Beautiful bedspreads and bedlinen are satisfying projects to undertake, or what about the newest homecraft—picture-making? There is some useful information about frame-making and refurbishing old frames to make delightful wall decorations.

Rugmaking is a craft that is always popular with families because everyone can join in. Rugmaking not only provides your home with luxurious furnishings but actually saves money too! Lampshade-making is a craft you are sure to want to try and if you like fine sewing and embroidery, *Home Handicrafts* includes some beautiful designs for table linen. Until you have tried making your own linens, you will not have experienced the thrill of a really good-looking table setting which you have planned yourself. Finally, especially for children, there is a section on toys, games, clothes and accessories. Soft toys, cuddly cushion animals, hand-made dolls, nursery wall panels—and if you like to make children's clothes there are some superbly designed patterns on graphs for you to try. Through the magic touch of your hands and originality of your own ideas, sparked off by the designs illustrated in these pages, you will be able to show your love for your family and the pride you feel in your home. Improving your home is a way of improving your life-style. Your surroundings reflect the kind of life you lead and, by making beautiful furnishings and accessories, designed to fit in with your colour scheme, your home becomes a statement about the kind of person you are.

And you will make your furnishings budget go further too!

Home Handicrafts is a book for home-lovers, planned to help you to make a lovely home.

To decorate your home

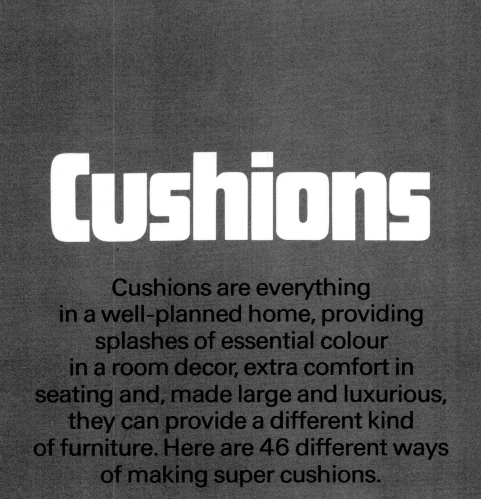

Cushions

Cushions are everything
in a well-planned home, providing
splashes of essential colour
in a room decor, extra comfort in
seating and, made large and luxurious,
they can provide a different kind
of furniture. Here are 46 different ways
of making super cushions.

Cushions and a quilt
in patchwork and appliqué

Mix and match patterns in black and white

Dress up a plain black
cushion with appliquéd strips
or fabric or ribbons
multi-patterned black and white.

Transform an old coverlet into a smashing patchwork quilt! Piece together squares from as many black-and-white fabrics as you can find, then sew the patchwork top to the coverlet. Add a patterned backing fabric and the quilt is finished. Extend the black-and-white theme to a circle cushion made of wedges in alternating light and dark patterns.

PATCHWORK CIRCLE

Draw a circle the size of your pillow. Fold the paper in half, then quarters, then eighths. Cut out one of the segments for a pattern, adding 1 cm ($\frac{3}{8}$″) seam allowance. Cut eight segments out of different fabrics. Join pieces to make four pairs. Join pairs to make two halves, then join the halves. Cut out backing the same size as pieced circle and join the pillow pieces, right sides together, leaving 15 cm (6″) open. Turn to right side, insert pillow, and slip-stitch closed. Edge with cording if desired.

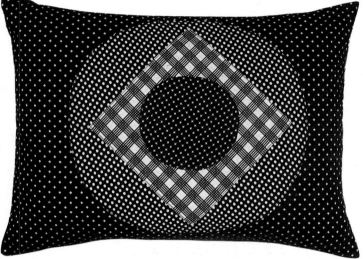

Build pattern on pattern in appliqués for a stunning complement to the quilt.

Materials Required: Pillows. An old coverlet. Fabrics: assorted remnants of black and white cotton prints; large piece of fabric for backing for each. Black sewing thread.

PATCHWORK COVER

Measure your quilt and divide the area into squares. Our coverlet is made up of 23 cm (9″) squares. Cut a cardboard template the size of the finished square, plus 1 cm ($\frac{3}{8}$″) seam allowance. Cut out required number of squares, using the template. Machine-stitch the squares into strips; press all seams to one side. Stitch the strips together and press. Place patchwork piece over coverlet, right sides up, and hand-sew to coverlet, sewing through patchwork and coverlet along all the seam lines. Place the backing on the patchwork, right sides together, and machine-stitch around three sides. Turn right side out and slip-stitch the opening closed.

APPLIQUÉ PILLOW

Cut two pillow pieces. Cut a large circle of contrasting fabric, adding 0.5 cm ($\frac{1}{4}$″) seam allowance. Appliqué circle in the centre of one pillow piece. Cut a square to fit inside the circle and a smaller circle to fit in the square. Appliqué the small circle in the square, then the square in the large circle. Place pillow pieces right sides together and stitch around three sides. Turn right side out and insert pillow. Slip-stitch closed.

Appliquéing

Lightly mark the pattern on background fabric. Mark pattern outline on the fabric, then mark a 0.5 cm ($\frac{1}{4}$″) seam allowance all around. Machine or hand-stitch on the design outline for a neat turning edge. Cut out piece along seam allowance outline. Clip all corners and curves. Turn in seam allowance just inside the stitching line and press. Slip-stitch to background.

New ideas for your sofa in
A wool-saving rug technique

Make short-pile cushions in glowing colours with this clever knotting technique.

The short, close pile of these cushions is made by knotting tapestry wool over a pile gauge or a knitting needle onto a background of double-thread canvas. The great advantage of this particular technique is that it is an economical use of wool, as the pile is shorter than on an ordinary hooked rug.

Using this same method, you can also make other items such as wall hangings or patterned rugs as long as you use the proper materials. Tapestry yarn is ideal for cushions, but you must use thicker yarn for a rug. Whatever materials you use, the thick pile will show up the design. The height of the pile depends on the thickness of the pile gauge or knitting needle. Use a larger size for longer pile. A pile gauge measuring 1 cm ($\frac{3}{8}$") gives a pile height of about 1.3 cm ($\frac{1}{2}$"), while a size 8 (Am) or 5 (Eng) knitting needle gives a pile height of 0.5 cm ($\frac{1}{4}$").

14

As a special feature
for long sofas,
these cushions have been
specially designed
so that when they are
placed in a row, they
form a continuous pattern.

Here are charts for two of the set
of three floral cushions.
Each square represents one knot made
over the pile gauge. Always begin
at the lower left corner.

1 Materials you will need to make the cushions: double-thread rug canvas measuring 46 cm (18″) square with 7 holes to 2.5 cm (1″) and tapestry yarn (13.7 m or 15 yd skeins) in the required colours and quantities.

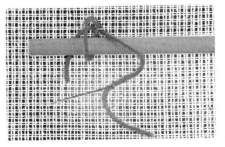

5 Use the pile gauge for the next knot. Make sure the two ends of yarn from the previous knot are pointing downward and place the pile gauge horizontally on top of them. Loop the yarn up and over to the left of the pile gauge. Insert the tapestry needle between the pair of horizontal threads one square to the right of the first knot.

9 Always work in rows from left to right and from bottom to top. The pile will be close and short, and will stand out from the canvas so that a beautifully clear design is formed, showing all the details. Follow the colours from the chart as you work each row. Each square represents one knot. For each new row, place the pile gauge over the pile from the row below and work the knots of different colours as before.

Knotting over a pile gauge

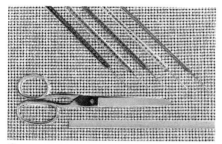

2 Tools you will need: a pile gauge or a knitting needle (use a pile gauge 1 cm ($\frac{3}{8}''$) wide for the correct pile length for the cushions), scissors, and a tapestry needle with a blunt point for each yarn colour.

3 To begin knotting: the first stitch is worked without the pile gauge or knitting needle. Insert the needle downward in between a pair of horizontal threads, then loop the yarn to the left over the loose end.

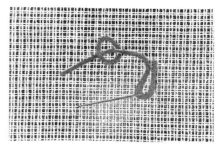

4 Now insert the needle under the upper horizontal thread. Pull the yarn tight to form a knot. The first knot has now been completed. All further knots are worked over the pile gauge.

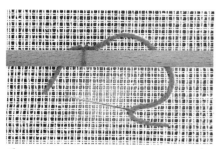

6 Take the yarn up and around again in a loop to the left, insert the tapestry needle under the upper horizontal thread and pull tight. Bring the yarn under the pile gauge. Repeat from step 5 for the next knot.

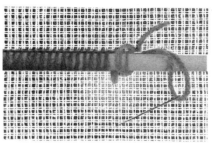

7 When starting a new colour, lay the end of the yarn under the pile gauge and begin by inserting the needle in between the horizontal threads. Make a knot as in step 4, then continue to knot as before.

8 When the pile gauge is full of knots, turn it so that it stands on its edge and pull it out, cutting the loops with a pair of sharp pointed scissors as you pull. Move it along to the right and continue knotting.

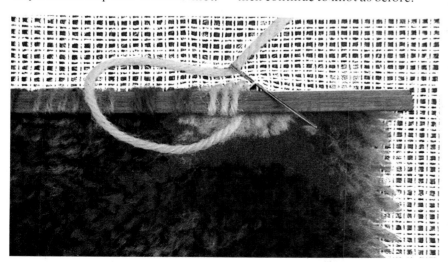

10 The chart can be enlarged onto graph paper so that it can be followed more easily. Make an envelope for the chart to serve as a row guide. Cut a piece of cardboard the width of the chart and stick a piece of stiff paper across it. As you work, push the chart down so the paper underlines the next row.

Here is a whole pattern for one floral cushion and a quarter-pattern for the geometric repeat. Each square represents one knot made over the pile gauge. Always begin at the lower left corner.

Following the charts

The knotted designs are easy to follow from the charts. For the three floral cushions, use the charts showing the complete design, beginning at the bottom left corner. For the other cushion, a chart showing a quarter of the design is given. Begin knotting at the bottom left corner and when you reach the center of the design on the first row, work the right half as a mirror image of the left half. Continue to work to the top of the chart. Work the top half as a mirror image of the bottom half.

Making the cushions

Cut the canvas to measure just under 46 cm (18″) square. This gives a cushion about 35 cm (13¾″) square with a 5 cm (2″) border of unworked canvas. Finish raw edges with tape or overcasting. Sew on a matching backing fabric around three sides. Insert a cushion and sew up the fourth side.

Shown below are the colours and quantities of tapestry yarn (13.7 m or 15 yd skeins) required for the three floral cushions:

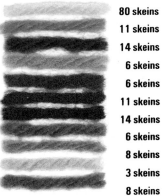

80 skeins
11 skeins
14 skeins
6 skeins
6 skeins
11 skeins
14 skeins
6 skeins
8 skeins
3 skeins
8 skeins

For the geometric-patterned cushion:

24 skeins
22 skeins
3 skeins
3 skeins
11 skeins

Patchwork potpourri

Dig down into your scrap-bag or pick up remnants of fabric from sales to make a variety of original and decorative cushions.

5

6

7

8

Making the cushions

Note: The measurements given are for each finished cushion, so add seam allowances of 1 cm ($\frac{3}{8}$") unless otherwise instructed. For filling the cushion covers, either buy cushion pads of the right size or cut five layers of washable wadding or batting to size and sew around the edges with overcasting stitches. Make up a lining, leaving an opening in the side of approximately 20–25 cm (8–9") for cushion. Slip-stitch closed. Where a cushion cover is made up of several pieces, it is advisable to make a paper pattern first.

Cushion 1: Size: 60 cm (23$\frac{1}{2}$") diameter. Materials Required: Two circles of fabric: 60 cm (23$\frac{1}{2}$") diam. Fabric for gathered edging: strip pieced to 190 cm (74$\frac{3}{4}$") long by 13 cm (5") wide. Narrow elastic: 1 m (1$\frac{1}{8}$ yds).
Stitch edging strip into a ring. Pin edging around one circle, right sides together. Baste the second circle on top, so that the circles are right sides together. Stitch around edge, leaving opening for cushion. Turn to right side. Insert cushion and sew closed. Press under seam allowance on the remaining raw edge of strip twice to make a casing. Stitch, then thread elastic through. Fold edging to right side over the cushion.

Cushion 2: Size: 46 cm (18$\frac{1}{2}$") square. Materials Required: Two pieces patterned fabric: 46 cm (18$\frac{1}{8}$") square. Floral frill: strip pieced to 210 cm (82$\frac{1}{2}$") long by 7 cm (2$\frac{3}{4}$") wide. Turn in raw edges of the frill and stitch. Pin frill into small tucks and then stitch onto the right side of one square of fabric 5 cm (2") from the edge. Place squares together, right sides facing, stitch edges, leaving an opening. Turn to right side. Insert cushion. Sew closed.

Cushion 3: Size: 43 cm (17") diameter. Materials Required: Two circles of floral fabric: 43 cm (17") diameter. Gingham frill: strip pieced to 240 cm (94$\frac{1}{2}$") long by 5 cm (2"). Stitch frill into a ring. Turn under one edge and stitch; gather the other edge. Pin gathered edge to one circle, right sides facing. Place the second circle on top, right sides facing, and stitch. Turn to right side. Insert cushion. Sew closed.

Cushion 4: Size: 46 cm (18") square. Materials Required: Two pieces of checked fabric: 46 cm (18") square. One piece of patterned fabric: 26 cm (10$\frac{1}{4}$") square. One button. Press under seam allowances on small square and stitch onto right side of one large square 10 cm (4") from edge. Stitch the large squares together right sides facing, leaving opening, then turn to right side. Insert cushion. Sew closed. Cover button. Sew to centre through all layers.

Cushion 5: Size: 45 cm (17$\frac{3}{4}$") square. Materials Required: Two pieces of floral fabric: 45 cm (17$\frac{3}{4}$") square. Eight strips of patterned fabric: each 51 cm (20$\frac{1}{8}$") by 3 cm (1$\frac{1}{4}$"). Stitch each set of four strips together diagonally across ends to make mitered corners. Stitch the two sets together around outer edge, right sides facing. Turn to right side. Press under seam allowances on squares. Baste squares together on 3 sides, wrong sides facing with border in between. Top-stitch. Insert cushion. Baste and top-stitch opening closed.

Cushion 6: Size: 40 x 58 cm (16" x 23"). Materials Required: Four patterned fabrics: 29 x 40 cm (11$\frac{1}{2}$" x 16"). Four patterned fabrics: 20 x 58 cm (8" x 23").
Make a template 40 x 58 cm (16" x 23") and cut diagonally from corner to corner. Use this to cut 8 pieces from different printed fabrics with 1 cm ($\frac{3}{8}$") seam allowances on all edges. Stitch 4 together to form large rectangle. Stitch two rectangles together, right sides facing. Turn to right side. Insert cushion. Sew opening closed.

Cushion 7: Size: 32 x 56 cm (12$\frac{1}{2}$" x 22"). Materials Required: Two pieces of floral fabric: 32 x 56 cm (12$\frac{1}{2}$" x 22"). Gingham: four strips 75 cm (29$\frac{1}{2}$") long and four 50 cm (19$\frac{5}{8}$") long, all 5 cm (2") wide at the centre and increasing to 10 cm (4") at the corners.
Cut a template for the scallops. Stitch two sets of two long and two short strips together to form rectangles, stitching diagonally across ends to form mitered corners. Baste borders together, wrong sides facing. Using the template, draw and cut out scallops around the edges. Stitch borders together along scallops with machine zigzag stitching. Turn under cover edges; baste the covers together, wrong sides facing, with borders in between. Top-stitch. Insert cushion. Top-stitch opening closed.

Cushion 8: Size: 48 cm (19") diameter. Materials Required: Fabric: Eight pieces 25 cm (10") square. One button.
Cut a circular template 48 cm (19") in diameter. Divide into four segments and use to cut out pieces from patterned and plain fabrics with seam allowances of 1 cm ($\frac{3}{8}$") on all edges. Stitch together to form two circles. Place circles together right sides facing, and stitch. Turn. Insert cushion. Sew closed. Cover button. Sew to centre through all layers.

Another bright idea for your home

Materials Required:
Ribbons. Cushions 40 cm (16″) square. Backing fabrics 44 cm (17½″) square. Cardboard.

Making the cushions
Stitch the ribbons together as directed. Cut out a template and then cut out the ribbons, adding 1 cm (⅜″) seam allowance on all edges. Arrange the pieces as illustrated and stitch.

Cushion 1: Stitch ribbons together to form a piece 30 cm (12″) by 120 cm (48″). Draw and cut a template 20 cm (8″) square. Fold the ribbons in half crosswise. Draw a diagonal line joining two corners of the template and place it along the ribbon stitching. Rotate the template so that the line is at a slight angle to the stitching. Cut through both layers. Cut the other two squares so that they match the first two exactly. Arrange the squares so that the ribbons form a diamond.

Cushions 2 and 3: Stitch the ribbons together to form a piece 160 cm (64″) by 22 cm (8¾″). Cut a template 40 cm (16″) square. Fold it diagonally and diagonally again to form right-angled triangles. Cut 4 triangles.

Cushion 4: Stitch the ribbons and cut the template to the same sizes as for Cushion 1. Draw a diagonal line joining two corners of the template. Place the line on the stitching of the ribbons. Cut four squares.

Cushion 5: When stitching the ribbons together, begin with the longest one diagonally across the centre, cutting it to 60 cm (24″) in length. Cut the ribbons on either side progressively shorter to form a 44 cm (17½″) square.

Finishing: Cut a backing piece 44 cm (17½″) square. Place the backing and top together, right sides facing, and stitch around 3 sides. Turn right side out, insert cushion, slip-stitch opening.

Country patchwork

Use up all those scraps of fabric you've been hoarding for so long to make a set of traditional patchwork cushions. They are machine-stitched so that they are made quite quickly. Our cushions are mainly floral, giving them a fresh country charm, but experiment with plain or geometric patterns for different effects. Try to use the same weight and quality of fabric for all the patches.

Sizes: Cushion 1 is a circle 48 cm (19") in diameter. Cushion 2 is a rectangle 42 x 56 cm (16½" x 22"). Cushion 3 has a side length of 23 cm (9"). Cushion 4 is 40 cm (15¾") square.

Materials Required: Scraps of fabric of same weight. Backing fabric to match. Thick polyester batting or wadding.

Making the cushions

The hexagonal patch is shown actual-

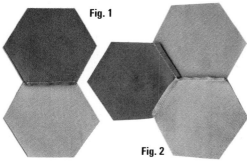

Fig. 1

Fig. 2

size in the lower right-hand corner. Make a template from cardboard with a 0.5 cm (¼") seam allowance. Cut out the patches from the appropriate fabric, using the template as a guide. In Cushions 1 and 2, the hexagons are stitched together in rows; in Cushions 3 and 4, they are stitched together in circles.

In rows: Stitch the hexagons together in straight rows as shown in Fig. 1, pressing each seam to one side as you finish

it. Then fit the rows together zigzag fashion. Stitch each seam up to the corner then, leaving the needle in the fabric, lift the presser foot and place the next 2 sides together for seaming. Repeat at each corner.

In circles: First stitch 2 hexagons together, then add a 3rd with one side against each of the other 2 hexagons as in Fig. 2. Keep the 3rd patch on top while stitching. Stitch up one side to the seam, lift the presser foot leaving the needle in the fabric, and place the next 2 sides together for seaming. Continue adding patches to form a circle.

When the patchwork is big enough, cut out the cushion shape with seam allowance. Make a paper pattern piece if necessary. Stitch the front and backing fabric together, right sides facing, leaving an opening for turning.

To make the cushion pad, cut out 4 layers of batting or wadding: 2 the same size as the cushion cover, 2 slightly smaller. Sandwich the smaller layers between the larger ones and overcast the edges together firmly. Stuff the cushion with this pad and sew up the opening by hand.

The hexagonal template is shown here actual size.

Cut the cost

Break away from the traditional three-piece suite by actually making your own sitting room furniture at half the cost. It's fun, practical and very comfortable.

For the cover fabric, we chose a strong, washable cotton velvet — plain and patterned. The inner cushions are made of unbleached cotton filled with kapok. Some of them have a quilted design on the front.

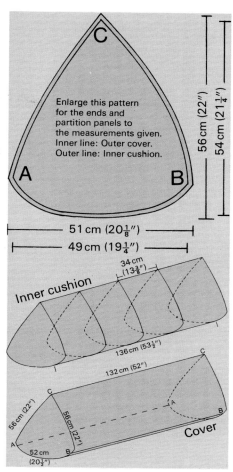

C

Enlarge this pattern
for the ends and
partition panels to
the measurements given.
Inner line: Outer cover.
Outer line: Inner cushion.

A B

56 cm (22")
54 cm (21¼")

51 cm (20⅛")
49 cm (19¼")

34 cm (13⅜")

Inner cushion

136 cm (53½")

132 cm (52")

C C A B

56 cm (22") 56 cm (22")

A B
52 cm (20½")

Cover

1 Back and side bolsters

Materials Required (for each):
Inner Cushion: 3.50 m (3⅞ yds), 140 cm (54") wide. Cover fabric: 5 m (5½ yds), 70 cm (27") wide. Zipper: 100 cm (40") long. Kapok: 7 kg (15 lbs).

Inner cushion: This is made larger in circumference as well as in length, so that the cover is well plumped out. It consists of 4 compartments, each 34 cm (13⅜") long.

Cutting out: Cut out 5 tear-shaped pieces (following outer line) and 4 rectangles 169 cm x 34 cm (66½" x 13⅜") plus 1 cm (⅜") all around for seam allowance. Make sure the long sides of the rectangles fit exactly around the circumference of the tear-shaped pieces before cutting them out accurately.

Sewing: Finish the 4 rectangles at the narrow edges. Stitch each rectangle to the next around the long sides, catching in a tear-shaped piece between them as a partition as follows: Beginning at point C, first pin the 3 seam allowances together. Then stitch and finish all 3 seams together. At the beginning and end

27

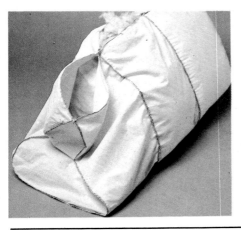

of the bolster, stitch on a tear-shaped piece. You then have an inner cover with 4 compartments (only 3 shown on our photograph on the left) which are open at the top. Stuff these as firmly as possible with kapok. Since kapok clings to fabric, it is advisable to do this job in a room such as the kitchen where there is no carpet or upholstery. Pin up the compartments at once and then sew together by hand.

Cover: Cut out 2 tear-shaped pieces (following inner line) plus 1 cm ($\frac{3}{8}$")

seam allowance. Cut 3 rectangular pieces each 132 cm (52") long, 2 of which are 56 cm (22") wide and 1 of which is 52 cm (20$\frac{1}{2}$") wide plus seam allowance (see diagram on previous page).
Sewing: First stitch seam B – B, right sides facing, for 16 cm (6") from each end. Stitch the zipper in seam opening. Then join seams A – A and C – C. Stitch a tear-shaped piece at each end. Press the seams, turn, and draw cover over the inner cushion.

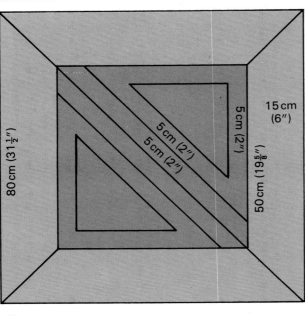

The pale green areas indicate the floral fabric: the dark green areas indicate the plain fabric. Enlarge the pattern to the measurements given.

80 cm (31$\frac{1}{2}$")

5 cm (2")
5 cm (2")

5 cm (2")

15 cm (6")

50 cm (19$\frac{5}{8}$")

2 Large square cushion
Materials Required for each:
Unbleached cotton: 1.65 m (1$\frac{7}{8}$ yds), 140 cm (54") wide. Plain fabric: 2.80 m (3$\frac{1}{8}$ yds), 70 cm (27") wide. Patterned fabric: 0.70 m ($\frac{3}{4}$ yd), 90 cm (36") wide. Batting or wadding for interlining: 0.60 m ($\frac{5}{8}$ yd), 90 cm (36") wide. Zipper: 60 cm (24") long. Kapok: 2.5 kg (5$\frac{1}{2}$ lbs).
Inner cushion: Cutting out: Cut 2 pieces 80 cm (31$\frac{1}{2}$") square plus 1 cm ($\frac{3}{8}$") seam allowance all around.
Sewing: Stitch the pieces together, leaving about 20 cm (8") open. Turn and fill firmly with kapok. Sew up the opening by hand.
Cover: For the back, cut out 2 pieces each 40 cm x 80 cm (15$\frac{3}{4}$" x 31$\frac{1}{2}$") plus 1 cm ($\frac{3}{8}$") seam allowance all around. For the front, cut a 50 cm (19$\frac{5}{8}$") square plus 1 cm ($\frac{3}{8}$") seam allowance all around. From the patterned fabric, cut 4 pieces as shown in the diagram with 1 cm ($\frac{3}{8}$") all around for the seam allowance.

From the interlining, cut a 52 cm (20$\frac{1}{2}$") square.
Sewing: First stitch the 2 back pieces together along one long side, right sides facing, and press the seam open. Then join the 4 patterned pieces along the diagonal edges, stitching only up to the seam

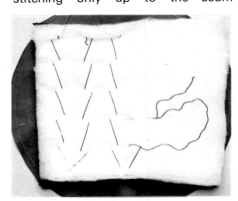

allowance at the inner edges. Press the seams open. Stitch in the square and press these seams open as well. Then top-stitch the front as follows:

Lightly draw in the lines shown in the diagram with the end of a piece of soap. Soap is used on velvet because the lines can easily be

removed later with a damp cloth. Baste the interlining to the wrong side under the area to be quilted (the demonstration photograph shows the technique on a different cushion). From the right side, stitch along the lines with a matching thread (for clarity, we used a lighter thread). Also stitch again along the seam lines around the square inset. Cut off the interlining up to the seamlines. Place the front and back of the cushion together, right sides facing, and stitch one side together 10 cm (3$\frac{3}{4}$") from each end. From the right side, stitch in the zipper invisibly. Then stitch the remaining 3 sides together.
Press the seams open. Turn to the right side and pull cover over inner cushion.

Cushions 3, 4, 5, 6, 7, 8, 9
Make these cushions, using the instructions for Cushion 2. Cut out according to the measurements given in the diagrams. The back of each cushion is cut from plain fabric.

Note: The two round cushions should be stuffed very firmly. The backs are each cut out in 2 halves, with the zipper inserted in this seam. We have not given any fabric requirements for the smaller cushions because you can make use of remnants for them. These cushions need not be stuffed quite as firmly as the large cushions.

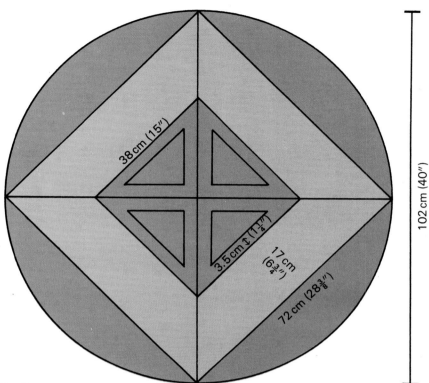

3 Round cushion with square inset

Materials Required: Inner cushion: 2.10 m (2¼ yds), 140 cm (54″) wide. Plain fabric: 2.80 m (3⅛ yds), 70 cm (27″) wide. Patterned fabric: 0.75 m (⅞ yd), 90 cm (36″) wide. Batting or wadding: 1.50 m (1⅝ yds), 90 cm (36″) wide. Kapok: 3 kg (6½ lbs). Zipper: 80 cm (32″) long.

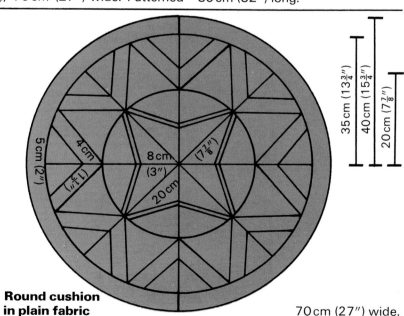

4 Round cushion in plain fabric

Materials Required: Inner cushion: 1.50 m (1⅝ yds), 140 cm (54″) wide. Plain fabric: 2.30 m (2½ yds), 70 cm (27″) wide. Batting or wadding: 1.65 m (1⅞ yds), 90 cm (36″) wide. Zipper: 60 cm (24″). Kapok: 2 kg (4½ lbs).

5 Square cushion with patterned corners

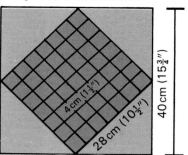

6 Rectangular cushion with diagonal stripes

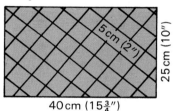

7 Rectangular cushion in patterned fabric

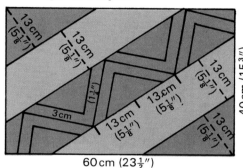

8 Square cushion in plain fabric

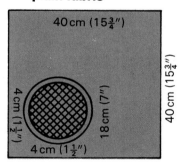

9 Round cushion with square inset

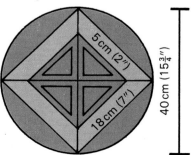

29

Try a new angle

canvaswork cushions worked in satin stitch

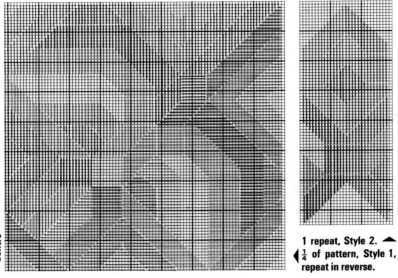

Centre

1 repeat, Style 2. ▲
◀ **¼ of pattern, Style 1, repeat in reverse.**

Size: About 32 cm (12¾") square.
Materials Required: Single-thread canvas: 45 cm (18") square, 14 holes to 2.5 cm (1"). Tapestry yarn: Style 1: 23 m (25 yds) yellow, 46 m (50 yds) lt. green, 39 m (42 yds) each gold and lt. brown, 36 m (39 yds) each dk. green and dk. brown, 10 m (10 yds) orange. Style 2: 62 m (67 yds) dk. pink, 59 m (64 yds) dk. green, 45 m (49 yds) rose, 37 m (40 yds) leaf green, 13 m (14 yds) each salmon pink and lime. Backing fabric 35 cm (14") square. Cushion to fit. Zipper.

Working embroidery and making cover

The cushions are embroidered in straight satin stitches. Follow the relevant chart and work over the number of threads shown. Where 2 colors meet, the yarns emerge from the same hole so that no canvas threads show. Begin each design at the centre of the canvas.

For Style 1, one quarter of the design is given; repeat the other quarters as mirror images. For Style 2, one repeat pattern is given. Repeat horizontally and vertically.

Trim canvas edges to 1.5 cm (⅝"). Stitch backing to canvas, right sides facing, on 3 sides. Turn. Sew in zipper on 4th side. Insert cushion.

Style 1

Style 2

Stitch, pad, and tack

Make your old chairs look like new and your new ones more valuable by giving them a 'face-lift'. Work these gay covers in geometric patterns using tapestry yarn on canvas. Even the simple striped design shown here is effective when worked in bright, clear colours.

Make your own fabric

1
MATERIALS REQUIRED

Tapestry yarn in rust, lilac,
green, pale blue, dark red,
salmon, and mauve.
Single-thread canvas:
14 threads to 2.5 cm (1"),
50 cm (20") wide.

2
MATERIALS REQUIRED

Tapestry wool in pale blue,
medium blue, burgundy, lilac,
rust, salmon, and green.
Single-thread canvas:
14 threads to 2.5 cm (1"),
50 cm (20") wide.

These lively geometric patterns – zigzags, squares and stripes – are very striking on chair seats.

Great impact with a simple stitch: work the designs in satin stitch over counted threads.

The effect is created by skilful colour co-ordination of various beautiful tapestry wools.

These ideas are meant to stimulate your imagination so that you can make your own designs.

3
MATERIALS REQUIRED

Tapestry yarn in lilac,
pale blue, green, salmon,
heather, and rust.
Single-thread canvas:
14 threads to 2.5 cm (1"),
80 cm (32") wide.
Note: The chair seat is cut out
on the bias, but the pattern
is worked straight on the canvas.

4
MATERIALS REQUIRED

Tapestry yarn: in salmon,
rust, mauve, lilac, green,
and pale blue.
Single-thread canvas:
14 threads to 2.5 cm (1"),
50 cm (20") wide.

33

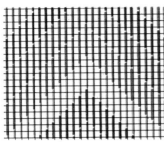

Stitch chart for chair 1

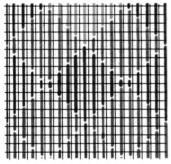

Stitch chart for chair 2

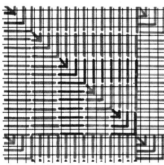

Stitch chart for chair 3

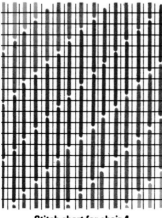

Stitch chart for chair 4

Bargello or Florentine stitch

Bargello or Florentine stitch is a form of satin stitch and is worked over counted threads of an evenweave fabric such as single-thread canvas or coarse linen.

1 Horizontal stitches: Insert the needle the given number of holes to the right and bring it out again one row down. The charts at the left indicate the number of threads to cover.

2 Vertical stitches: Insert the needle the given number of holes up and bring it out again one hole to the left to begin the next stitch. The stitches formed on the back are slanted.

3 Be sure to make all abutting stitches touch. Whether the stitches are vertical or horizontal, always take the needle back through the same hole to ensure that the canvas is covered.

4 Slanting stitches: Insert the needle the given number of holes up and over. To join another pattern, work the abutting stitches into the same holes so that the canvas is covered.

Upholstery the easy way

When you have finished your seat cover, you will wish to mount it professionally. We'll show you how, step by step. Take the measurements directly from your chair and cut all of the materials accordingly.

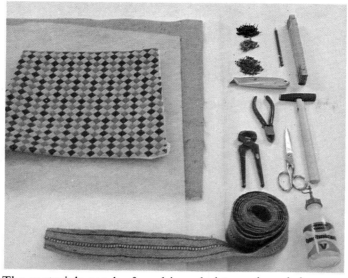

The materials can be found in upholsterers' workshops or in do-it-yourself shops: webbing, burlap or sackcloth, upholstery batting or wadding, foam rubber 2 cm ($\frac{3}{4}$″) thick, tacks, staples, ornamental nails, and fabric glue. Tools required: hammer, pliers, pair of scissors, ruler, mat or craft knife, pencil.

7 Stick the glued narrow edge of the foam down onto the seat. Cut the next layer from batting or wadding; dot with adhesive and stick.

8 Turn under excess canvas and slip-stitch it to the back. Line up the piece carefully on the chair seat; stretch over the padding for a well-rounded effect.

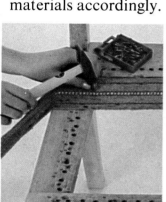

1 Turn under one end of the webbing, pinch it flat and nail the turned-under end to one side of the chair frame. Then stretch it over to the other side.

3 Turn the edge of the webbing over and tack down. Repeat for parallel webs. Weave the other webs across; staple and tack.

5 Cut a piece of foam rubber to fit over the chair seat. Dot adhesive all over the back of the foam rubber and burlap or sackcloth. Press the layers together.

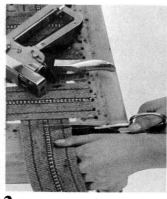

2 Pull the webbing tight, holding it down on the floor with your foot, and staple. Cut the excess webbing off, allowing for the turning.

4 Cut a piece of burlap or sackcloth to fit the seat of the chair, allowing extra for turnings. Staple in position, then tack down firmly.

6 Spread adhesive all along the narrow edges of the foam and along the edge of the burlap or sackcloth to create a rounded edge.

9 Tack down the canvas at the corners and at the middle of each side. Hammer ornamental naïls closely around the edges.

The designs are geometric, the colour combinations are unusual. These striking cushions are worked in tapestry yarn using variations of couched filling stitches which gives them a woven appearance.

Geometric patterns for canvas

Cushions with a woven look

Sizes: The cushions measure approximately 48 x 56 cm (18" x 21") and 40 cm (15") square.

Materials Required: Tapestry yarn in the colours and quantities given overleaf. Single-thread canvas: 18 or 20 holes to 2.5 cm (1") in size of cushion, plus 2.5 cm (1") seam allowance all around. Matching fabric for cushion back. Cushions, measuring 5 cm (2") larger all around than covers.

Basic Stitches: The cushions are worked in various couched filling stitches which give a woven fabric appearance.

Working the cushions

Cut the canvas to the correct size, adding a 2.5 cm (1") seam allowance all around. Place tape around the raw edges to prevent the canvas from fraying. Draw the pattern onto the canvas with a ruler and waterproof felt pen. Diagrams showing the reduced patterns are given on the following page. All four patterns have been reduced to the same scale, so 1 cm ($\frac{3}{8}$") on the diagram represents 8 cm (3") on the finished cushion. First draw the outline of the cushion, then draw the horizontal and vertical lines. Finally, draw in the diagonal lines. Work each colour area separately. To change colours,

bring the new colours out in the holes where the previous colour ended. To work the diagonal areas, follow the slope of the pattern line when making the couched stitch.

The following instructions, which indicate the direction to work the stitches, are also shown in the illustrations overleaf.

Design 1: Work from one short side to the other.

Design 2: Work the diagonal areas from the outer edge to the straight centre area. The stripes are worked from one short side to the other.

Design 3: Work from one long side to the other.

Design 4: Work the centre square horizontally and all the others vertically.

Making the cushions

To block the piece, cover a softwood surface with brown paper. Draw the canvas outline on the paper and place the piece face down on the outline. Fasten the canvas edges with rust-proof thumb tacks, making sure the corners are true right angles. Cover with a damp cloth and leave until completely dry.

Cut the backing fabric to the correct size and pin it to the canvas, right sides together. Stitch around three sides, clip corners, and turn to the right side. Insert cushion; slip-stitch opening.

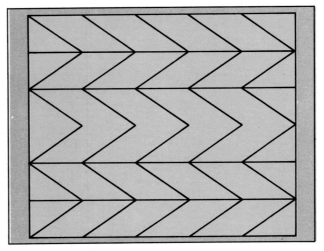

Design 1: This cushion is worked in a slanted couching stitch (see pictures 4 and 5 opposite).

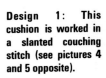

green
11 skeins
pink
11 skein
orange
6 skeins
maroon
6 skeins

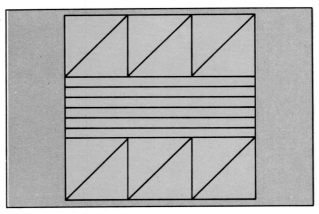

Design 2: Use slanting stitches (see pictures 4, 5, and 6 opposite).

green
8 skeins
pink
8 skeins
orange
8 skeins
maroon
11 skein
turquoise
8 skeins
lilac
8 skeins

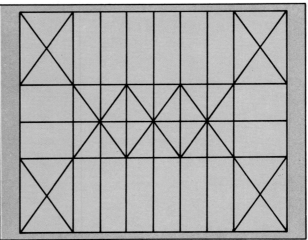

Design 3: This is worked in interlocking slanting stitches (see picture 7 opposite).

green
8 skeins
pink
6 skeins
orange
6 skeins
maroon
16 skein
turquoise
8 skeins
blue
6 skeins

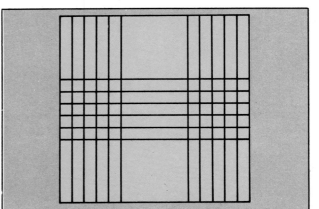

Design 4: Use small straight stitches for this cushion (see pictures 1, 2, and 3 opposite).

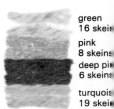

green
16 skein
pink
8 skeins
deep pi
6 skeins
turquois
19 skein

Couching stitches on canvas

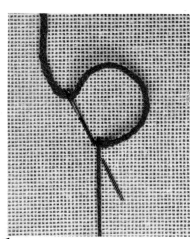

1 Bring the needle out at the lower edge of the colour area to be covered, take the yarn up to the top of the area, and insert it at the upper edge. Bring the needle out on the right side of the yarn, 2 canvas threads down, and insert it again 2 threads across and to the left of the yarn. To begin the next stitch, bring the needle out 4 threads below the last stitch.

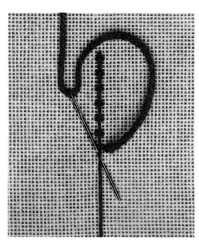

2 Work down the whole length of the couched stitch with straight stitches 4 threads apart. At the end of the row, bring the needle out 2 threads to the left of the first long stitch, ready to begin the next one.

3 In the next row the over-stitches are staggered with those of the previous row. For the first overstitch therefore, bring the needle out 1 thread to the right at the top of the couched stitch. All the following stitches should be 4 threads apart.

4 For the first row of slanting stitches, bring the needle out 1 thread to the right at the top of the couched stitch, then insert it 4 threads down and bring it out 1 thread to the left. Begin the second stitch 5 threads below the top of the first one. Continue down the row in this way.

5 On all further rows, place the couched stitch 2 canvas threads to the left of the previous one. Work the slanting stitches over it as for picture 4, so that they lie side by side.

6 The rows of slanting stitches can be worked so that they slope in alternate directions to give a chain stitch effect. Work the first row as in picture 4. To begin the stitches of the second row, bring the needle out 1 thread to the left of the couched stitch and insert it into the same thread as the base of the stitch beside it. Repeat these two rows.

7 To achieve a staggered pattern with the slanting stitches, work the first row as in picture 4. To work the first stitch of the following row, bring the needle out at the right of the second couched stitch, 2 threads above the base of the stitch beside it. Make a slanting stitch over the couched stitch as before, beginning the next stitch to the right and 1 hole down. Each row will be 2 threads apart, but the stitches will appear to interlock.

Relax luxuriously among
soft scatter pillows made in easy
knit-and-purl patterns.
Follow the charts at right for the
four designs shown here.

Quick and easy knitted geometrics

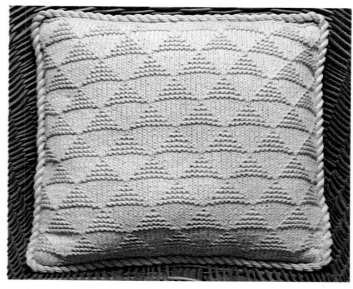

Size: 40 cm or $15\frac{3}{4}''$ square.

Materials (for each):

350 gm or 13 oz [50 gm = 80 m or 87 yds]. Knitting needles size 5 (Am) or 8 (Eng). Thick white cording,

1.7 m or $1\frac{7}{8}$ yds. Matching thread. Foam pillow or pieces for stuffing.
Tension: 18 sts and 30 R = 10 cm or 4″.

DIRECTIONS

Cast on 72 sts and work desired pattern for 232 R. Pattern charts are given below. Each symbol repre-

sents a stitch and solid lines indicate the end of the pattern repeat. When you have knitted to the line, go back to the beginning of the chart and begin the pattern again. Cast off stitches loosely.
Finishing: Fold in half, right sides together, and sew together along 2 sides

with backstitch. Turn to right side. Insert pillow and sew opening closed with slip stitch worked in each knitted stitch, leaving 2.5 cm or 1″ open for cord ends. Sew cording around edge with slip stitch. Overlap ends so cord looks continuous. Push ends into opening; slip-stitched closed.

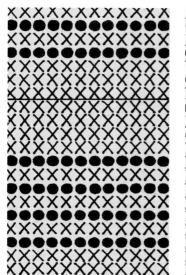

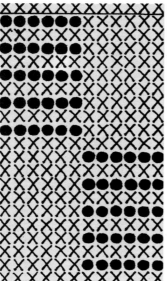

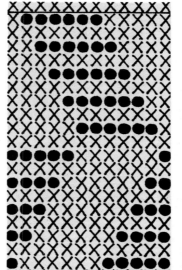

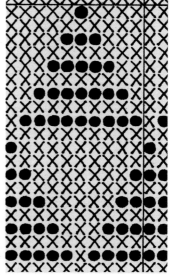

Stitch charts: Each symbol represents 1 stitch. Dots = purl stitches and Xs = knit stitches. The solid lines indicate the end of a pattern repeat.

Bedspreads

Haven't you always wanted
to own a real family heirloom? Here is
your chance to start one.
Make a bedspread which you will love to
use now and which will be treasured
for years to come.

Charming, old-fashioned atmosphere

Crochet

BEDSPREAD

Size: 180 cm x 235 cm or 72" x 93½".

Materials Required:

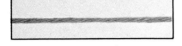

1600 gm or 57 oz white. Crochet hook size 3.00.

Basic Pattern: Follow Crochet Diagram, repeating R 1–12. For odd-numbered rows, read diagram from right to left and for even-numbered rows read from left to right.

Tension: 26 sts and 12 R = 10 cm or 4".

Abbreviations: Ch = chain. St(s) = stitch(es). Tr = treble stitch. R = row(s).

DIRECTIONS

Bedspread: Make 496 ch; follow diagram, working 1st dc into 3rd ch from hook, then follow diagram to end of R – 494 sts. The diagram consists of 82 sts which are repeated 6 times across R, with 1 extra edge st at each end. Work R 1–12 18 times in all. Fasten off.

Lace Edging: For the first edging, make 60 ch: follow and work in pattern as for diagram, working 1st tr into 3rd ch from hook, and working over the 58 sts to arrow showing end of first edging. *Keeping end of odd-numbered R straight,* increase 2 sts at other edge on 2nd to 7th R, working extra sts into tr. Then, keeping continuity of pattern, decrease 2 sts on same edge on next 6 R. Continue thus until 18 repeats of pattern have been worked. Fasten off. Work second lace edging to match, working in reverse and beginning where arrow indicates on the diagram.

Finishing: Press well. Sew edgings across short ends.

CUSHION

Size: 38 cm or 15" in diameter.

Materials Required:

150 gm or 6 oz old rose. Crochet hook size 3.50.

For the cushion ruffles, several double trebles are worked into the front of the stitches in that round.

Each short end of the bedspread is edged with a pointed lace pattern which is worked from the same crochet diagram below.

Crochet diagram: 82 stitches and 12 R form 1 repeat. For the odd-numbered rows, read the diagram from right to left; read even-numbered rows from left to right.

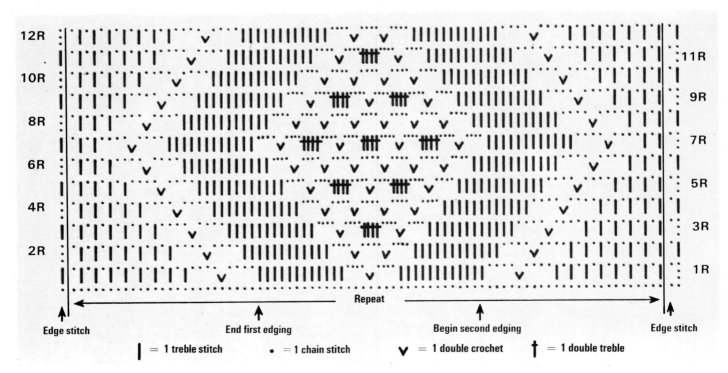

12R · · · 11R
10R · · · 9R
8R · · · 7R
6R · · · 5R
4R · · · 3R
2R · · · 1R

Repeat

Edge stitch   End first edging   Begin second edging   Edge stitch

| = 1 treble stitch   **·** = 1 chain stitch   **v** = 1 double crochet   **†** = 1 double treble

Basic Pattern: Tr and dtr worked in rounds.
Tension: 20 sts and 9 R = 10 cm or 4″.
Abbreviations: Ch = chain. St(s) = stitch(es). Tr = treble. Dtr = double treble. Rnd(s) = round(s).

DIRECTIONS

Front: Make 5 ch and join into a ring with a slip st. Rnd 1: With 3 ch as 1st tr, work 14 tr into ring. Join all rounds with a slip st into the last st of 1st ch. Rnd 2: 4 ch for 1st dtr. In this and all following dtr rnds, work dtr into the front loop of the previous rnd, 2 dtr into 1st st, then 3 dtr in each st. Rnd 3: Work behind the 2nd rnd into the back loop, *1 tr into 1 st, 2 tr into next st, repeat from * all around. Rnd 4: With 3 ch as 1st tr, work 2 tr into each tr. Rnd 5: Repeat the method of Rnd 2, working into the front loops of last rnd. With 4 ch as 1st dtr, work * 2 dtr in each of next 2 tr, 3 dtr in next tr, repeat from * all around. Rnd 6: Repeat Rnd 3, working into back loops of Rnd 4. Rnd 7: With 3 ch as 1st tr, work tr on tr. Rnd 8: With 4 ch as 1st dtr, work *2 dtr into next 2 tr, 1 dtr in next tr, repeat from * all around. Rnd 9: Repeat Rnd 7, working into the back loop of Rnd 7. Rnd 10: With 3 ch as 1st tr, work * 2 tr in each of next 2 tr, 1 tr in next tr, repeat from * all around. Rnds 11–22: Repeat Rnds 8–10 4 times. Fasten off.
Back: Make 5 ch, join into a ring with a slip st, and work in rounds of tr, increasing to match Front until the Back is the same diameter as the Front. Then fasten off the yarn.
Finishing: Press, then join Back and Front together from wrong side with double crochet, leaving opening for cushion. Turn to right side. Insert cushion. Sew the opening closed.

Crocheted ruffles

1 The circular ruffles of double trebles are worked by crocheting into the front loops only of the previous treble round.

2 In the next round, fold the double trebles toward you and work trebles into the back loops of the last treble round.

3 In the following round, the trebles are worked in the usual way, crocheting into both loops of the previous round.

4 When joining the front and back, place them right sides together and work a partial round of double crochet. Turn and insert cushion.

Creamy cobwebs

<u>Size:</u> 170 cm x 240 cm or 67" x 95".

<u>Materials Required:</u>

2000 gm or 71 oz white cotton. Crochet hook size D.

<u>Basic Pattern:</u> <u>Motif:</u> Make 6 ch and join into a ring with a slip st. <u>Rnd 1:</u> 2 ch, *1 small puff st by yarn around hook 3 times, insert hook into ring, draw up a loop, then yarn over and draw through 6 loops, yarn over and draw through remaining 2 loops, repeat from * 5 times more. Join this rnd and Rnds 2 and 3 with a slip st into top ch at beginning of <u>rnd. Rnd 2:</u> 3 ch as 1st dc, * then 3 ch, 1 dc in between the next 2 clusters, repeat from * 4 times more, 3 ch. <u>Rnd 3:</u> 2 ch, *1 large puff st by yarn over hook 5 times, insert hook into ch space of previous rnd, draw up a loop, yarn over and draw through 10 loops, yarn over and draw through 2 loops, 3 ch, 1 large puff st into same ch space, 3 ch, repeat from * 5 times more. <u>Rnd 4:</u> *3 ch, 1 sc in between the next 2 puff sts inserting hook around the ch loops of Rnds 2 and 3, 3 ch, then 1 sc into the next dc of Rnd 2 inserting hook round the ch loop of Rnd 3, repeat from * ending 1 slip st into 1st ch.

In Rnds 5–10, always work 3 ch as 1st dc. <u>Rnd 5:</u> 5 dc in 1st ch loop, *3 ch, skip 1 ch loop, 5 dc in next loop, repeat from * ending 3 ch, join with a slip st. <u>Rnd 6:</u> 2 dc, 3 dc in next dc, 2 dc, 2 ch, repeat from * all around, join with a slip st. <u>Rnd 7:</u> *2 dc, 3 dc in next dc, 1 dc, 3 dc in next dc, 2 dc, 2 ch, repeat from * all around, join with a slip st. <u>Rnd 8:</u> *3 dc, 3 dc in next dc, 3 dc, 3 dc in next dc, 3 dc, 2 ch, repeat from * all around, join with a slip st. <u>Rnd 9:</u>

46

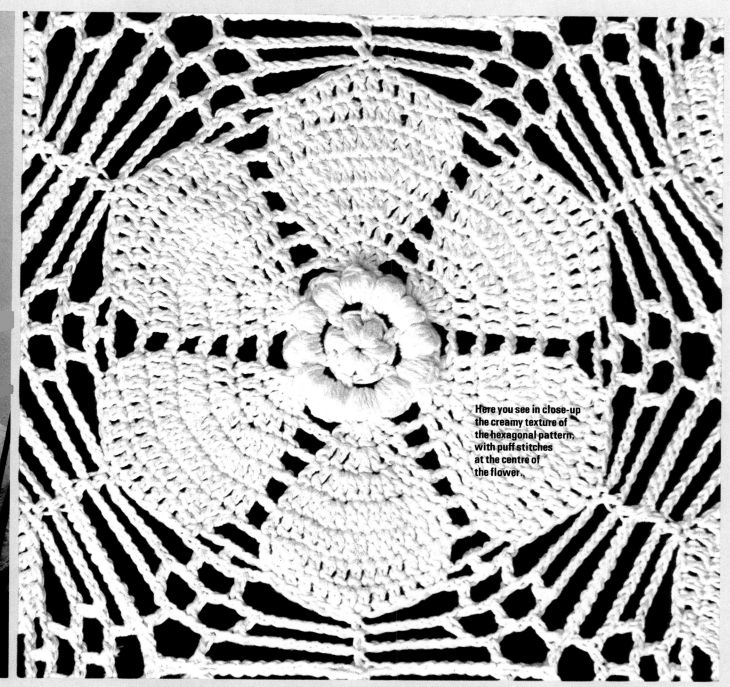

Here you see in close-up the creamy texture of the hexagonal pattern, with puff stitches at the centre of the flower.

*15 dc, 2 ch, repeat from * all around, join with a slip st. Rnd 10: 1 dc, 1 half-worked dc in next 2 sts and loop off together, 9 dc, 1 half-worked dc in next 2 sts and loop of together, 1·dc, *5 ch, 1 dc, 2 half-worked dc as before, 9 dc, 2 half-worked dc, 1 dc, repeat from * all around, 5 ch, join with a slip st. Rnd 11: *1 sc into 2nd st of group, 1 hdc, 8 dc, 1 hdc, 1 sc, 3 ch, 1 dc into 3rd of 5 ch, 3 ch, repeat from *, join with a slip st to sc. Rnd 12: Slip-st over the first 6 sts, *9 ch, 1 dc into 1st ch-loop, 3 ch, 1 dc into 2nd ch-loop, 9 ch, 1 slip st into the 6th and 7th sts, repeat from * ending last repeat of round with slip st into the 6th slip st. Rnd 13: *9 ch, 1 dc into the 8th of 9-ch loop, 3 ch, 1 dc into the 2nd ch of the small ch-loop, 3 ch, 1 dc into the 2nd ch of large ch-loop, 9 ch, 1 sc in between the 2 slip sts, repeat from * all around, slip st to sc.

join with a slip st. Rnd 14: *11 ch, 1 dc into the 2nd ch of 1st small ch-loop, 5 ch, 1 dc into the 2nd ch of next ch-loop, 11 ch, 1 sc in sc, repeat from * all around, join with a slip st and fasten off. These 14 rnds make one complete motif.

Tension: Each motif measures about 22 cm or 8½".

Abbreviations: Ch = chain. Sc = single crochet. Dc = double crochet. Hdc = half dc. Rnd(s) = round(s).

DIRECTIONS

Make 95 motifs as given in Basic Pattern.

Finishing: Pin out motifs and steam-press lightly. *Join 1 row of 11 motifs together neatly, then in between them on next row join 10 motifs joining the 2 rows together. Repeat from * 3 times more, then add a final row of 11 motifs. Cut lengths of cotton yarn about 26 cm or 10¼" long. Knot into point and joins of outer motifs.

Made on a knitting machine
Set the mood with bold hexagons

Size: Approx. 250 x 260 cm or 98½″ x 102½″. Each hexagon measures about 30 cm or 12″ across and 26.5 cm or 10½″ high.

Materials Required:

750 gm or 27 oz each dark blue and bright blue, 500 gm or 18 oz pale green, 400 gm or 15 oz dark green, 350 gm or 13 oz rust [50 gm = 200 m or 220 yds].

Basic Pattern: Stocking or stockinette stitch.

Tension: 28 sts and 40 R = 10 cm or 4″.

Abbreviations: St(s) = stitch(es). R = row(s).

DIRECTIONS

Make 105 hexagons: 30 each in dark blue and bright blue, 20 in pale green, 15 in dark green, and 10 in rust. Also work 10 half hexagons in rust.

Bring 42 needles down into

Sew pieces together with backstitch.

D position and cast on by hand. With needles in working position, continue thus: *increase 1 st at beginning of next 8 R. Work 2 R straight. Repeat from * 3 times more. Now increase 1 st at beginning of next 10 R. Work 3 R straight. (Half hexagon completed – 53 R.) Now work in reverse, working 3 R straight, and decreasing 1 st at beginning of next 10 R, then continue to match first half in reverse until 42 sts remain – 106 R. Cast off.

For the half hexagons, work the 53 R to centre and cast off the 84 sts.

Finishing: Pin out and press well. Join all hexagons with backstitch. Sew 6 strips of 10 motifs, alternating dark blue and bright blue. Sew 5 strips of 9 motifs in the following order: pale green, dark green, rust, pale green, dark green, pale green, rust, dark green, and pale green. Alternate the 6 strips so that one begins with a dark blue hexagon and the other with a bright blue hexagon, then place the 5 strips between. Stitch neatly in position as shown in the photograph. At each side, sew on the half hexagons to form a straight edge. Turn in a narrow hem around all edges and stitch down. Press seams.

Whipped cream coverlet

Size: 130 x 240 cm (51" x 94½").
Materials Required:

2700 gm or 96 oz white. 5 double-pointed needles size 2 (Am) or 11 (Eng).
Stitch Pattern: See chart.
Abbreviations: St(s) = stitch(es). R = row(s). K = knit. P = purl. Inc = increase. Rnd(s) = round(s).

DIRECTIONS

For the bedspread you will require 45 squares and 22 triangles.

Squares: Each square is worked in rnds on 5 double-pointed needles. The chart gives ¼ of the square, so the pattern must be repeated 4 times in each rnd. Follow the chart for the odd-numbered rnds and knit every even-numbered rnd, working the 1st st of each repeat in twisted knit stitch. Cast on 8 sts, placing 2 sts on each of 4 needles. Work Rnds 1–48, then P 2 rnds. Cast off.

Triangles: Cast on 7 sts. Work back and forth across the rows. Work the odd-numbered R from the chart, beginning each R with an edge st, then working the pattern 2 times, and ending with a K st and an edge st. P the even-numbered R, working twisted purl st into the twisted knit sts.

Border: Cast on 9 sts. R 1: K 1, *inc 1, K 2 together in

twisted knit st, repeat from * 3 times. R 2 and all even-numbered R: K 1, inc 1, K to end. R 3: K 2, then repeat from * of R 1. R 5: K 3, then repeat from * of R 1. Continue thus until there are 16 sts. Next even R: Work as for R 2. Next odd R: Cast off 7 sts, K to end. Continue to repeat from R 1 until the work measures 7.5 m or 8¼ yds. Cast off.

Finishing: Pin out the squares and triangles, cover with a damp cloth, press lightly, and leave to dry. Join on wrong side with backstitch. Begin at lower edge by sewing 3 squares in between 4 triangles, then add 4 and 3 squares alternately to end. Sew 4 triangles at the other end and 7 triangles along each side. When all squares and triangles have been joined, sew on the border neatly.

Patterned motifs are joined for the coverlet and a border finishes the edge.

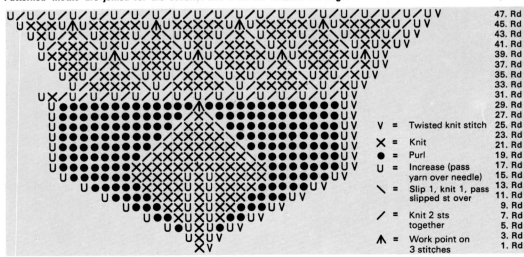

V =	Twisted knit stitch
X =	Knit
● =	Purl
U =	Increase (pass yarn over needle)
\ =	Slip 1, knit 1, pass slipped st over
/ =	Knit 2 sts together
∧ =	Work point on 3 stitches

Rows (right side): 47. Rd, 45. Rd, 43. Rd, 41. Rd, 39. Rd, 37. Rd, 35. Rd, 33. Rd, 31. Rd, 29. Rd, 27. Rd, 25. Rd, 23. Rd, 21. Rd, 19. Rd, 17. Rd, 15. Rd, 13. Rd, 11. Rd, 9. Rd, 7. Rd, 5. Rd, 3. Rd, 1. Rd

Pattern repeat: Each symbol represents one stitch of the odd-numbered rows. See the directions for the even rows.

Create an optical illusion

The optical trick is simple. Diagonal stripes in light and dark shades of the same colour are placed side by side in a zigzag pattern. Two shades of any colour will produce the same effect.

The zigzag of alternating light and dark stripes gives a three-dimensional effect.

Size : 130 x 225 cm (51¼" x 88½").

Materials Required :

100 gm or 4 oz each of red, dark green, purple, blackberry, dark grey, blue, rust, burgundy, light burgundy, green, lilac, old rose, light grey, light blue, light brown, dark yellow, beige, pale yellow [50 gm = 188 m or 205 yds]. Knitting needles size 5 (Am) or 8 (Eng).

Basic Stitch : Stocking or stockinette stitch. The diagonal pattern is produced by increasing at one side and decreasing at the other side of the same R.

Colour Sequence of Dark Stripes : 23 R light brown, *20 R each of dark yellow, red, burgundy, dark green, purple, blackberry, dark grey, blue, light brown, repeat from * 2 times, then work 23 R dark yellow.

Colour Sequence of Light Stripes : 23 R beige, *20 R each of pale yellow, rust, light burgundy, green, lilac, old rose, light grey, light blue, beige, repeat from * 2 times, then work 23 R pale yellow.

Tension : 23 sts and 34 R = 10 cm or 4".

Abbreviations : St(s) = stitch(es). R = row(s). K = knit. P = purl.

DIRECTIONS

Dark Stripes (5 required) : Using light brown, cast on 40 sts and K 3 R.

R 4 : Work in front and back of next st, then K to last 3 sts, slip 1, K 1, pass slip st over, K 1. R 5 : P.

Repeat these 2 R until 23 R of light brown have been worked. Continue in Colour Sequence, working 20 R in each colour. When the dark yellow has been worked in the last sequence, K 3 more R in dark yellow. Cast off in dark yellow.

Light Stripes (5 required) : Using beige, cast on 40 sts and K 3 R.

R 4 : K 1, K 2 together, K until 2 sts remain, K into front and back of next st, K1. R 5 : P.

Repeat these 2 R until 23 R of beige have been worked. Continue in Colour Sequence, working 20 R in each colour. When the light yellow has been worked in the last sequence, K 3 more R in light yellow. Cast off in light yellow.

Finishing : Block strips wrong side up, then press with a warm iron over a damp cloth. Arrange the dark and light stripes alternately and sew together on the wrong side with backstitch. Press seams.

The diagonal stripes in each strip are produced by increasing at one side and decreasing at the other side of the same row.

Easy enough to knit without looking

Of course you can knit while watching television! Actually, the more exciting the story is, the faster your needles will click. Try it with something easy like our bedcover. It's worked in garter stitch so all the rows are knitted. With no effort at all, the knitted rows create a crinkly texture.

Your family and friends will want to join the fun, each knitting a strip in a favourite colour.

Once you have knitted all the strips, make a pleasing colour arrangement and join them with a row of crochet. Finish the outer edges with three rows of crochet in the same colour as used for joining.

Strip Size: Required length x 10 cm or 4″ wide.

Coverlet Size: Coverlet at left is 22 strips long x 140 cm (55″) wide. Coverlet at right is 14 strips wide x 220 cm (86½″) long.

Materials Required: Use same thickness of yarn throughout. Your colour sequence will determine the amount of yarn required in each colour. [50 gm or 2 oz = a strip 10 cm x 48 cm or 4″ x 19″.] Knitting needles size 10 (Am.) or 3 (Eng.). Crochet hook.

Basic stitch: Garter stitch (knit every row).

Colour sequence: Be creative! Work a coverlet in various shades of your favourite colour, or use up left-over yarn in a pleasing multi-coloured arrangement.

Tension: 16 stitches and 26 rows = 10 cm or 4″.

Note: It is important that

The vertical stripes of this bedcover are worked in shades of red and orange.

A knitted coverlet is warm and cosy and will be wonderfully versatile.

Strips are joined with a row of crochet in a contrasting colour.

each strip has the same number of rows, because the strips are crocheted together row by row.

Making the strips
Determine size of coverlet and whether you want horizontal or vertical stripes. Make a sketch of the colour sequence. Cast on 16 stitches for each strip and knit to required length. Knit desired number of strips in desired colours.

Joining the strips
See the illustration at lower left. Insert crochet hook into a stitch at edge of each strip, pass yarn over hook and draw it through first two loops on hook, pass yarn over and draw it through the other two loops. Repeat along length of the strips. We used black yarn between the strips for contrast. When you have joined all the strips, finish the coverlet edges with three rows of crochet all around in the same colour as used for joining. Work two or three stitches in each corner stitch so that the corners will lie flat.

Worked in garter stitch

Featherweight snuggle rug

Mohair is so soft, warm, and lightweight that you will barely feel this cover. It's ideal for cold days when you want to curl up with a good book, or as a blanket on your bed.

Size: 130 cm or 52" square. Each square is about 30 cm or 12".

Materials Required:

300 gm or 11 oz beige, 200 gm or 8 oz each of blue, orange, and green [40 gm = 106 m or 115 yds]. Knitting needles size 8 (Am) or 6 (Eng).

Basic Stitch: Garter stitch (K every R).

Colour Sequence: Cast on with green, then work 11 R green, 12 R each of beige, orange, blue, green, beige, orange, 11 R blue, cast off in blue.

Tension: 15 sts and 32 R = 10 cm or 4".

Abbreviations: St(s) = stitch(es). R = row(s). K = knit.

◀ The squares are sewn together with the stripes running in alternate directions. The edging is worked as one long piece and sewn on.

The cover can also be made in ▶ a two-colour combination. You will need 400 gm or 15 oz of each colour plus 100 gm or 4 oz for the border.

DIRECTIONS

The Squares (16 required): Using green, cast on 45 sts and work in garter stitch in Colour Sequence. Cast off.

The Edging: Using beige, cast on 8 sts and work in garter stitch for 120 cm or 48".

Shape corner: Leave last st unworked at end of next R, turn, increase 1 st by passing yarn over the needle, K to end. Continue thus, leaving 1 more st and increased st unworked at the end of alternate R until only 2 sts remain on right hand needle. Next R: K 2, K together the increased stitch with next st, turn and K to end. Continue thus, working together the increased st with the following st until all sts are worked. Continue to work in garter stitch for 120 cm or 48", then shape next corner. Repeat for the other 2 sides. Cast off. Join cast on and cast off edges together.

Finishing: Sew 4 squares together to make a strip, and sew the 4 strips together, reversing the direction so that the stripes are alternately horizontal and vertical. Sew the edging in place.

In Tunisian crochet
Blanket coverage

Curl up and relax in style with the aid of this handsome rug crocheted in pure wool and embroidered with cross-stitch designs.

Size: About 130 cm x 210 cm or 51" x 83".

Materials Required:

900 gm or 32 oz green, 800 gm or 29 oz white, 700 gm or 25 oz rust, 650 gm or 23 oz brown [50 gm = 102 m or 112 yds]. Tunisian crochet hook size 6. Large eyed, blunt tipped needle.

Basic Pattern: Tunisian stitch. On right side, draw a loop through each upright st of the previous R. Do not turn work. Yarn over and draw through 1 st, then *yarn over and through next 2 sts, repeat from * to end. This is counted as 1 row.

Embroidery Pattern: Each colour sign = 1 cross stitch over a Tunisian stitch. Grey represents white.

Tension: 16 sts and 15 R = 10 cm or 4".

Abbreviations: St(s) = stitch(es). Ch = chain. Dtr = double treble. R = row(s). Dc = double crochet.

DIRECTIONS

The coverlet is worked in separate strips which are sewn together afterward.

Rust Strip (make 6): Work 13 ch and, working into 3rd ch from hook for 1st st, work 199 R in Basic

Pattern. Fasten off.

Green Strip (make 2): Work 51 ch and work 199 R in Basic Pattern. Fasten off.

Brown, White, Brown Strip (make 3): Using brown make 14 ch, using white make 21 ch, then with another ball of brown work 16 ch (last 2 ch for turning ch). Work in Basic Pattern and at colour changeover, always work last st in the following colour. Work to the second half of the 4th R, then work to 1 st before colour changeover, make 1 dtr 3 R lower (see right), then at beginning of the white strip make another dtr back into the 1st R. Work other colour changeover in the same way. Work dtr every 3rd R, and work 199 R in all. Fasten off.

Finishing: Embroider the green strips following the large cross-stitch diagram (21 sts and R form one complete pattern). Work 1 cross-stitch over 1 Tunisian st, working from the 15th–35th sts across. Begin the 1st motif in the 9th R from lower edge, and 6 more motifs each 6 R apart.

Next embroider the rust strips, following the small motif (5 sts and R form one complete pattern). Work motif on 4th–8th sts across and begin in the 10th R from lower edge. Work motif alternately in green and white 17 times with 6 rows between each motif. Now work around all strips using rust and working in dc.

Place strips in colour sequence thus: rust, brown-white-brown, rust, green, rust, brown-white-brown, rust, green, rust, brown-white-brown, rust. Overcast all strips together with double rust strand, picking up both threads of dc. Finally dc all around the outer edge to give a neat border.

The rug is easy to assemble, as it is crocheted in separate strips and then sewn together.

Right: Large motif for the dark-green strips.
Below: Small motif for the rust strips.

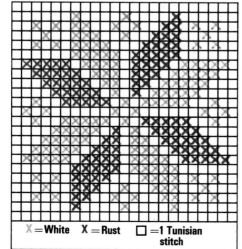

X = White   X = Rust   □ = 1 Tunisian stitch

Accentuated colour change

Double trebles are worked at the beginning and end of colour areas in every 3rd row of the Tunisian crochet. Begin to work the double trebles in the 4th row. Work to last loop of 1st colour, yarn over twice and continue as shown below, but work under upright thread of stitch 3 rows below the previously worked stitch.

1 For double trebles worked in the left-hand colour, insert the hook under the upright thread of the stitch in front of the previously worked double treble.

2 Work the double treble. With the new colour, work the last loop of the old colour with the first loop of the new colour.

3 For the double trebles worked in the right-hand colour, always work under the first upright thread of the stitch behind the previously worked double treble.

Five subtle tones have been used here to attractive effect. The scallops are worked in strips and the separate strips are joined together afterward. This avoids having to cope with the increasing weight of working the cover in one piece.

In thick, natural wool

A hint of rustic charm

Size: 180 cm x 208 cm or 71" x 82".

Materials Required:

700 gm or 25 oz off-white, 600 gm or 22 oz each in pale grey, dark grey, nut brown, and black [50 gm = 150 m or 164 yds]. Crochet hook size H.

Basic Pattern: See instructions given on the next page.

Colour Sequence: *5 R each in off-white, pale grey, dark grey, black, and brown, repeat from *.

Tension: 1 scallop is 18 cm or 7" wide and 8 cm or 3¼" deep.

DIRECTIONS

Strips: Crochet separate strips in Basic Pattern, repeating each Colour Sequence 5 times, then work another scallop in off-white. Fasten off.
Work 10 strips in all.

Finishing: Press work lightly on wrong side. Using the strand of yarn left hanging at end of each scallop, join strips. Match colours on each strip and join on wrong side with overcasting stitches, catching in only 1 thread of each stitch.

Here the effect of joining the scalloped strips can be seen clearly.

Making scallops

1 To begin, use off-white to make 13 chains. <u>R 1</u> (wrong side): Into the 9th chain from the hook, work 1 treble stitch, 4 chains, then work 1 double crochet into the last chain.

2 Make 3 chains to turn. <u>R 2</u>: Work 9 treble stitches into first loop in R 1, 1 treble stitch into the treble stitch and then work 10 treble stitches into the second loop.

3 Make 6 chains to turn. <u>R 3</u>: Work 1 treble stitch into the third treble stitch, *skip 1 treble stitch, make 2 chains, 1 treble stitch into the next treble stitch, repeat from * ending with 2 chains, 1 treble stitch into the turning chain, and 3 chains for turning. <u>R 4</u>: *Work 3 treble stitches into the loop, 1 treble stitch into the treble stitch, repeat from * ending 3 treble stitches into the loop of the turning chain and 1 treble stitch into the turning chain. <u>R 5</u>: Repeat R 3. This completes one scallop. Leave a length of yarn hanging for sewing the strips. When the strips are sewn together, each pair of scallops is joined with this hanging thread.

4 The new colour is begun on a wrong side row. <u>R 6</u>: Work 1 double crochet into the second treble stitch before the centre (11th) treble stitch, make 4 chains, work 1 treble stitch into the centre treble stitch, make 4 chains, then 1 double crochet into the following second treble stitch.

5 Before beginning the next row, work 2 chains and then slip-stitch into the next treble stitch of the previous scallop. Make 3 chains to turn. Continue, alternating right and wrong sides.

6 <u>R 7</u>: Work 9 treble stitches into the 4-chain loop, 1 treble stitch into the treble stitch, 10 treble stitches into next 4-chain loop, join to the next treble stitch of the previous scallop with a slip stitch, end as for the end of R 6. Turn with 6 chains. <u>R 8</u>: *Make 2 chains, work 1 treble stitch into the second treble stitch, repeat from *, joining with a slip stitch. Make 3 chains to turn. <u>R 9</u>: * Work 3 treble stitches into loop, 1 treble stitch in treble stitch, repeat from *, join with slip stitch, make 6 chains to turn. <u>R 10</u>: Repeat R 8. Continue thus, repeating R 6–10.

Start with one and you're on your way

Flowers bloom in abundance on this colourful cover. Three-dimensional roses are worked in Irish crochet in bright rose-like colours or in wild combinations to make fantasy flowers.

Joining squares

With double crochet:
Working from the
right side, insert the
hook under the
lower threads of the
edge stitches in each
square and work
double crochet in the
usual way.

With chain stitch:
Working from the
wrong side, insert
the hook under the
upper threads of the
edge stitches in each
square and work
chain stitch in the
usual way.

With overcasting:
Working from the
wrong side, insert
the needle under the
upper threads of the
edge stitches in each
square and work
overcasting stitches
in the usual way.

IRISH ROSE SQUARES

Abbreviations: St(s) = stitches. Rnd(s) = round(s). Ch = chain. Dc = double crochet. Htr = half treble. Tr = treble.

DIRECTIONS

Make 8 ch and join into a ring with a slip stitch. <u>Rnd 1</u>: 6 ch, *1 tr into ring, 3 ch, repeat from * 6 times more. Join with a slip st into 3rd of 6 ch (8 spaces). <u>Rnd 2</u>: (1 dc, 1 htr, 4 tr, 1 htr, 1 dc) into each 3-ch space (8 petals). Slip st along back of 1st petal to lower edge of 1st tr. <u>Rnd 3</u>: (work into the back of rnd 2) *5 ch, 1 dc into 1st tr of next petal, inserting the hook into the back of the stitch, repeat from * all around. <u>Rnd 4</u>: (1 dc, 1 htr, 6 tr, 1 htr, 1 dc) into each 5-ch space. <u>Rnd 5</u>: *7 ch, 1 dc into 1st tr of next petal, inserting the hook into the back of the stitch, repeat from * all around. <u>Rnd 6</u>: (1 dc, 1 htr, 6 tr, 1 htr, 1 dc) into each 7-ch space. <u>Rnd 7</u>: Join yarn to space between petals, (3 tr, 1 ch, 3 tr) into same space, *2 ch, 1 dc into centre of next petal, 2 ch, 3 tr into space between petals, 2 ch, 1 dc into centre of next petal, 2 ch, (3 tr, 1 ch, 3 tr) into space between petals, repeat from * 3 times, omitting last 3 tr, 1 ch, 3 tr. Join with a slip st in top of 1st tr and slip-stitch along to next 1-ch. <u>Rnd 8</u>: *(3 tr, 1 ch, 3 tr) into 1-ch space, (2 ch, 3 tr) into next 4 2-ch spaces, 2 ch, repeat from * all around. Join with slip stitch.

In all following rnds, work 3 tr, 2 ch into each 2-ch space along each side and 3 tr, 1 ch, 2 tr into each corner.

Patchwork can be made up of a wide variety of squares and still give a unified effect of colour or design.

66

Table linen

Good housekeepers and wives
used to be judged by the richness of
their linen cupboards.
Hand-made and embroidered table linen
sets a touch of distinction
on your home.

This cross-stitch tablecloth adds elegance to a simple table setting. The effect is enhanced by fine white china.

Black and white simplicity

Size: 138cm (54½") square.
Materials Required:
Stranded embroidery cotton: 22 skeins black. White evenweave linen: measuring 140 cm (54") square. Thread.

Working the embroidery

Mark out a square measuring 100.5 cm x 100.5 cm (39⅝" x 39⅝") with thread. This outlines the outer boundary of the embroidery. The design pattern shows a corner with one repeat before it and two repeats after it. Work this section first, then add four single repeats on the side where there are already two repeats. Continue in this manner until the border is complete around the square. The border can easily be made rectangular by adding more repeats on the long sides.

Each cross-stitch is 0.5 cm ($\frac{3}{16}$") square and there are approximately 5 crosses to 2.5 cm (1"). Calculate the number of threads over which to work each cross according to the weave of the linen (*ie*, with a weave of 20 threads to 2.5 cm or 1", each cross is worked over 4 threads). Work the crosses with 6 strands of cotton and be sure that all crosses cross in the same direction. To finish, make a double hem of 1 cm ($\frac{3}{8}$").

A detail of the cross-stitch border. Each cross-stitch is 0.5 cm ($\frac{3}{16}$") square.

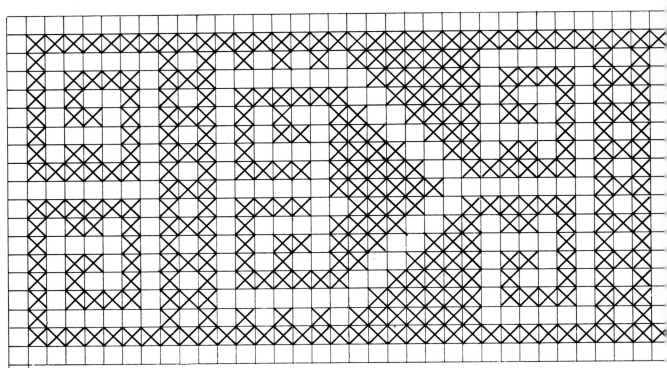

Dramatic border

Work this bold pattern to mark the
outline of your table top on a crisp
white cloth. Follow the charts for the
repeats of the pattern and the corners.

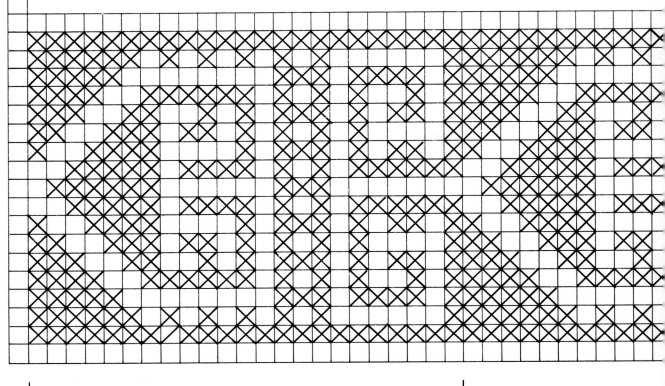

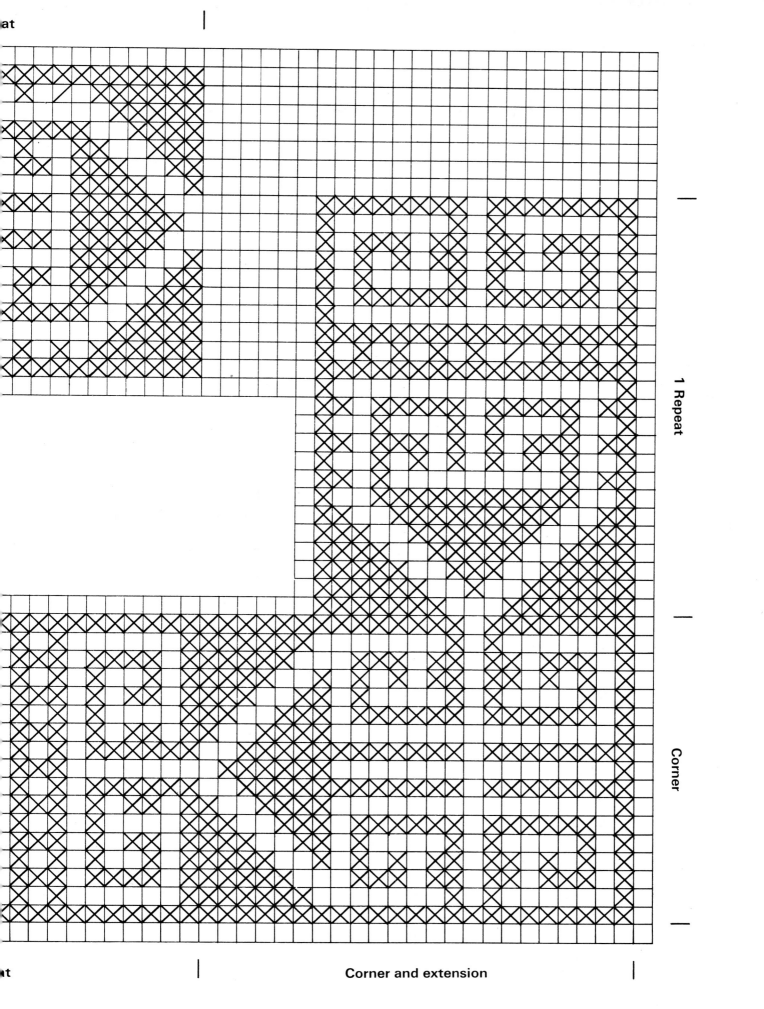

1 Repeat

Corner

Corner and extension

Here you can see exactly how the lines of braid cross one another.

A detail of the corner motif of the design.

Arabesque borders

Beautifully braided

Decorative braid work is a lovely old technique often found in traditional peasant embroidery.

Size: The cloth illustrated measures 177 cm x 136 cm (69¾" x 53½").

Materials Required:
Linen: 1.85 m (2 yds), 150 cm (60") wide. White cotton braid: 0.5 cm (¼") wide, 62 m (68 yds).

Preparing the cloth
Cut out the cloth to the correct size, adding a 4 cm (1½") hem allowance all around. Mark the horizontal and vertical center with lines of basting stitches. Onto tissue paper, trace 3 corner motifs and enough side motifs to form one short and one long side. Using the photograph as a guide, place the motifs along two sides of the cloth. When you have found the correct position, mark guide lines all around the cloth between which the design will run. Use basting stitches for these lines, following the grain of fabric. Check that the border fits into the other 2 sides correctly. Now transfer the motifs to the cloth with dressmaker's carbon paper.

Attaching the braid
Stitch on the braid with backstitch as shown on the right, following the lines of the design. In spite of the complicated appearance of the curving pattern, there are, in fact, only four interlocking lines and you begin a new length of braid only four times. Simply follow through with a long strip until you come back to where you started.
Sew two straight lines of braid 1 cm (⅜") apart 2 cm (¾") from the inner and outer edges of the pattern. These lines can be stitched on by machine.

Finishing
Turn under the hem twice, mitring the corners, and sew in place. Two more strips of braid can be sewn around the outer edges of the cloth, but additional braid will be required.

◀ The interlaced lines of braid make a graceful border pattern.

Embroidery with braid

For this kind of decoration, choose any braid which is flexible enough to apply in curved lines.

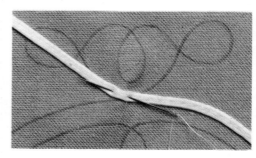

1 Place the braid along the lines of the design and sew it on with small, widely-spaced backstitches. Do not stretch the braid or the fabric will pucker.

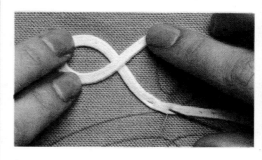

2 On the small, tight curves, it is advisable to shape the braid along the line first, holding it down flat with your fingers as you work.

3 Sew the beginning and end of the braid together, keeping them flat. Make sure that they meet where they will be covered by another line of braid.

Graceful border pattern

The flowing lines of this design make an elegant border for a table cloth. The traced lines are covered with narrow braid which is sewn on with small backstitches.

Two joined side repeats
▼

Corner motif with two side repeats ▶

In a morning mood

Size: 35 cm x 50 cm ($13\frac{3}{4}$" x $19\frac{3}{4}$").

Materials Required: (For 3 table mats) Stranded cotton: 2 skeins brown, 2 skeins light grey. Linen blend, even-weave fabric: [26 threads to 2.5 cm (1")] 1.30 m ($1\frac{3}{8}$ yds), 90 cm (36") wide in salmon pink. Embroidery hoop.

Tracing the motif

Although this is a counted-thread design, it will help to trace the motif onto the fabric first. Half the motif is shown actual size on the right. Trace the whole motif with its centre line. Also, mark this centre line on the fabric with sewing thread along a straight woven thread.

Transfer the motif to the mat with dressmaker's carbon paper, making sure that the centre lines correspond exactly and the grain is absolutely straight. Position the centre line of the motif so that it begins and ends 5 cm (2") from each long edge, running parallel to one of the narrow sides and 10 cm (4") away from it.

Embroidering motif

Stretch the fabric in an embroidery hoop.

The two-tone embroidery motif is composed of intricate intertwined lines worked in double running stitch, or Holbein stitch as it is also known. This is a counted-thread stitch. For the place mats, it is worked over 4 threads of the weave or diagonally over 4 crossed threads using undivided stranded cotton.

Work as shown in the photographs on the right.

Making the mats

For each mat, cut out a piece of fabric 43 x 58 cm ($16\frac{3}{4}$" x $22\frac{3}{4}$"). Turn under a 2 cm ($\frac{3}{4}$") hem twice, mitre corners, slip-stitch. Press from the wrong side with a moderate iron.

These traditional mats enhance a lovely wooden table and elegant china. The geometric motif is worked on an easy-to-wash linen blend fabric.

Half the motif is given actual size with its centre line. Complete when tracing.

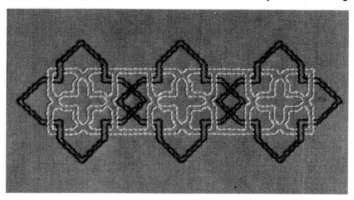

Here is a detail of the whole motif showing the interlaced lines in double running stitch. Make sure they cross one another correctly for a uniform pattern.

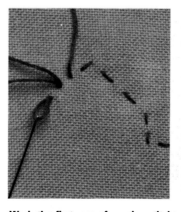

Work the first row of running stitch over 4 threads of fabric horizontally and vertically and over 4 crossed threads of fabric diagonally.

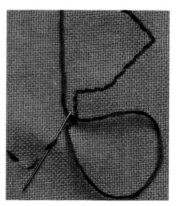

With the second row of running stitches, fill in the spaces left by the first row, inserting the needle into the fabric as shown.

77

In cut work

Heirloom embroidery

A fine tablecloth worthy of the true connoisseur of embroidery. This form of cut work is also called Richelieu embroidery after Cardinal Richelieu, Minister to King Louis XIII of France.

Size: 125 cm (49″) square.
Materials Required:
Stranded embroidery cotton: 3 skeins white. White linen: 140 cm (54″) wide, 1.90 m (2⅛ yd).

Making the cloth
Cut a 110 cm (43″) square; the rest is for the border. Trace and transfer the motifs onto the fabric, positioning them 7 cm (2¾″) from the edges. Centre the main motif on each side, placing the pointed motif at the corners and the linking motifs in between.
Work the preliminary outline stitches and the bars (including the stitches over the bars) with one strand of cotton. Cover the outlines with closely worked buttonhole stitch, using two strands of cotton. Finally, cut out the centre of the motifs with bars and the large oval in the main motif.

Making the border
Cut four strips, 18 cm (7″) wide, the length of the cloth plus 18 cm (7″) for the corners. Stitch the strips onto the cloth, right sides together, with a 1 cm (⅜″) seam allowance. Mitre the corners very accurately. Fold the strips in half lengthwise, and finish on the wrong side of the cloth by turning under the raw edges and slip-stitching to the seam by hand.

Cut work

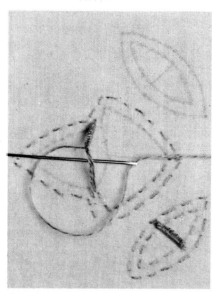

1 Outline the motifs with 2 rows of running stitches. On coming to the position for a bar, take the thread across the motif and back 3 times. Work the bar in buttonhole stitch to make it firm.

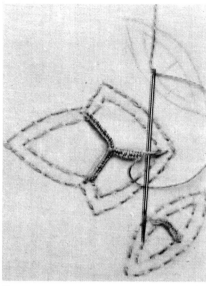

2 On completing the first bar, continue working running stitch to the next bar. Fasten this connecting bar to the centre of the already completed bar and buttonhole stitch around it as before.

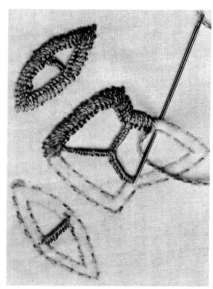

3 Embroider the outlines of the motifs with closely-worked buttonhole stitch, thus covering the preliminary running stitches.

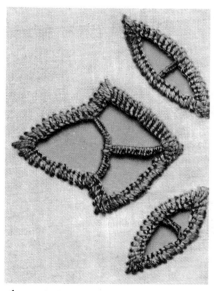

4 After completing all the motifs around the cloth, cut away the fabric from the centre very carefully with sharp-pointed scissors.

Linkin

Corner Motif

Motif

Main Motif

Cutwork border

Embroider this delicate pattern around the edge of a tablecloth and create a beautiful family heirloom to treasure.

For clothes, tablecloths, and bed linen **Add a coloured border**

If you are a romantic at heart, then these embroidered borders will appeal to you. Choose your favourite motif—the simple flowers, the intricate arabesques, or the stylized bouquets — then add a scalloped border.

The petals and leaves of these small flowers are worked in satin stitch. They look charming around the yoke of a dress or blouse and can be repeated at the edge of the sleeves.

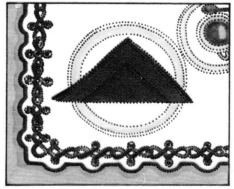

A border of arabesques has a timeless beauty. It looks decorative on place mats, but could equally well be worked all around the edge of a tablecloth. The border is worked in satin stitch.

Plain white pillows are given an individual touch with a border of stylized bouquets worked in lazy daisy or detached chain stitch. They would make a guest room look charming and inviting.

These sprays of roses are worked in satin stitch, the rows of dots around the edge in French knots. They make a delightful border on the turn-over of a sheet for a child's bed. The scalloped edge on the borders is worked in buttonhole stitch.

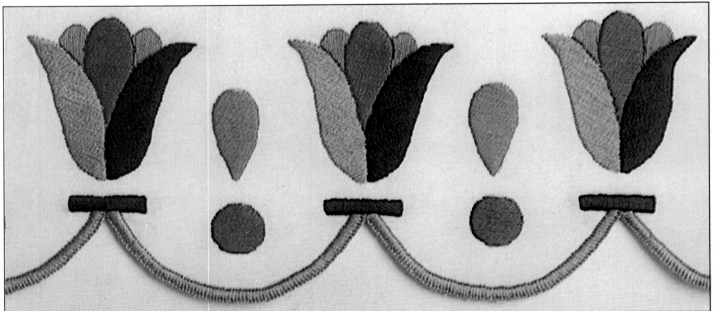

The stylized tulips are worked in satin stitch, using several different colours of stranded cotton. The decorative scallops are worked in buttonhole stitch.

84

Materials Required:

Stranded embroidery cotton in the following colours and quantities for 40 cm (15¾") of border. Purple border: 1 skein purple, ½ skein green. Red border: 2 skeins red. Blue border: ½ skein each of pale blue and dark blue. Pink border: 1 skein salmon pink, ½ skein green. Tulip border: 1 skein each of pale blue, dark blue, pale green, and dark green. Fabric: Any closely-woven cotton or linen.

Tracing the borders

The pattern shows a section of each border including a corner. Before you transfer the border onto the fabric, work out the required length and adjust so that the repeated motifs meet exactly at the corners. Transfer with dressmaker's carbon paper.

Working the embroidery

Purple border: Work the petals and leaves in satin stitch with 2 strands, the stems in stem stitch with 3 strands and the dots in French knots.

Red border: Work in satin stitch with 2 strands.

Blue border: The petals and leaves are lazy daisies, the dots are French knots, all using 2 strands. The inner scallops are worked in satin stitch with 3 strands.

Rose border: Work the petals and leaves in satin stitch with 2 strands, the French knots with 3 strands.

Tulip border: All the motifs are worked in satin stitch with 2 strands. Use diagonal stitches for the outer petals, horizontal stitches for the centre petal and the small motifs, and vertical stitches for the small petals and the lines above the scallops.

Scalloped edges: The outer edges are worked with 3 strands in buttonhole stitch over a running stitch outline filled with padding stitches. Cut away fabric carefully close to stitches.

Embroidery on borders

Looped motifs in satin stitch

1 Work around the double lines of the motifs, but where one line crosses under another, leave a space and continue on the other side. The space will be filled in later.

2 As you continue around, you will meet lines that are already embroidered. Do not embroider over them, but continue working on the other side of them. Where the lines cross, the stitches will lie in opposite directions, to give the impression of a looped ribbon.

Lines of French knots

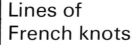

1 Bring the thread through the fabric and wind it three times around the needle tip from front to back. The working thread must be held taut while making the knot.

2 Still holding the thread, insert again close to where it first emerged. Bring the needle out at the next dot and continue as before.

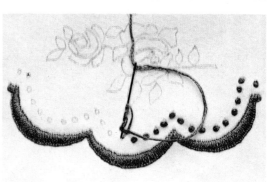

Scalloped borders

Give a colourful finish to clothes and linens with one of these five decorative edgings.

Potato printing on tablecloths, place mats, napkins

Colour and imagination are all you need

Two rows of apples edge the place mat. A subtle effect is produced by using a stamp several times without dipping it in the paint.

◀ Print place cards with the same motif as the tablecloth.

Potato printing is an effective way of making pretty designs from simple shapes. The most obvious shapes to work with are straight-sided geometric ones such as squares, rectangles, triangles, stars, or bars. But with a little more care you can cut round or oval motifs into the potatoes. The effect is created by the regular repetition of the shapes, which can be placed on top of or beside each other.

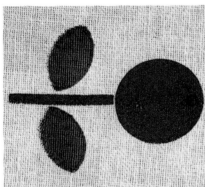

Choosing the materials

To make the stamps, choose large potatoes which are really firm and fresh. You can print onto most kinds of fabric and paper. The most suitable fabric for a tablecloth is cotton or a cotton/linen blend. Coarse weaves or very textured fabrics will distort the design. Fabric with dressing or sizing on it should be washed before being printed because part of the colour will dissolve along with the dressing or sizing at the first wash and the design will become fuzzy at the edges.

Cover the working surface with a plastic cloth or a large clean sheet of paper.

For the stamp pad, stretch a piece of felt over half the area of a wooden board; the other half can be used as a cutting board for the potatoes.

Arranging motifs

Potato printing is especially decorative on place mats, napkins, tablecloths and runners, curtains, or cards, where the motif appears several times. In repeat patterns — where the motif recurs at regular intervals — mark the position of each motif with light pencil lines and a ruler. Or baste a strip of paper along the edge of the fabric, just below the border, marking on it the shapes and colours.

◀ Here are some motifs for a children's party table. They are all made up of simple shapes which you can draw and transfer onto a paper template with dressmaker's carbon paper before cutting into the potato stamp.

Materials for potato printing:
1. A small sharp knife.
2. Very fresh potatoes.
3. Permanent fabric printing colours.
4. Turpentine.
5. Several small pots for mixing paints (egg cups, yoghurt pots, etc.).
6. A glass for the turpentine – to clean the brushes between colours.
7. Fabric scraps for printing tests.
8. Inexpensive paint brushes: one for each colour.
9. A fine-tipped pen.
10. White paper. Paper towels.
11. A ruler and compass for marking the position of the motifs. Scissors.
12. A clean working surface.
13. Tracing paper and dressmaker's carbon paper for transferring the motifs.
14. Pins or tacks to secure fabric.
15. Various shapes (pastry cutters, film tins, etc.)

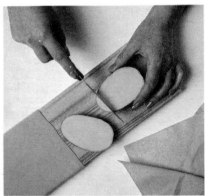

4 Cut the potato straight down the middle, round it off, and leave it to dry on paper towels.

8 Print one shape close to the next one until the motif is complete. Let each layer dry before overprinting.

Potato printing

1 Permanent fabric printing colours come in a wide range of shades which will create bright motifs.

2 Assemble all of the working materials. Use large kidney-shaped potatoes for the printing.

3 The motif can be sketched or transferred onto white paper. Draw round it and cut out.

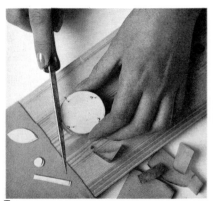

5 Pin the paper design to the flat surface of the potato and cut around it for a cleanly-shaped stamp.

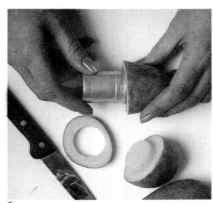

6 For a circle, dig an old film tin into the potato. Cut away the surrounding ring of potato.

7 Spread paint onto the felt; allow it to be absorbed. Press the stamp onto the felt, then onto the fabric.

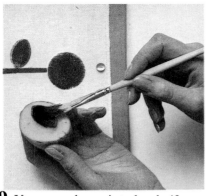

9 You can also print clearly if you paint the colour onto the stamp with a paint brush.

10 Press the printed parts on the wrong side with a hot iron. This fixes the colour to the fabric.

Hints

Keep a different stamp for each colour, to avoid creating muddy-looking mixtures of colours.

Printing errors: slightly irregular motifs can look just as pretty as very regular ones. Obvious mistakes can be painted with white fabric colour and reprinted when dry.

Submerge potato stamps in cold water to keep them fresh. They will keep for one to two days in the refrigerator.

Let freshly-cut stamps dry for a while before beginning to print. Dry stamps print more clearly.

Hemstitch is now rarely used in its
original form to simply sew
a hem. Instead, it is used as
a decorative stitch
in drawn-thread embroidery.

Drawnwork to enhance beautiful linens

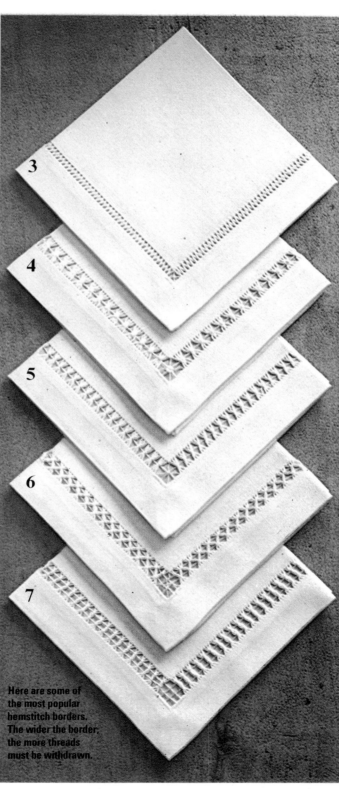

Here are some of the most popular hemstitch borders. The wider the border, the more threads must be withdrawn.

Hemstitch and needle-weaving are the two techniques used in drawnwork.

It gives a distinctive decorative finish to table linens, clothes, and accessories.

Size: The finished size of the place mats is 30 x 40 cm (11¾" x 15¾"). The napkins are 30 cm (11¾") square. Cut out the pieces along the grain of the fabric to measure 40 x 50 cm (15¾" x 19¾") and 40 cm (15¾") square respectively. This includes twice the 2.5 cm (1") hem allowance to make a double turning. The first turning can be slightly narrower if necessary.

Materials Required: Medium-weight even-weave linen. White stranded embroidery cotton (use 4 strands or match the thickness of the linen threads).

Drawing the threads

Mark the position of the hem and the drawn-thread areas on the wrong side of the fabric with pins or fine pencil lines. The outer drawn threads will be about 7.5 cm (3") in from the edges. The width of the drawn-thread areas on Nos. 1–3 is 0.5 cm (¼"), on Nos. 4–7, 1 cm (⅜").

Draw out the threads. On the place mats, the drawn threads cross at the corners and extend to the edges of the fabric, so draw the threads from the outside inward. On the napkins and inside the place mats, where the drawn threads do not extend to the edges, cut the outer thread in the middle and draw out to both sides as far as the marks. Continue withdrawing threads until the open area is the required width. Either weave in the ends of the threads invisibly or cut off the fabric thread ends and finish the edges with buttonhole or overcasting stitch. Mitre the corners; turn under the hem.

Embroidering

Work hemstitch along the top and bottom of the drawn-thread areas. In Nos. 2 and 3, group four threads together; for the rest, group three threads together. In No. 1 use ladder hemstitch. The squares inside the border are worked in overcast bars. No. 2 is overcast ladder hemstitch. No. 3 is zigzag hemstitch. For Nos. 4–7, the thread groups are tied in a decorative way. Three groups are connected in Nos. 5 and 7, four in Nos. 4 and 6.
Fill in the empty corners on the narrow designs with crossed threads. The larger corners are filled in with several crossed threads in a design matching the style of the work. Do not pull these threads too tight.

Making the hem

Turn under the hem before working the outer row of hemstitch. The hem edge is then caught in with the stitching. On the place mats, work the small designs inside the main border areas, then work the border and the hem. At the corners, the hemstitching or overcasting will be worked over three layers of fabric.

Drawn-thread embroidery

Plain hemstitch

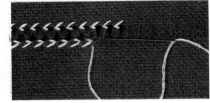

1 Work from left to right on the wrong side of the fabric. Pass the needle from right to left behind the required number of threads.

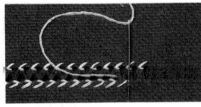

2 Insert the needle at the same point, going two fabric threads down. For ladder hemstitch, repeat on the other side with the same groups.

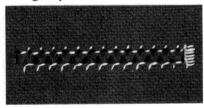

3 Zigzag hemstitch (right side): work over an even number of threads. On opposite side, each group is made up of ½ the threads from two adjacent groups.

4 Corners are finished with close buttonhole stitch. To fill corners, stretch the thread over crosswise several times and buttonhole-stitch over middle to form a cross.

Hemstitch variations

1 Gather several groups of threads together and fasten them with a slip knot. To do this, form a loop with the thread and, with the needle above the loop, pass it behind the groups. Bring it out inside the loop and pull the thread carefully to tighten the knot so that the distance between the groups is equal. You can work this stitch from either side of the fabric.

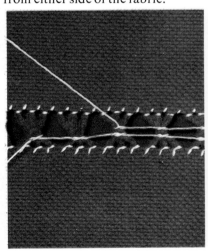

2 Work two rows of slip knots in the same way. Work from right to left and from either side of the fabric at equal intervals. Napkin border No. 7 is worked with this decorative stitch.

Mark the length and width of the drawn-thread areas on the wrong side of the fabric. Draw out the threads, then embroider the remaining threads with hemstitch variations.

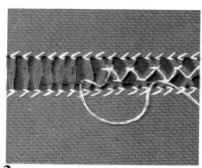

3a For a double zigzag effect, thread groups are joined in a staggered formation. Because the working thread runs from one slip knot to another, the stitches must be worked from the wrong side. Pass the needle behind two thread groups about one third up from the base to begin this stitch.

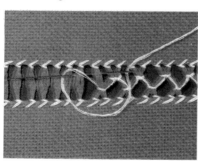

3b Loop the thread up and around to form another slip knot, passing the needle behind the last group and the next group along, about two thirds up from the base. Pull the knot tight.

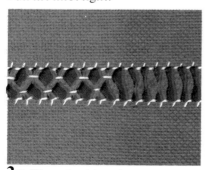

3c The double zigzag as seen from the right side of the fabric.

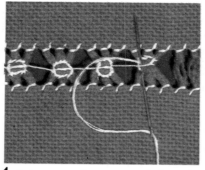

4 Join several groups of threads with slip stitches, then work small circles in the centre in stem stitch or backstitch.

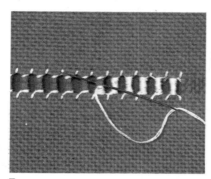

5 The groups of threads in ladder hemstitch can be closely overcast to form wrapped bars.

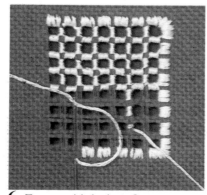

6 For a grid design, first overcast the raw edges closely. Then overcast the remaining horizontal and vertical threads firmly to form wrapped bars, giving a trellis effect.

Forming hem and corners

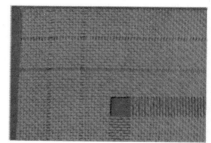

1 Allow three times the required width of the hem (for the double turning and the front). Mark the fold lines on heavy linen by drawing a thread along them and on fine linen with a pencil line. Withdraw the threads.

2 To mitre the corners neatly, fold them in once so that the marked lines meet. Cut off the corner points evenly at the inner turning line.

3 Now turn the hem under twice and baste it in place. Slip-stitch the mitred corners together. Catch in the edges of the hem as you work the hemstitch.

The traditional blue onion design has been reproduced for you as an embroidery pattern for a white tablecloth. Set a festive table with a pretty blue-and-white tea set.

Embroidery in blue

Materials Required: Stranded cotton: 11 skeins dark blue, 5 skeins pale blue. Linen tablecloth.

Embroidering the motifs
Mark the centre of the cloth with horizontal and vertical lines of basting stitches in pastel-colored thread. Trace the motifs and transfer them onto the linen with dressmaker's carbon paper. The large floral motif is positioned in the centre and the small onion motifs form a border. On the cloth illustrated, the distance from the centre to the border is 44 cm (17½") on the long sides and 25 cm (10") on the short sides. The onion motifs are about 2 cm (¾") apart. Arrange the small flower motifs inside the border. Work the outlines in stem stitch and fill in the leaves and flowers with satin stitch worked in the colours shown in the illustrations.

The graceful flower motif is worked with subtle shading in only two blues.

Traditional floral motifs

The graceful forms of the blue onion pattern make a striking decoration when used singly or as border repeats.

Curtains and Blinds

If you can sew, you can make curtains,
but here are some ideas
which are different for window coverings.
Try making a bead curtain
for instance – or a roller blind.
Or, if crochet is your craft, make your
own curtain mesh or a beautiful lace
edging for fabric curtains.

Three edgings to crochet
Beautiful borders

For the prettiest windows imaginable, why not trim the edges of your curtains with one of three crocheted edgings, made in cotton.

Edging 1: The band and scallops are worked together in one continuous piece.

Size: The edgings measure about 10 cm or 4″ wide.

Materials Required:

Crochet cotton. These can be worked in various thicknesses but the amounts of cotton will vary from 35–50 gm per metre or 1–2 oz per yard, depending on the thickness. For No. 5 cotton, use a 1.00 crochet hook.

Basic Pattern: As shown in each Crochet Diagram.

Abbreviations: Ch = chain. Dc = double crochet. Tr = treble. R = row(s).

DIRECTIONS

Work a test piece first. Pin it out well in length and width and dampen it lightly. This is the best way to judge the length you will require.

Edging 1: Follow Crochet Diagram 1. This shows the edging from the right side, so follow the diagram in the direction of the small arrows. At the end of R 4, begin first scallop thus: Make 6 ch. In R 5 work 1 tr into the last tr of the 4th R. In R 6 work 13 tr into ch loop, joining the last one with a slip stitch onto the last tr of R 4. Now work over the turning ch of R 3 with slip sts and work back in pattern as shown in diagram. In this way the scallop is enlarged up to R 9. Work R 10–15, then repeat from R 6.

Edging 2: The border is worked first in a straight strip in tr and ch and the pointed picot edge worked on one side later. Owing to the increases at the points, this edging has the appearance of a frill. Work from Crochet Diagram 2. Crochet the straight strip, repeating R 2 and 3 of diagram and follow the direction of the arrows. Then crochet the pointed edge, working in R. Note that the beginning and end of R are given, with the center repeated the number of times required.

Edging 3: Follow Crochet Diagram 3. This shows edging from the right side, so follow the diagram in the direction of the small arrows. Work to end of R 8, then make 14 ch and join with a slip st to R 6. Now make 2 ch and work 1 dc into turning ch of R 5. Work 24 tr in ch loop and join to R 9. Continue thus, increasing the scallop to R 13. Repeat R 2–13 as required.

Crochet Diagram 1: The diagram shows the edging from the right side, so follow the diagram in the direction of the small arrows. Begin to work the scallop at the end of R 4, enlarging it to R 9 as shown. Work R 10–15 as shown, then repeat from R 6 to work the next scallop as before.

✳

Symbols for all diagrams

- • = chain
- ⌒ = slip stitch
- ᐯ = double crochet
- ꓲ = treble
- o = picot (4 chain, then 1 double crochet back into the first chain)

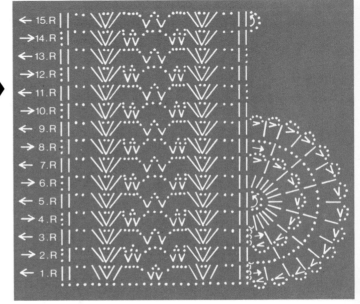

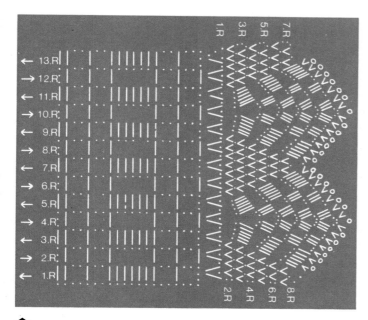

Crochet Diagram 2: First, crochet the straight band by repeating R 2 and 3 of the diagram. The diagram shows the edging from the right side, so follow the diagram in the direction of the small arrows. Then, crochet the pointed edge, working back and forth in rows. The Crochet Diagram gives the beginning and end of each row; repeat the center as many times as required.

Crochet Diagram 3: The diagram shows the edging from the right side, so follow the diagram in the direction of the small arrows. Begin to work the scallop at the end of R 8, enlarging it to R 13 as shown. Work R 14–20 as shown, then work the next scallop as before, to length required.

Edging 2: The straight band is worked first, then the pointed picot edge is added.

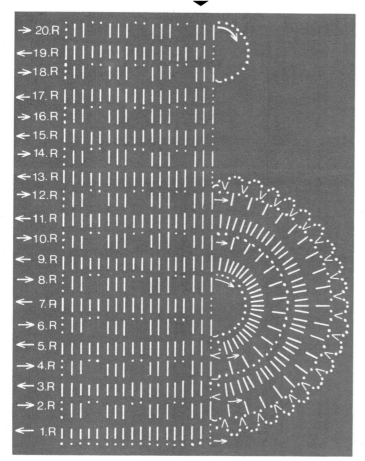

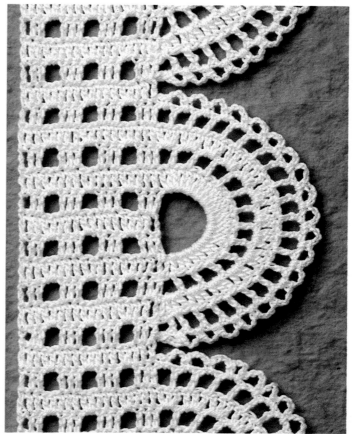

Edging 3: This design is worked as one continuous piece; see diagram left.

Pretty and practical
Give your home a face lift

Roller blinds are an attractive alternative to curtains and are often more practical for kitchen and bathroom windows or windows of an awkward shape. The most suitable fabrics are smooth, firm ones such as linen, canvas, and cotton, although finer fabrics can be successful if handled with care. Plastic fabrics are ideal for kitchens and bathrooms as they withstand splashes and can be wiped clean. Loosely-woven or very thick fabrics should be avoided.

Roller blind kits are available complete with a roller, a lath for the lower edge, brackets, and fittings. To calculate the width required, decide first whether it is to hang inside or outside the window recess. If it hangs inside the recess, measure the recess area. If it is to hang outside, add about 15 cm (6") to the outside measurement of the window frame. The fabric width should be about 2.5 cm (1") less than the roller, so that it does not catch on the brackets at either side. For the length, add 8–10 cm (3–4") to allow for the roller and 4–5 cm (1½–2") for the lath casing. When making up the blind, be sure to fix it to the roller the correct way. Usually the fabric hangs close to the window and behind the roll, but, with special brackets, the position of the spring can be altered to allow the fabric to roll the other way. The 'acorn' or ring by which the blind is pulled down may be attached to the lath or to the casing with a cord or a strip of matching fabric.

Making the blinds

1: **Materials Required:** Main fabric: Cotton/linen mixture to fit width of window. Insertion: Strips of cotton lace.

Cut out the main fabric to size, allowing 1 cm (⅜") at each side and at the lower edge, and 8–10 cm (3–4") at the upper edge. For the lath casing, cut a strip of fabric, 8 cm (3") wide and long enough to fit the width of the blind plus 2 cm (¾") seam allowance. Pin the strips of lace insertion at regular intervals to the right side of the fabric and stitch along the outer edges. From the wrong side, cut the fabric behind the lace centrally up its length and press apart. Stitch over the edges from the right side, this time with zigzag stitch, then cut away the fabric close to the stitching on the wrong side.

Finish the raw edges at the top and sides with zigzag stitch. Turn the sides under once and stitch down. On the casing for the lath, press under 1 cm (⅜") on the short sides. Stitch to the blind, right sides together, with a 1 cm (⅜") seam allowance. Fold the casing in half, turning under the seam allowance at the back. Stitch down 0.5 cm (¼") from the seam allowance fold edge.

2: **Materials Required:** Striped canvas or ticking.
Cut out the fabric as given for the main fabric for Style 1. Then calculate the number of complete scallops required for the width of one window.

Make a template for one scallop and mark the scallops along the edge of the fabric. Add a 0.5 cm ($\frac{1}{4}$″) seam allowance at the lower edge. Cut a facing for the scalloped edge, wide enough to form a case for the lath at the upper edge of the scallops. Finish the upper edge, the sides, and the casing with zigzag stitch. Turn under sides and stitch. Stitch the facing to the scalloped edge right sides together and turn to the right side. Join the upper edge of the casing to the blind.

3: Materials Required:
Flower-printed cotton.
Allow an extra 1 cm ($\frac{3}{8}$″) at the sides, 4 cm ($1\frac{5}{8}$″) for the hem and 8–10 cm (3–4″) at the top. Finish the raw edges at sides and top. Turn the sides under and stitch. Make a casing 3 cm ($1\frac{1}{4}$″) wide for the lath and attach as for Style 1.

4: Materials Required:
Cotton lace curtain fabric.
Cut out as for main fabric, Style 1, allowing an extra 8–10 cm (3–4″) at the top. The fabric illustrated does not fray if the lace motifs remain intact in cutting out. The casing here is made from a row of motifs. Turn under a hem on each side and stitch to the wrong side of the blind, leaving a scalloped edge of motifs at the bottom. With a fraying fabric, a casing made as for Styles 1 or 3 would be more suitable.

5: Materials Required:
Gingham-check fabric.
Follow the instructions for Style 3.

106

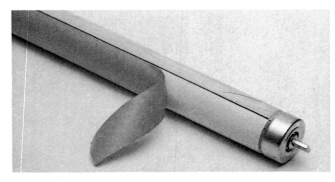

To secure the fabric initially, stick double-sided adhesive tape to the length of the roller. Remove the paper backing and line up the edge of the fabric with the edge of the tape. Press the fabric down firmly.

Secure the fabric to the roller with closely-spaced tacks, making sure that the fabric will roll up and down in the correct direction for the position of the spring.

Insert the lath into the casing at the lower edge of the blind. The lath ensures that the fabric hangs well and gives a rigid support when raising or lowering the blind.

The brackets are fixed to each side of the window frame. The spring tension at the side of the roller may need to be adjusted at first. The roller blind shown here rolls away from the window, but many roll toward the window.

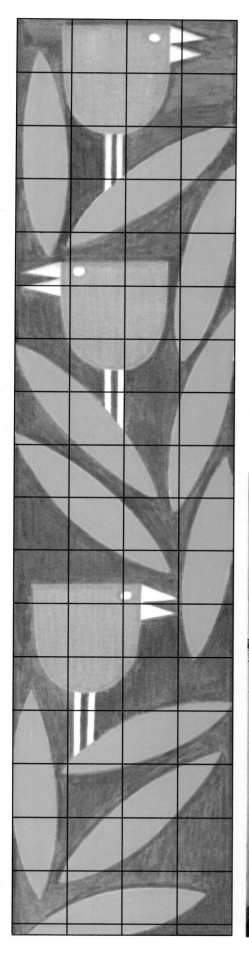

A bead curtain to let in fresh air

A bead curtain is marvellous for summer. Hang it in the doorway to your garden or balcony and it will allow the air to circulate while keeping the flies out. Or use it indoors to partition rooms with a bold splash of colour. Our bead curtain has a design of stylized birds and leaves. The pattern is created by threading the beads of different colours onto lengths of string over an actual-size drawing. It's a simple technique and even children will love to try it.

The method of working the bead curtain is explained overleaf.

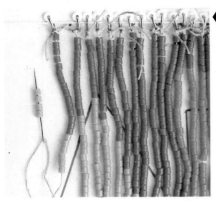

The lengths of fine string are knotted onto the runners or hooks. The beads are threaded with a needle, following the design which lies underneath. Try to keep the shapes as near as possible to the pattern.

For a good overall impression as the curtain progresses, work only 50 cm (19½″) at a time. After threading each group of strings, hold them together in bundles, winding the strings around a nail.

Secure the strands by bringing up each string and tying a knot between the last bead and the bead before it.

Here is a detail of the curtain showing part of a bird's head. The strands should lie close together during the work.

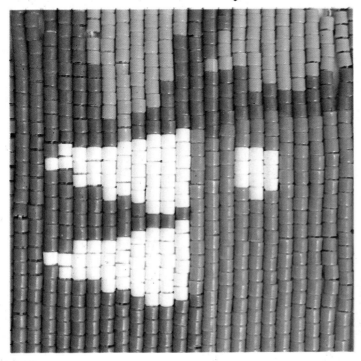

Size: When pushed closely together, the bead curtain measures 2.10 m (2¼ yd) long by 48 cm (19″) wide. If it is hung loosely, it will cover a doorway measuring 70 cm (27½″) wide. For a closer pattern or for a wider doorway, just add a few more rows of background.

Materials Required: Curtain rail measuring the same as width of the doorway. Curtain runners or hooks. Strong, fine string. Large-eyed needle. A few long nails. Cylindrical porcelain beads in dark blue, medium blue, pale green, and white.

Making the curtain

Enlarge the design from the graph pattern. The actual-size pattern will lie underneath the strings for a guide as you work. The curtain is most easily worked on a large piece of board or on the floor. Spread out the pattern and fasten the curtain rail at the top end with a few nails so that it does not shift.

Cut the string into lengths which measure the same as the height of the doorway, adding about 30 cm (12″) for the knots at beginning and end. Fasten the strings to the runners or hooks with double knots, then slide them onto the curtain rail and attach stoppers at either end. To prevent the strings from getting tangled as you work, divide them into small groups and wind the ends round a nail when you are not using them (see the second picture on the left). The runners or hooks should be up against one another as you thread the beads.

Beginning at one side, take one string from the first group and thread the beads according to the pattern underneath until the string of beads is 50 cm (19½″) long. Keep pushing the beads firmly upward. Work strand after strand of the first group in this way. Then wind the strings back around the nail. Continue threading beads onto all the strings of the other groups until each strand of beads is 50 cm (19½″). Thread a further 50 cm (19½″) on each string and continue in this way until the whole curtain length has been completed. As you work, keep comparing the strands of beads with the design.

When all the beads are in place, push the beads on each strand firmly upward. Bring each string up and tie a secure knot between the last bead and the bead before it, as shown in the third picture, left. Do not cut off the string at the bottom of the strands immediately. When the curtain has been hanging up for a while, the string will stretch slightly and then you can make any necessary adjustments.

To keep the strands equi-distant, knot the runners or hooks together at 1 cm (⅜″) intervals.

The curtain rail can be painted so that it blends in with the door frame.

Enlarge your pattern for the bead curtain from the graph page 107. Divide a large piece of paper, measuring about 2.10 m (2¼ yd) long by 0.5 m (½ yd) wide, into 12 cm (4¾″) squares. Draw the outlines of the design onto the paper, so that they cross the squares in the same places as on the graph pattern.

Rosy nostalgia

Old-fashioned roses crocheted into curtain panels add a touch of nostalgia to windows.

A pair of curtains look pretty on a front door, adding an old-fashioned touch. They can also be lengthened or widened to any size by simply adding more motifs.

Size: 28 cm (11") wide and 58 cm (22¾") long.

Materials Required:

150 gm or 6 oz white [50 gm = 300 m or 330 yds]. Crochet hook size 2.00.

Basic Pattern: For the bar and space pattern, tr and ch are worked alternately. For the blocks, work in tr substituting tr for ch to fill in the spaces.

Tension: 35 sts and 17 R = 10 cm or 4".

Abbreviations: St(s) = stitch(es). R = row(s). Ch = chain. Tr = treble stitch.

DIRECTIONS

Make 101 ch. R 1: Work tr into 4th ch from hook and in each ch to end — 99 sts. Turn with 3 ch. R 2 (right side): 1 tr, (1 tr, 1 ch, skip 1 tr) 5 times, 6 tr, (1 tr, 1 ch, skip 1 tr, 10 tr) 5 times, 1 tr, 1 ch, skip 1 tr, 6 tr, (1 tr, 1 ch, skip 1 tr) 5 times, 3 tr, turn with 3 ch. R 3–6: Follow photograph for pattern, turning each R with 3 ch. R 7: 8 tr, 1 ch, skip 1 tr, 4 tr, then (1 tr, 1 ch, skip 1 tr) 35 times, 5 tr, skip 1 tr, 1 ch, 9 tr. Continue to follow photograph, working the Rose pattern 3 times (or more if a longer curtain is required), then work border in reverse (in other words, from 7th–1st R). Fasten off. Block and steam lightly.

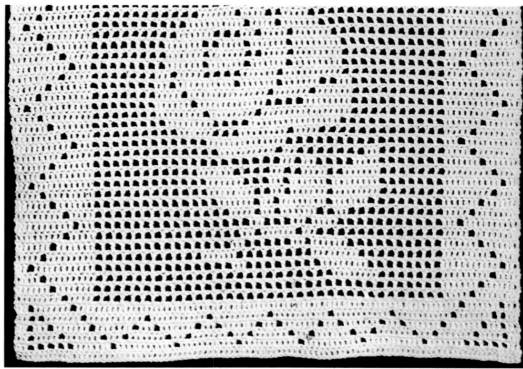

You can easily work the border pattern and rose design repeat by counting the stitches in this photograph row by row.

A window on the world

Curtains give character to a room, and our mesh pattern will prove invaluable as a filter for sunlight without shutting you off from the world.

Size: 200 cm x 160 cm or 79" x 63".

Materials Required:

650 gm or 23 oz white. Crochet hook size 3.00.

Basic Pattern: Number of ch sts divisible by 5, plus 2 and an extra 3 ch for turning. R 1: Work 1 tr into 4th ch from hook, then 1 tr into each ch to end, turn with 5 ch. R 2: 1 long-tr (yarn over hook 4 times, and work off 2 loops at a time) into next tr. * 5 ch, skip 4 tr, 1 long-tr into next tr, repeat from *, ending 1 long-tr into last tr, turn with 5 ch. R 3: 1 long-tr into next long-tr, *5 ch, skip 5-ch space, 1 long-tr on long-tr, repeat from *, ending 1 long-tr into top of turning ch, turn with 5 ch. Repeat R 3.

Tension: 22 sts and 3½ R = 10 cm or 4".

Abbreviations: Ch = chain. St(s) = stitch(es). Tr = treble. R = row(s).

DIRECTIONS

The curtain is worked crosswise. Make 425 ch and work 160 cm or 63" straight in Basic Pattern, then work 4 tr into each ch-loop and long-tr on long-tr. Fasten off.

Finishing: Pin out curtain, dampen, and leave to dry.

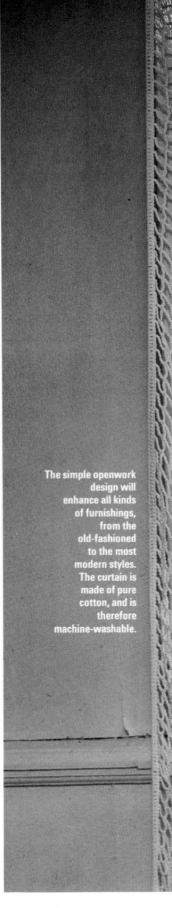

The simple openwork design will enhance all kinds of furnishings, from the old-fashioned to the most modern styles. The curtain is made of pure cotton, and is therefore machine-washable.

The pattern of bars is simple to crochet and produces a very durable curtain despite the delicate outer appearance.

Kitchen
curtains in

Barber pole stripes

The finished size of *each* curtain of the pair should be the same as the height by the width of the area to be covered (this allows for fullness when the curtain is closed). Make a diagram of the two curtain halves, side by side, so the stripes will be continuous when the curtains are pulled across the window. Enlarge the diagram to actual size and make tissue paper pattern pieces, adding 1 cm ($\frac{3}{8}$″) seam allowance, 2 cm ($\frac{3}{4}$″) for sides and top, and 4 cm (1$\frac{1}{2}$″) for hem at bottom. To determine the amount of fabric required for each colour, arrange strips side by side and end to end to work out the most economical width and length of fabric to use. Pin pieces along the lengthwise threads of the fabric and cut out the strips. With right sides together, pin and stitch the strips. Finish all raw seam allowance edges with zigzag stitch. Press seam allowances toward the darker color.

Turn in allowance at side edges, turn under raw edge, and stitch in place. <u>Caution!</u> The fabric is cut on the bias along the outside edges, so don't stretch the fabric when stitching. Turn in allowances at top and bottom as for sides and stitch in place. If you wish to gather the curtains along the top, cut two pieces of elastic or bias tape which measure a little more than half the width of each curtain half. Pull one piece through the casing formed at the top of each curtain half and stitch to curtain half at each end. Arrange gathers evenly and sew on curtain rings.

Plan the curtains carefully before beginning. Draw diagrams of the curtains side by side so the stripes will be continuous when the curtains are closed.

114

Pictures to sew

Picture-making is a new craft.
Here are some delightful pictures for
you to work and frame
and some new and novel ideas
for refurbishing old frames and
bringing them up to date.

Canvaswork picture
Painting with a needle and yarn

Canvaswork has had a great
revival in popularity. But
don't stick to the well-worn
traditional designs; try your
hand at this winter scene.
All you need is canvas,
a needle, and a colourful yarn.

The picture is shown here on a graph:
Each square represents one stitch.
The materials required are double-thread
canvas and stranded embroidery cotton.

118

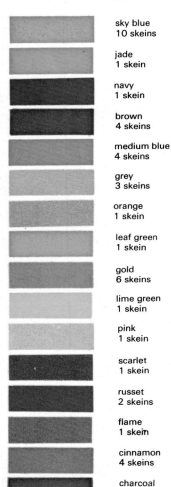

sky blue
10 skeins

jade
1 skein

navy
1 skein

brown
4 skeins

medium blue
4 skeins

grey
3 skeins

orange
1 skein

leaf green
1 skein

gold
6 skeins

lime green
1 skein

pink
1 skein

scarlet
1 skein

russet
2 skeins

flame
1 skein

cinnamon
4 skeins

charcoal
1 skein

white
12 skeins

120

Stretching the canvas on a frame

To ensure that the canvas keeps its shape, it is advisable to work on a frame. The right hand guides the needle above the frame, the left hand works beneath it.

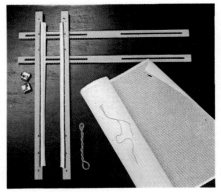

1 To work a canvaswork picture you will need canvas, an adjustable frame, and some strong thread.

Working tent stitch (without turning canvas)

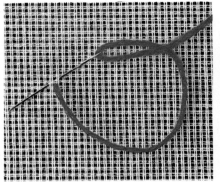

1 Right to left: insert the needle one hole up to the right.

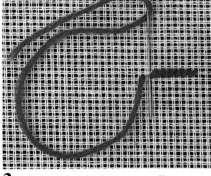

3 Row change: bring needle out at the base of the stitch before last.

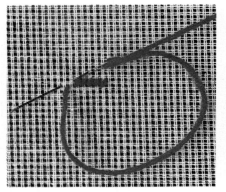

2 Bring needle out two holes down to left. Repeat across.

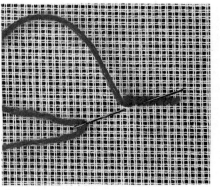

4 Left to right: needle goes in one down to left and out two up to right.

Canvaswork—Tent stitch, Preparing a tapestry frame

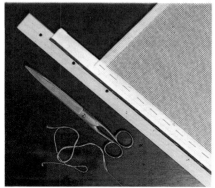

2 Turn under the canvas edges and sew the top and bottom edges to the taped bars, following the grain.

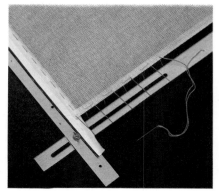

3 Assemble the frame and lace the canvas to the side bars of the frame, using strong thread.

4 Before beginning your picture, be sure that the canvas is taut and that the grain is straight.

Working a corner

5 Row change: bring the needle out at the hole below the last stitch.

1 Diagonally to the left: for a row change at the right, bring the needle out one hole down to the left.

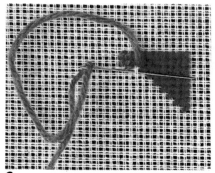

3 Diagonally to the right: for a row change, bring needle out one hole to the right.

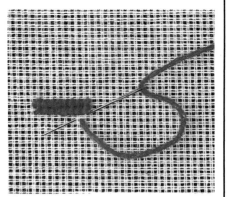

6 Continue as before, repeating steps one through five.

2 For a row change at the left, bring needle out at the base of the last stitch.

4 Continue by inserting the needle one hole down to the left, then two holes up to the right.

This idyllic country scene is embroidered in cross-stitch, following the chart overleaf. Surround it with a decorative border, and it's ready to frame and hang up.

Here's a delightful picture for you to embroider. The country scene has all the appeal of 'primitive' art with its bright colours, simple shapes, and bold composition. Give your friends a chance to appreciate your creative talents by framing your picture and hanging it in a prominent position.

*

Size: About 39 cm (15½'') wide by 25 cm (10'') high.

Materials Required: Stranded embroidery cotton: 1 skein each of the colors listed in the key overleaf. White Hardanger fabric or an even-weave fabric: 24 pairs of threads to 2.5 cm (1''). Heavy cardboard and ordinary straight pins for mounting.

Basic Stitch: The picture is worked in cross-stitch, using 2 strands of stranded cotton. Each square on the chart represents 1 cross-stitch worked over 2 double threads in height and width.

Making the picture

Cut out the fabric, adding 5 cm—10 cm (2''—4'') all around the picture area for turning back. Mark the centre of the fabric horizontally and verti-cally with running stitches. Work the picture according to the chart over-leaf, beginning at the centre. The colours are given on the key; white squares represent fabric which is not embroidered. When the main picture is complete, work the side panels and the border around the edge.

Mounting the picture

Press the embroidery from the wrong side on a well-padded surface. Press lightly so that the stitching will not be flattened.

Stretch the embroidery over the card-board and place pins into the edges at each corner to hold it in place. Pin the centres of the four sides, but do not push the pins all the way in until the piece has been completely moun-ted. Continue to pin the edges, dividing and subdividing the spaces between the pins until there is a border of pins around the cardboard 1 cm (⅜'') apart. Use a ruler to check that the lines of stitches are straight; adjust the pins if necessary. When the embroidery is in place, drive in all of the pins. Tape the fabric edges at the back or lace them together with long zigzag stitches. Frame the picture as desired.

Worked in cross-stitch

A pastoral scene

124

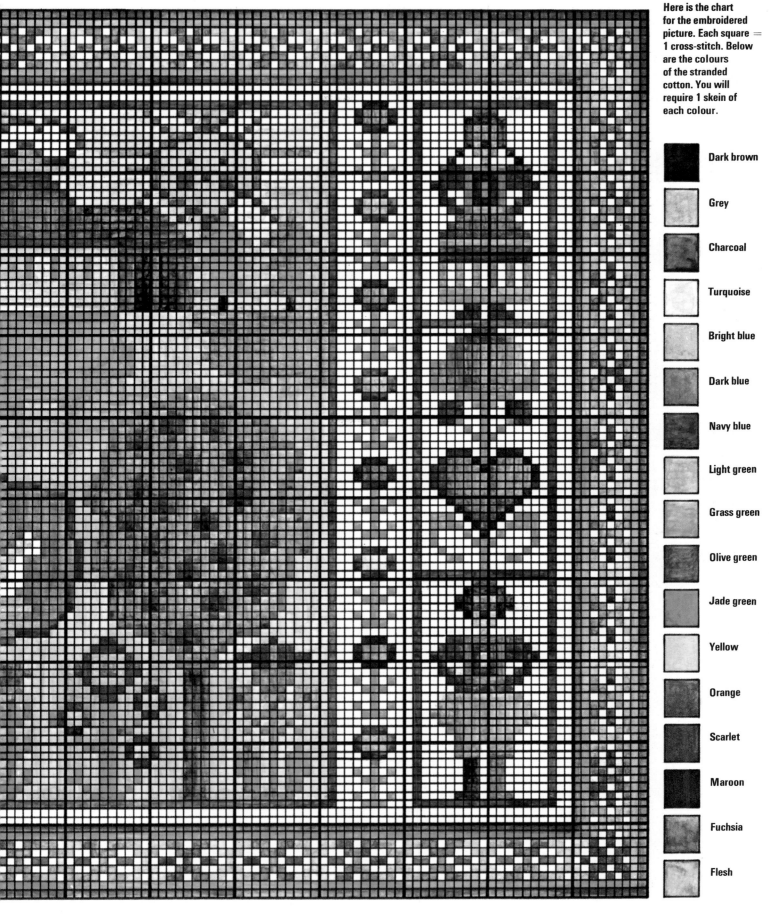

Here is the chart for the embroidered picture. Each square = 1 cross-stitch. Below are the colours of the stranded cotton. You will require 1 skein of each colour.

Dark brown

Grey

Charcoal

Turquoise

Bright blue

Dark blue

Navy blue

Light green

Grass green

Olive green

Jade green

Yellow

Orange

Scarlet

Maroon

Fuchsia

Flesh

125

3

It's a frame-up

7

8

12

13

16

Here are lots of bright ideas for revamping old picture frames or decorating new frames by picking out the colours in favourite pictures or photographs. We have ideas for all shapes and sizes of frame. All you need are enamel paints, brushes, a ruler, a pencil, masking tape, cardboard, and scissors.

1 Outline the inner edge of the frame with a narrow band of blue and a wide band of green. The rest of the frame is painted white with a blue surround.

2 First paint the yellow sides, then the dark green ones. The green stripes at the corners are painted over the yellow. Stick masking tape along the edges for straight lines.

3 Paint as for 1, using pink on the frame to pick out the pink dress in the picture.

4 Paint the whole frame green. Draw lines with a pencil and ruler and fill in the pink stripes.

5 Paint the whole frame green, then draw pencil lines all around it about $0.5\,\text{cm}$ ($\frac{1}{4}''$) apart. Fill in the stripes radiating from the center in black.

6 Paint the frame pale blue, then draw in the graduated stripes. Fill in the stripes with dark blue paint. The pale blue paint can be mixed from dark blue and white in equal proportions.

7 First paint the background in yellow, then stick masking tape on the frame in a zigzag pattern and paint over it in green. Remove the tape.

8 An attractive idea for a square frame. Paint the frame yellow. Then draw in diagonal lines with a pencil and ruler, and fill in the stripes in red.

9 Paint the background yellow. For the border, make a diamond-patterned stencil and fill in with red paint.

10 Divide the frame into quarters and, sticking masking tape where the edges meet, paint two quarters light green and two quarters dark green.

11 First paint the central area magenta, then the outer red parts. Stick masking tape at either side for the stripes and fill in with yellow paint.

12 For this unusual frame, first paint the background blue. Then cut a stencil for the star motif and paint on the white stars evenly around the frame.

13 Paint the whole frame green for the background. For stripes, stick on masking tape and fill in with blue.

14 Paint the frame green, then scatter little flowers over it by dotting them on in white and yellow with a fine brush.

15 Another idea for a square frame. Paint the background yellow, then stick two evenly-spaced rows of masking tape around it, stopping short at the outer corners. Fill in the stripes in purple.

16 First paint the frame pale blue. Then, using masking tape to outline the triangular shapes, fill in the medium blue areas next and finally the dark blue areas in the center.

Note: After painting your frame, leave it to dry, then give it a protective coat of varnish. Insert the picture and hang.

Rugmaking

Rugmaking is a homecraft
for all the family. Rugs can be hooked,
knotted, crocheted on canvas,
embroidered or braided in sisal.

Simply decide which technique you want
to try and then choose one of
these brilliant designs.

Rug tiles to sew together

A carpet crocheted on canvas

Colour variation: make a carpet in this sophisticated colour range of beiges and brown. It fits in well with both modern and traditional furniture and would complement a neutral decor. Here all of the tiles are in the same colour sequence. ▼

Size: The rug measures approximately 150 cm x 200 cm (60" x 80"). One complete tile measures approximately 25 cm (10") square.

Materials Required: Skeined rug yarn: 1500 gm or 53 oz dark green, 950 gm or 34 oz almond green, 750 gm or 28 oz beige. Crochet hook size H (Am) or 5.00 (Eng). Rug canvas: 120 cm

(48") wide, 3.60 m (4 yds).

Basic Pattern: Chain stitches crocheted onto a base of rug canvas. The working thread always remains underneath the canvas.

Colour Sequence 1: From the centre, work 7 rounds beige, 3 rounds each dark green, beige, dark green.

Colour Sequence 2: From the centre, work 7 rounds

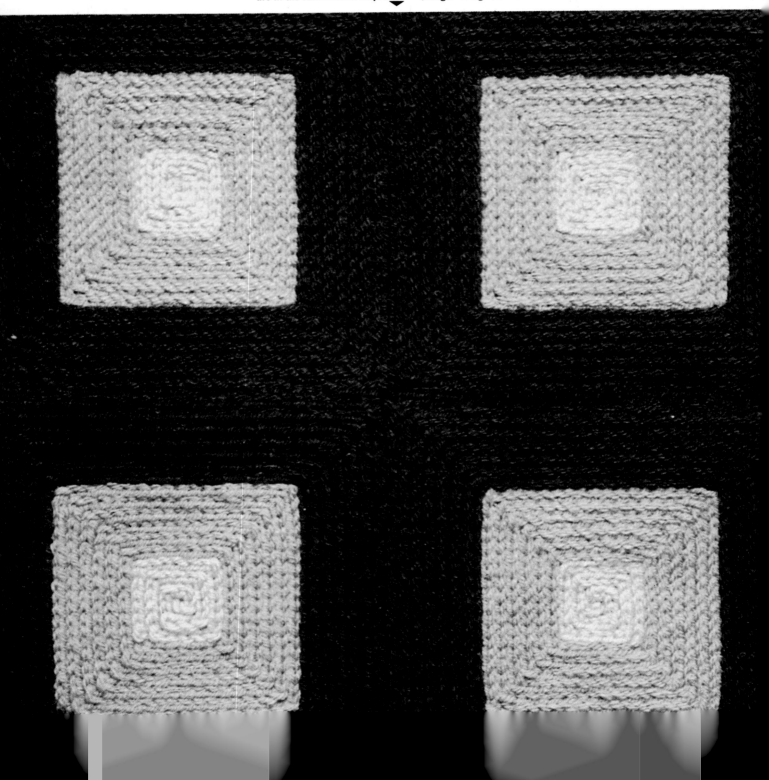

dark green, 3 rounds each almond green, dark green, almond green.

Making the rug

Cut out 48 pieces of canvas measuring 30 cm (12") square from the rug canvas. Work 24 tiles in each of the two colour sequences, turning under the edge in the last round and crocheting through the double layers of the canvas (see Crocheting on canvas How-to). Trim excess canvas, leaving one row of unworked squares all around.

Sew the completed tiles together from the wrong side, with overcasting stitch. Work with the appropriate yarn colour, splitting it into two strands, and passing it through each square of canvas along both edges.

Alternate the two colour combinations and make a rug six tiles in width and eight tiles in length.

Colour variation: the carpet shown here is worked in a more striking range of colours—black, maroon, and pink. This would be a dramatic floor-covering in a modern setting featuring chrome and glass-topped furniture.
▼

Crocheting on canvas, Joining squares

This unusual technique of crocheting carpet tiles on rug canvas is basically the same as tambour work embroidery on a large scale. The tiles, which are quick to work, are interchangeable and can be sewn together in any order to make a beautiful, hard-wearing floorcovering.

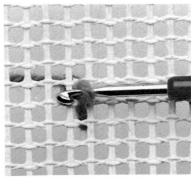

1 First make a slip knot and hold it under the canvas. Draw the loop through to the right side with the crochet hook.

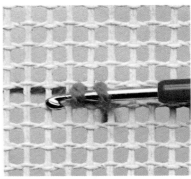

2 Insert the crochet hook into the next hole along and catch the yarn, drawing it through the first loop to make a chain stitch.

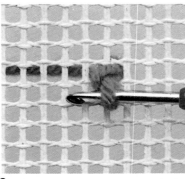

3 This is what the first chain stitch looks like. Draw the next loop up through the hole below. Work rows in a spiral.

4 Colour change: after the last stitch of the colour, cut the yarn; draw the end through the loop, and then through the next hole.

5 Begin the new colour in the hole above the last chain stitch. Tie the two yarn ends together and draw the new colour through.

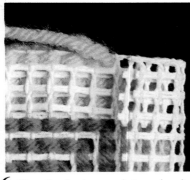

6 For the last round, turn back the unworked canvas, so that there is one row of unworked holes all around the piece.

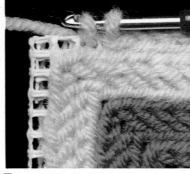

7 Work the chain stitches through all thickness of canvas. Weave in the yarn ends and slip-stitch the canvas in place.

8 Finally, sew the edges of the tiles together on the wrong side, using an overcasting stitch worked with split yarn.

4-movement Smyrna knot

Deep-pile rugs can be made by knotting short lengths of rug yarn into a canvas base with a latch hook (also called latchet hook). The Smyrna knot can be made in two ways – the 4-movement and 5-movement methods. The 4-movement knot, which is shown here, is quicker to work than the 5-movement knot.

These two knots create pile which lies in opposite directions. When two people are working on the rug at the same time (one at each end), by using both methods, the pile will all lie in the same direction when the knots meet in the middle of the canvas. The 5-movement knot is explained on page 144.

1 Rug yarn for making latch hook rugs can be bought in packs, pre-cut and ready to use.

2 Fold the yarn in half and loop it around the shank of the latch hook, holding the ends together. Insert the hook into a hole, under the horizontal threads, then push it out through the hole above. The yarn is below the horizontal threads.

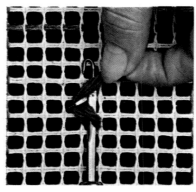

3 Turn the hook slightly and pull the yarn ends across the open latch. Draw the hook back through the canvas. This will close the latch and pull the yarn ends through the loop. Be careful not to split the yarn with the latch when it closes.

4 Tighten the knot by pulling the ends. (The knot will be easier to make if you keep the yarn very loose while working and tighten it after you have finished). Work knots from left to right across each horizontal row, following illustrations 2–5.

5 For an evenly knotted rug, work completely across canvas before beginning next row. Work design by following colour chart (each square represents a knot on the canvas). Place a few strans of yarn in each colour close at hand. This will speed up the pace of your work.

Rugmaking with a latch hook is an easy craft to learn and an absorbing way to make a strong, good-looking rug with a rich pile. Here is a clever motif which can be arranged and rearranged in dozens of different rug designs!

A geometric puzzle rug

Try sixteen squares laid in the same direction.

Turn two rows to create a different pattern.

Four squares turned to the centre make a circle.

Alternating squares make four wavy diagonals.

Waves run across the rug at the top and bottom.

Turn all the squares and it's different again!

135

The yarn is knotted into every mesh of the canvas, working from left to right across each row. Since the yarn pieces are all the same length, a lush, even pile is achieved.

The fun of having a puzzle rug never ends. If you get tired of your design, you can simply rearrange the motifs. Or, try a complete change by assembling the motifs so the rug is a completely different size and shape. Make a runner for a hall two squares wide and eight squares long or a hearth rug three squares wide and five, six, or seven squares long.

Size: Using $3\frac{1}{4}$ mesh per 2.5 cm (1″), each motif will be 39.5 cm (15½″) square and a 16-square rug will be 158 cm (62″) square. Using 4 mesh per 2.5 cm (1″), each motif will be 32.5 cm (12¾″) square and a 16-square rug will be 130 cm (51″) square.

Materials (for each motif): Rug canvas: 44.5 cm (17½″) square of $3\frac{1}{4}$-mesh canvas or 38 cm (15″) square of

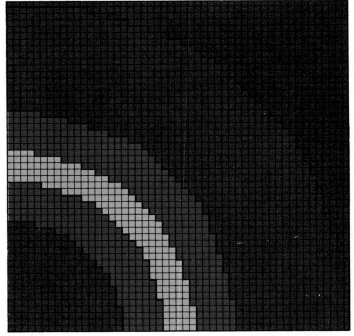

Colour chart for the puzzle rug motif. Each square represents one knot. Begin at the lower left corner and follow the chart row by row.

4-mesh canvas. Pre-cut rug yarn: 4 packs dark red, 2 packs brown, 2 packs pink, 1 pack yellow. Latch hook. Rug binding. Carpet thread. Upholsterer's needle.

Estimating yarn amounts

The number of strands in pre-cut packs varies with the brand. We used packs containing 320 pieces per pack. To determine the number of packs required, count the squares of the chart to determine the number of pieces of each color required. Multiply each number by the number of motifs you plan to make, then divide by 320 or the number of pieces in your packs to determine the number of packs needed to complete a large rug. Our 16-square rug requires: 68 packs dark red, 28 packs brown, 25 packs pink, 10 packs yellow.

Planning the design

Decide the size and shape of rug you need and then draw your rug design on paper, arranging the motifs in a way which pleases you. Based on the number of motifs you have used for your design, determine the yarn and canvas needed.

Working the squares

Cut canvas to the proper

size, always making sure there are 51 holes across and 51 rows, plus a 1″ margin all around. Begin working at the lower left corner of the canvas, 1″ in from each edge. Follow the chart at left to work design (each square represents 1 knot on the canvas). Work across rows rather than working colour areas to achieve even blending and avoid separation of pile into colour areas.

Joining rug pieces

Trim away excess canvas at the corners of each square. Turn canvas margins to the back and sew in place. The squares are joined by the diagonal basting stitch used for flat-joining in dress-making. Place two squares side by side, pile side down. Using curved upholsterer's needle and carpet thread, sew squares together, matching meshes. Following your design sketch, join the squares in strips, then sew the strips together to complete the rug. Sew rug binding over the joinings and around the edges. When the rug is finished, run your hand in one direction over the pile to remove any loose fibres. Trim any uneven ends.

Alternative colour schemes for the puzzle rug

Colour requirements vary according to the style of the furniture and the amount of light in the room.

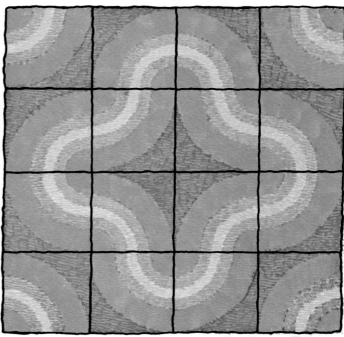

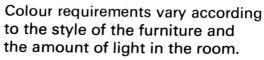

This is the scheme shown on the previous pages. Warm colours go well with transparent materials such as plastic and glass.

For rooms which need a touch of coolness, choose colours in the blue to green range. Lime green will sharpen up the softer tones.

Yellow gives a feeling of warmth and light to a sunless room. Modern wood furniture goes well with yellow hues.

Rich green and brown, plus a singing red, complement antique furniture and brass and copper accessories.

Oriental charm

Chinese carpets were originally made only in silk and used to decorate the imperial palaces and temples. Although they are just as sumptuous as the better-known Persian carpets, they are very different in design and colouring. The central area is usually a single light colour, while the border, rich in symbolic designs, is worked in darker colours. Twigs and flowers, especially the lotus blossom, are a prominent feature of Chinese carpets which are always delightfully graceful in design. Our rug combines the elegance of Chinese design with the hard-wearing quality of a latch hook rug worked with pre-cut rug wool.

Size: 137 cm x 198 cm (54" x 78"). The rug is 180 knots wide, 260 knots long.

Materials Required: Rug canvas: 10 holes to 7.5 cm (3"), 2.10 m (2¼ yds) each of 90 cm (36") and 65 cm (24") wide. Rug wool in pre- cut packs (320 pieces per pack) in colors and quantities shown overleaf. Latchet hook. Wide black carpet binding tape.

Joining the canvas
As the rug canvas is 90 cm (36") wide, 2 separate pieces of canvas are required to make up the width, one of 90 cm (36") wide, the other of 65 cm (24") wide. Cut off the selvedge on each piece along the edge to be joined. Overlap the edges by 2.5 cm (1"), matching up the holes and threads precisely, and sew together along each raw edge. The overlap will be hidden in the pile when the carpet is complete.

Working the design
Follow the chart and colour key over- leaf; each square equals one knot. Work with the full length of canvas stretching away from you, leaving a border of at least 4 cm (1½") of canvas all around.
Using the Smyrna knot technique, work in rows across the canvas from left to right (or right to left if left- handed). Do not work in patches of one colour because the pile will not blend together evenly, and it is easy to miss a hole in the thick pile.

Binding the edges
When the rug is complete, trim the excess canvas to 4 cm (1½"). Turn under the border and stitch down at the back. Sew carpet tape over the raw edges, mitring the corners.

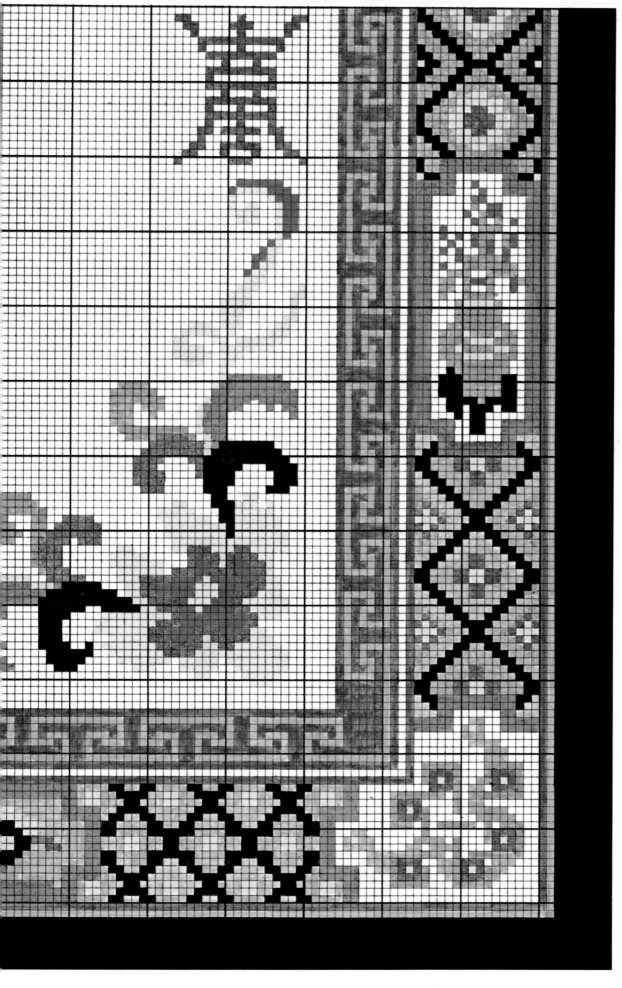

Light blue-green

Dark green

Medium green

Black

Dark blue

Bright blue

Medium blue-green

Sky blue

Orange

Gold

The colour key for the
Chinese carpet is given
above. The quantities
required are:
  2 packs Light blue-green
  3 packs Dark green
  6 packs Medium green
25 packs Black
19 packs Dark blue
15 packs Bright blue
  3 packs Medium blue-green
54 packs Sky blue
  2 packs Orange
  2 packs Gold
Each square on the chart
represents one knot. The
border is 8 squares wide
and is worked in black.

Variations on a theme

The colour scheme is up to you

Play up the design with warm shades of red, pink, gold, orange, and brown.

You can be the proud owner of beautiful rugs like these. Adapt the colours to your decor, or even better, design your own rug so that it will be exactly the size and colour you need.

Use neutral colours to tie in with a more traditional mood. Add life to the scheme with a rich crimson and a sunny yellow.

Colour your canvas in cooler tones to create a totally different effect with the same design of zigzag and straight lines.

142

You'll find that it is great fun to design your own rug, so why not let the whole family get involved? Give everyone sheets of squared paper and some coloured pens or pencils — you can work out the general colour scheme ahead of time. It is probably easiest to begin with a geometric design, but after a while, you will become accustomed to working with curved lines on the squared paper and you can make representational shapes such as fish or flowers.

Designing is much easier than you think. The important thing is to have fun with it and let your imagination run free. You'll be surprised by the results.

Designing a rug

First, determine the shape and size of the rug you wish to make.

Draw this outline on your graph paper. Each square of the graph paper represents one horizontal bar of the canvas and there is one knot per horizontal bar. Fill in the outline with your design, making sure the size and shape of the design are appropriate for the size and shape of the rug.

Transferring a design

Cover a large, flat surface with several layers of newspaper and place the canvas on top. Being sure to leave 5 cm (2″) margins on each side, transfer the design with waterproof paints or marking pens as shown at right. Be sure to let the paint or ink dry thoroughly before starting to knot.

5-movement Smyrna knot

This is the reverse of the 4-movement knot. By using both, rows worked from opposite ends will lie in the same direction.

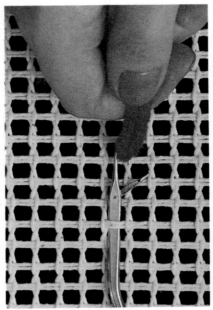 

1 Insert the hook under the threads of the canvas. Open the latch and slip a piece of rug yarn onto the hook.

2 Hold the yarn ends even. Pull the hook back through the canvas until the yarn is halfway through the hole.

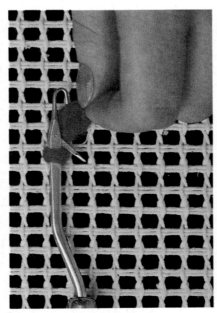

3 Push the hook back through the loop until the latch is above the loop and open. Turn the hook slightly so the latch is more toward you.

4 Pull the yarn across the hook and pull the hook down. The latch will close and pull the ends through the loop. Pull the knot tight.

Designing, Painting the canvas

Work out your own design on graph paper –
you may be impressed with your artistic ability.

1 Smyrna knots are worked on 3⅓ or 4 meshes to 2.5 cm (1″) double-thread canvas. The horizontal threads are held in place by the twisted vertical threads.

2 Thick rug wool is used with this canvas. The yarn can be bought in ready-cut packs or bundles and it is available in a wide range of colours.

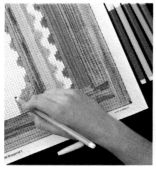 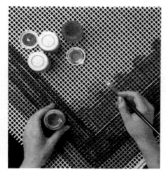

3 Work out your design on graph paper with felt-tipped pens.

4 Transfer your design to the canvas with waterproof paints or markers.

5 Each square of the graph represents one knot on the canvas. Be careful to transfer the design to the canvas so that the colour is clearly marked on every mesh.

6 Work knots into each mesh across the row, with yarn which corresponds in colour to the painted canvas. Watch the design come to life as you fill in the colours.

**Floral
fantasy**

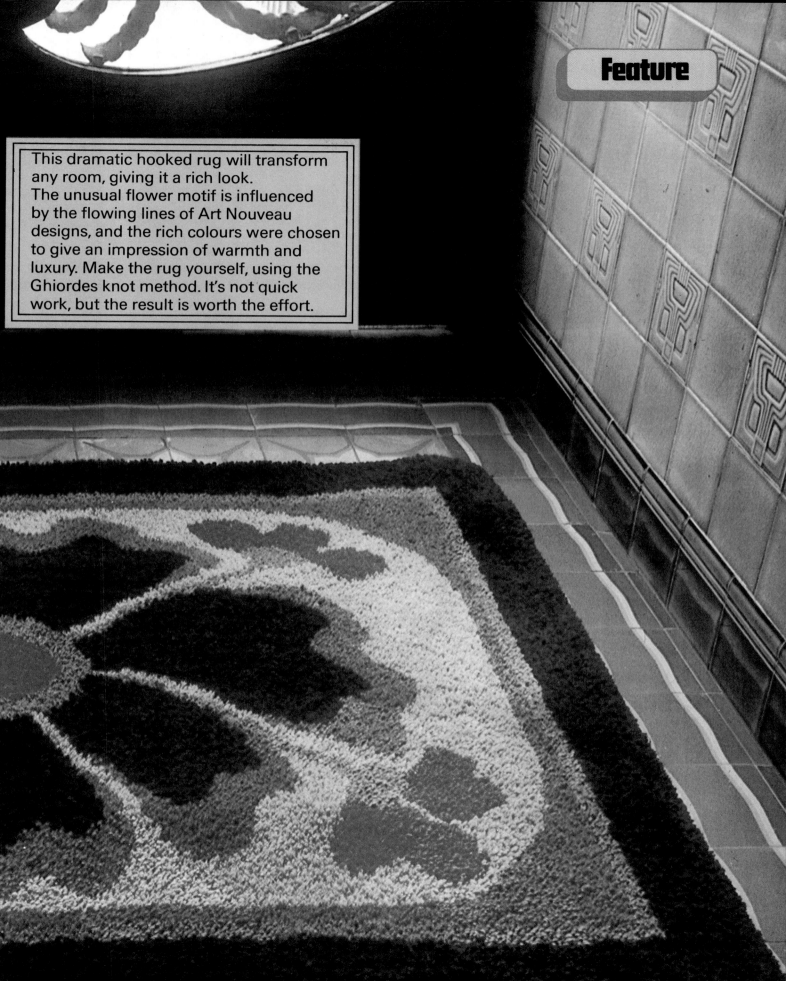

This dramatic hooked rug will transform any room, giving it a rich look.
The unusual flower motif is influenced by the flowing lines of Art Nouveau designs, and the rich colours were chosen to give an impression of warmth and luxury. Make the rug yourself, using the Ghiordes knot method. It's not quick work, but the result is worth the effort.

Size: On $3\frac{1}{2}$ meshes to 2.5 cm (1"): 110 x 150 cm (44" x 60"). On 4 meshes to 2.5 cm (1"): 90 x 125 cm (36" x 50").

Materials Required: Double-thread rug canvas: 1.6 m ($1\frac{3}{4}$ yd), 122 cm (48") wide. Rug yarn in uncut skeins or pre-cut packs:

Color	Skeins (in gms)	Packs
Pink	1,300	23
Old rose	450	8
Violet	1,050	18
Burgundy	2,240	40
Grey	650	11

For border edging: 200 gm skeined wool in burgundy. Latch hook. Wool cutter for skeined wool (optional).

Choosing the yarn

The rug can be made either with skeined yarn or pre-cut packs. The most economical length of yarn for the Ghiordes knot is 5–5.5 cm (2"–$2\frac{1}{4}$"). With a yarn cutter, you cut the skeins to this length. A simple yarn cutter can be made at home. Use a 10 cm (4") piece of wood about 0.6 cm ($\frac{1}{4}$") thick and 2 cm ($\frac{3}{4}$") high. Cut a groove along one long, narrow edge. Wind the yarn around it several times, then cut it along the groove with a razor blade. Longer lengths of yarn will give a slightly deeper pile.

Choosing the canvas

For this rug which is worked with the Ghiordes knot you will need double-thread canvas as a base. It usually has coloured checks woven into it marking off every 10 holes to simplify counting. The canvas is available in several different widths.

Skeined yarn can be cut to size with a yarn cutter.

Working the rug

If you are using skeined yarn, cut it into the 5–5.5 cm (2–$2\frac{1}{4}$") lengths required. It is a good idea to keep each colour in a separate transparent bag. Using the chart, count the number of squares along the length and width of the rug and thread-trace the outline on the canvas with a length of knitting yarn. Before beginning to knot, finish the edges of the rug by trimming the margins to 2 holes all around and turning under the surplus canvas. Work edge stitch in the border color along the edges as shown opposite. Begin working the Ghiordes knots from left to right across the rows, beginning in the lower left-hand corner (or vice versa if left-handed). Follow the chart from bottom to top, remembering that each square on the grid represents 1 knot on the canvas. Always work across the canvas in rows, not in separate colour areas. In this way the knots will blend evenly from colour to colour.

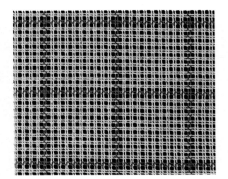

1 Insert the latch hook under the lower horizontal (weft) thread and loop the wool over the hook.

1 Rug canvas often has coloured checks woven in so that it is easier to count a pattern from a chart.

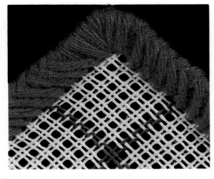

4 Neaten the corners of the rug with enough overcasting stitches to cover the canvas completely.

Ghiordes knot

The Ghiordes knot is worked on double-thread canvas with rug yarn in pre-cut packs or uncut skeins.

Working the knot

2 Draw about ⅔ of the yarn under the thread with the hook and turn the short end toward the left.

3 Insert the latch hook under the top horizontal (weft) thread and place the yarn across the hook.

4 Draw the yarn through to finish the Ghiordes knot. Stroke the knot downward. Continue in this way.

Making the rug

 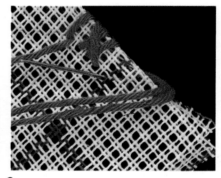

2 With a wool cutter, you can cut skeined yarn to the required length. For the Ghiordes knot, the most suitable yarn length is 5–5.5 cm (2″–2¼″). A home-made wooden yarn cutter can also be used.

3 Trim the margins of the canvas. Turn under 2 squares all around and work edge stitch over edges.

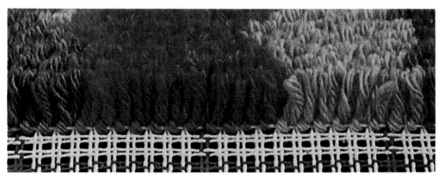

5 This is what the Ghiordes knots look like when worked in rows on the canvas. The different colours do not separate, but blend together. The pile of the rug will vary with the length of wool you use.

Working edge stitch

Work edge stitch from left to right. Begin with 3 adjacent vertical stitches worked over 3 holes, with the needle going from back to front. Bring the needle out through the 4th hole, then through the 1st hole again. Bring the needle out through the 5th hole, with the yarn looped below the needle as shown, then through the 2nd hole again. Continue in this way, alternating 1 stitch forward and 1 stitch worked 3 holes back.

Work the rug by following this chart which indicates the number of knots and the colours to use. Each square of the chart represents one knot. The first three burgundy rows are covered with edge stitch. Begin at the bottom left-hand corner and follow the design.

It is easy to design a pattern on graph paper

Here are just a few designs – you will think of dozens more!

Working a design

Leaving a 5 cm (2") margin all around, cut away any excess canvas. Place the canvas on a flat working surface and weight the far end if necessary. Fold margin of the end closest to you to the back.

Begin at the lower left corner and work the knots through both layers of the canvas. Work a complete row before beginning the next one.

At the other end, fold back the margin and work through both layers as at the beginning. Turn in the raw edges at the sides and stitch in place. Cover the raw edges with rug binding.

When working on a large rug, two people can work on the rug at the same time if one starts at one end with the 4-movement knot and the other works at the opposite end with the 5-movement Smyrna knot. When the two ends meet, the pile will be lying in the same direction along the entire rug.

ZIGZAG RUG

Size: On 3⅓ mesh canvas: 80 x 120 cm (30" x 47½"). On 4 mesh canvas: 66 x 99 cm (26" x 39").

Our rugs are 104 knots wide and 157 knots long. The outer border is 5 knots deep and the inner contrasting border is 8 rows deep.

Amounts of yarn required:
Natural colour scheme:
20 packs brown
24 packs beige
8 packs olive green
7 packs white
8 packs crimson
8 packs rust

4 packs yellow
Red and orange colour scheme:
9 packs gold
7 packs bright red
9 packs white
11 packs orange
11 packs pink
24 packs dark red
19 packs brown
Blue and red colour scheme:
17 packs turquoise
24 packs dark blue
9 packs red
7 packs pale blue
11 packs light blue
15 packs medium blue
6 packs pink

Cross-stitch on canvas

For home and hearth

This rug has a beautiful, stylized pattern of coloured animals on a dark background, with wide panels and borders. Symbolic animal and bird motifs have always been popular in all types of needlework, and have been traditionally used in rug designs for many centuries.

Size: The rug measures about 1 m x 1.56 m (39½" x 61½").

Materials Required: Rug canvas: 1.70 m (1⅞ yds), 115 cm (44") wide, 10 holes to 7.5 cm (3"). Skeined rug yarn (25 m or 25 yds per skein): 20 skeins navy blue + 2 skeins for border; 4 skeins rose; 6 skeins off-white; 6 skeins copper; 3 skeins brick red; 2 skeins sand. These yarn quantities may vary slightly according to whether you work lightly or loosely. Large-eyed needle with rounded tip.

Making the rug
Work the rug by following the detail, overleaf, counting the stitches from the illustration. Before you begin, mark the outline of the design area (128 double threads by 205 double threads) or paint in the design area with waterproof felt-tipped marking pens. <u>Note:</u> There are 2 rows of black stitches beyond the white lines at the sides and 2 rows of black stitches beyond the copper lines at the ends. Trim the excess canvas to 3 cm (1¼") all around (ie 4 holes). Turn half of the border under so that 1.5 cm (⅝") remains showing (ie 2 holes). To bind the edge, overcast closely with navy blue yarn, inserting the needle into each hole of the canvas and between the double threads.

Use cross-stitch throughout, working each stitch over one pair of threads of canvas. Work the first diagonal stitch of the cross from the lower left hole to the upper right hole, continuing along the row from left to right until the colour changes. Then work back along the row from right to left, making the second diagonal stitch of the cross from the lower right hole to the upper left hole. In this way, the crosses will all be crossed in the same direction.

Finish each area of one colour before beginning the next colour and make sure that the loose ends are fastened off securely. The yarn in the needle should not be longer than 1 m (1 yd).

Preparing the canvas; working the cross-stitch

1 The design is worked in six colours of rug wool with a thick, blunt-tipped needle. Work the design, following the illustration, opposite. If you wish, the design can be copied on the canvas with felt-tipped pens.

2 Either mark the whole design on the canvas, or just the outline if you prefer to count the stitches from the illustration as you work. The design area is 128 double threads wide by 205 double threads long. Mark four holes beyond the outer edge of the design all around with a felt-tipped pen or a piece of wide masking tape. Cut off the excess.

3 Fold the margin in half so that there are two layers of canvas, two holes wide at the

edges and four layers at the corners. To bind the edges, overcast them, inserting the needle into each hole and between the double threads.

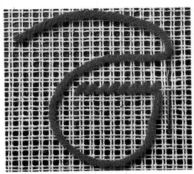

4 The design is worked in rows of cross-stitch. First, work across the row from left to right for the required number of stitches. Work each stitch over one pair of threads of the canvas, bringing the yarn out at the lower left hole of the first stitch of row to begin. Then insert the needle in the hole diagonally up to the right and bring it out directly below.

5 Now work back along the same row from right to left, bringing the yarn out at the lower right hole to begin. Then for all other stitches, insert the needle in the hole diagonally up to the left and bring it out of the hole directly below. Crosses must cross in the same direction.

6 Work each area of color separately. Work back and forth in rows, always being sure that the stitches have been crossed in both directions before going on to the next row. Use strands about 1 m (1 yd) long.

7 Here you can see a section of the rug which has been partially worked. The colour areas are being worked separately, following the painted areas of the canvas or the detail on the right. When working vertical rows, be careful that the crosses are worked in the same direction as other stitches. Fasten the loose ends of yarn on the wrong side by running them under several stitches.

Work the design,
following the
illustration
for the number
of stitches to
work in each
colour. The
design area is
128 stitches by
205 stitches.
There are 2
rows of black
stitches beyond
the white lines
at the sides
and 2 rows of
black stitches
beyond the copper
lines at the ends.

Colour key

Rose

Off-white

Navy blue

Copper

Sand

Brick red

A braided sisal rug is ideal as a doormat—it's colourful and hard-wearing.

Here's a new craft to try!

Braided sisal in the round

Sisal braiding is easy — even children can do it — and here is a fascinating way of using sisal to make attractive rugs and mats. Lengths of sisal are first braided and then twisted and stitched into flat rounds. Finally, the rounds are stitched together to make decorative patterns.

Sisal is a practical material for making rugs. It is extremely hard-wearing, and easy to clean, as the finished structure of a braided rug is rather open and dirt falls right through. This makes them ideal for hallways, children's rooms, and places where the foot traffic is likely to be heavy. Braided sisal can also be used to create beautiful table mats and covers. Hot plates won't harm the table and, after a meal, the mat is simply shaken to remove food fragments. Give free rein to your

Rounds can be stitched into a formal arrangement for a stunning hearth rug.

3-strand braiding

The technique is illustrated with pairs of strands in three colours so you can see where to place the strands. The rug rounds were braided in a single colour, but tri-colour rounds could certainly be used to produce a tweed. <u>Note:</u> It is important to keep the tension even.

Making the rounds

Six strands of 2-ply sisal were used to make the rounds for the rugs. Sisal is available in natural and a range of attractive colours. Cut the strands approximately $1\frac{1}{3}$ times the length of the required braid. A 30″ braid will make a round 9 cm ($3\frac{1}{2}$″) in diameter. A 60″ braid makes a 12.5 cm (5″) diameter round and a 90″ braid makes 15 cm (6″) diameter round.

creativity when planning the designs. Sisal can be obtained in bright colours but if you find that only the natural sisal is available, dye it to the colour you require. Follow the manufacturer's instructions.

Planning the design
Before starting to braid, draw a plan of the rug or mat on squared paper, indicating the colours to be used. Each circle must touch adjacent circles so that the sisal rounds can be stitched together.

Making a rug or mat
Make the rounds, laying them out according to your pattern. Stitch rounds together as shown at right.

158

Braiding and stitching sisal rounds

1 Knot three pairs of strands (2 red, 2 green, and 2 white) at one end and hang them from a hook. Place red pair to the right, green pair in the middle, and the white pair to the left.

2 Holding the red pair in your right hand and white pair in your left, bring the red pair to the middle over the green, being careful to keep the strands flat (do not let them twist).

3 Bring the white pair to the middle over the red. Continue to braid in this way by bringing outside strands from alternate sides to the middle. Knot or bind the braid at the end.

1 Cut lengths of sisal and knot them together at one end. Holding the strands by all the ends, dampen the strands in water to make them more pliable. Do not dampen ends.

2 Bind the cut ends of the sisal with tape. This not only prevents fraying, but makes the strands easier to handle. The tape can be easily removed when the braiding has been completed.

3 Hang the knotted strands from a hook while braiding as this helps to achieve an even tension. If a hook is not available, the knot can be shut in a drawer to secure it.

4 At about 10 cm (4″) from the end, cut away one strand of each pair to reduce the bulk of the braid. Continue to braid with three single strands. Tie ends with a cut-off strand.

5 Starting from the tied-off end, bend the braid into a round and begin to stitch the braid to itself, using a heavy-duty thread. Use flat joining stitch and stitch on the wrong side of the work.

6 Work in a circle, making sure that the stitches are not pulled too tightly so that the round will not become distorted.

About 5 cm (2″) from the end of the braid, turn the knotted end toward the center of the round on the wrong side and cut it off straight across.

Stitch down the raw ends on the wrong side, making sure that no stitches show on the right side of the round.

159

The finishing touch

The decorations are done,
the curtains and loose covers are made,
and the rugs are down.
Now for the finishing touches which
make a room special. Lampshades
can provide an essential touch of
colour in a decor, book covers
and painted boxes provide
conversation pieces, hand-embroidered
towels show that you care.

Four bright ideas

Lampshades made to measure

It can be difficult to find ready-made lampshades that harmonize well with the furnishings in your home. If you make them yourself, you can choose styles and fabrics to match the surrounding decor perfectly, whether it is modern or traditional. There is a wide range of frames available, from the simplest drum shape to the pretty, feminine Tiffany shade.

The choice of fabric depends on the shape of the frame to some extent; a light fabric that stretches slightly is more suitable for a soft shade, while a firmer weave such as furnishing fabric or cotton can be used for a hard shade.

The edge of a lampshade can be finished off attractively with braid, binding or fringing. We give you four ideas for trims on the Tiffany

161

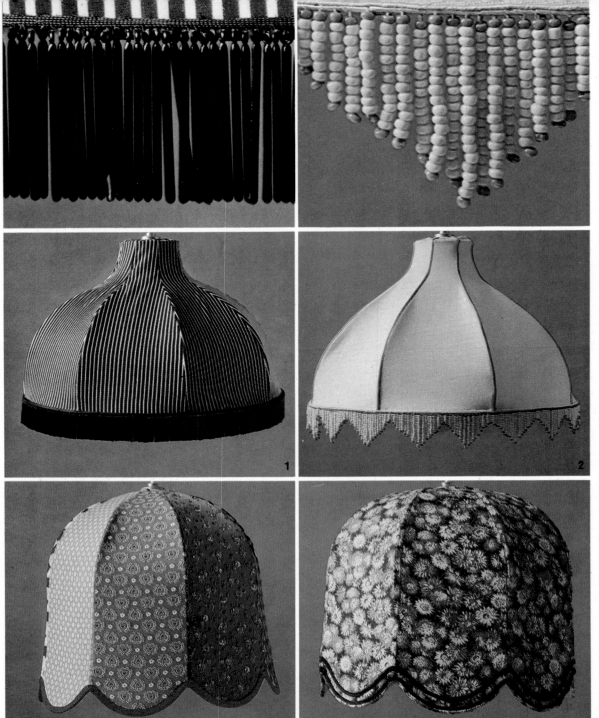

lampshades shown above. The instructions for covering lampshades are given on the next page.

Style 1: The fringed effect shown here can be achieved by sewing little plastic rods to a narrow silk braid. This is then pinned exactly over the stitching line and sewn on by hand. However, a strip of ready-made fringing will give a very similar effect.

Style 2: Differing lengths of strung beads create a zigzag border around this shade. This effect is accentuated by the contrasting colour of the first and last beads. To use this idea for any shade, first measure the circumference, then divide this into a regular number of sections for the zigzags. Make a template for the zigzags and thread the beads in strings to conform to this shape. Sew the strings of beads onto narrow braid and edge the shade with the braid. Finally, sew narrow braid to match the colour of the beads over the seams.

Style 3: This shade is worked in panels of different printed fabrics and trimmed with wide bias binding.

Style 4: Two strips of braid follow the lines of the scalloped edge to trim this floral lampshade.

Making a tailored cover for a lampshade

Lampshade frames come in a variety of shapes and sizes, but the method of making the shade is the same for all of them. The pattern sections should be exactly the right size, so that the fabric is taut when it is stretched onto the frame.

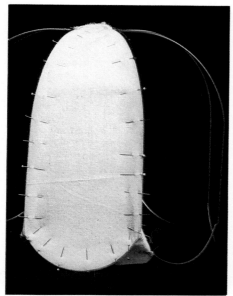

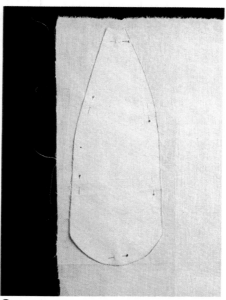

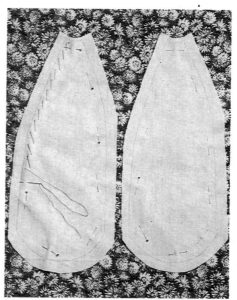

1 First make a pattern piece by wrapping a piece of fabric around the struts and pinning it tightly all around. Trace the outline of the struts and cut out the section.

2 To give warmth to the light, the shade is lined with unbleached cotton. Cut out each section with a seam allowance of 1 cm ($\frac{3}{8}$") at the sides and 1.5 cm ($\frac{5}{8}$") at the bottom.

3 Pin the cotton sections to the wrong side of the fabric and secure with diagonal basting stitches. Then cut out the sections, cutting exactly around the lining.

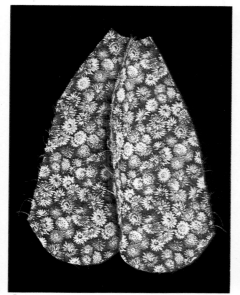

4 Baste the cover together along the seamlines and try it on the frame. Then stitch the sections together with French seams. Neaten the upper edge with bias binding.

5 Draw the cover over the frame, making sure that the seams lie exactly over the struts. Turn under the lower edge of the cover and pin firmly all around.

6 Sew this edge by hand from the right side with small backstitches. To finish the raw edge on the inside, a bias cotton strip is sewn over it by hand as shown above.

1

Lighting-up time

Shady looks

Finding the right lighting for your home is not always easy, because lamps can be very expensive and may not suit your taste or decor. An obvious answer is to make your own lampshades in pretty fabrics which fit in with your requirements exactly. In this way, old lamps can be given a new lease of life, and second-hand bargains can be renovated to individual taste. Choose a fabric to match the curtains, wallpaper or furniture, and a lampshade frame to complement the shape of the lamp base.

1 The lamp base is straight and slender, so a straight-sided frame has been chosen to match it. The fabric is a muted floral print for a soft light.

2 This lamp base fans out toward the bottom, requiring a wider, flatter shade to balance it. The flower-patterned fabric sheds a warm light.

3 This lamp is perfect when a good bright light is needed. The fluted base and boldly-patterned lampshade would fit in well with most decors.

4 A geometric pattern has been chosen for this unusual lampshade. The lines of the design run spirally around the shade because of its conical shape.

Making lampshades

The photograph at the bottom on the far right shows all four lamps together, so that you can see their comparative sizes. The largest is 65 cm (25½″) high, the smallest 28 cm (11″).

The most important item for making a hard shade is adhesive parchment. This is treated on one side so that fabric can be pressed onto it.

1 <u>Materials Required</u>: Lampshade frame, adhesive parchment, fabric, cotton bias binding in a matching colour, clear glue, clothes pins or pegs for holding.

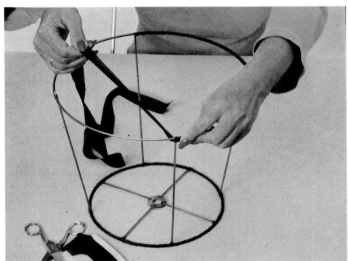

2 Cover the frame with bias binding around the upper and lower rings, spreading the wire with glue segment by segment. The binding does not require sewing.

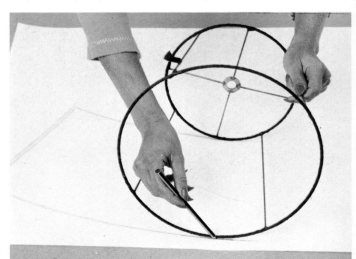

3 Spread the parchment, adhesive side down, and roll the frame carefully along it completely around its circumference, marking cutting lines at top and bottom.

4 Check the pattern by rolling the frame over it again. Add 1--1.5 cm ($\frac{3}{8}$"--$\frac{5}{8}$") to the length for the overlap. Draw a circle round the top for the cover. Cut out.

7 Use clothes pins or pegs to hold the parchment while the glue dries. Spread glue on the overlap and press in place carefully, so there are no open edges.

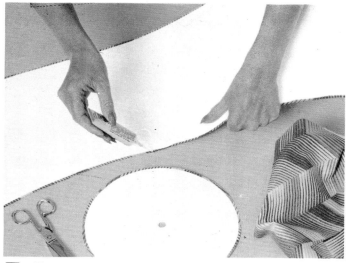

5 Place the fabric on the adhesive side of the parchment. Trim the fabric to 0.5 cm ($\frac{3}{16}$") all round the parchment and glue under.

8 Finally, glue the top cover onto the binding in the same way as for the main part of the shade. Cut a hole in the center so that the fixture can be fitted.

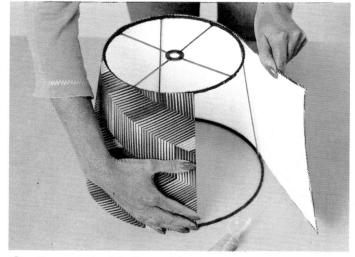

6 Spread the binding with glue and press the parchment onto it. Place the shade on a firm surface while you work, as shown above, to prevent it from slipping.

New looks for books

Protect your recipe books from kitchen splashes and stains with a smart new cover in vinyl-coated cloth.

Notebooks, address books, recipe books, diaries, albums — all those books which are in constant use will benefit from a strong, protective covering. Or you may want to give your favourite book an attractive face-lift, or make a very individual present.

Books which suffer a lot of wear and tear, such as the recipe books shown in the large photograph, will last longer if they are bound in vinyl-coated cloth. They will look brighter and can simply be wiped clean.

The selection of books on the right have been covered in different ways to suit their contents. Here we left the spines free and covered only the front and back surfaces. All kinds of materials can be used — a beautiful fabric, a photograph, an art postcard, a favourite picture from a magazine.

It is very important to work neatly for a professional finish. Use a metal ruler and sharp craft knife for cutting. If using fabric, turn in edges to stop fraying. On rounded corners snip fabric several times so that it lies flat. Whatever you use as a cover, stick it on with a good adhesive.

Many materials such as magazine illustrations, wallpaper, printed fabrics, and old photographs can be used to cover your books.

1 Draw the outlines of the book onto the wrong side of the fabric and mark the width of the spine.

2 Cut the fabric around the shape, adding 1 cm (3/8″) extra all around. Cut wedges on either side of the spine.

3 Apply fabric adhesive thinly onto one outside cover. Place the book onto the fabric and press down firmly.

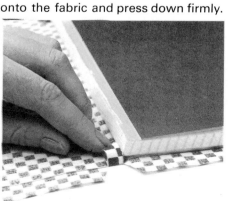

4 Apply adhesive to the book spine and turn the tabs to the inside. Press on the fabric. Glue the other side.

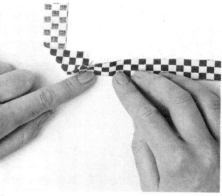

5 Turn the excess fabric to the inside of the cover and glue in place. Mitre the corners neatly.

6 To make the book look neat from the inside, paste the first and last pages over the edges of the fabric.

Painted wood

Razzle dazzle boxes

These colourful and decorative containers were once plain wooden boxes bought from a crafts shop. Painted and filled with little surprises like sweets or nuts, they make original presents. They are also useful about the house for storing those odds and ends that never seem to find a home, like games pieces, paper clips, pins, rubber bands, etc. Plain wooden boxes come in many shapes and sizes, and can be made from thin wood like the ones shown here, or from sturdier wood with hinged lids.

If you like pop motifs, these boxes are for you. Instructions for transferring the motifs to the boxes are given opposite. If these designs are not to your taste, look out for other ideas in children's comics, magazines, and on posters if you are not confident enough to draw your own.

170

The repeat pattern
around the base
of the red box can
be developed from
the border pattern
on the lid.
▼

▲
Half the floral
design is
shown. Transfer
the other half
in reverse.

A quarter of
the star
design.
▼

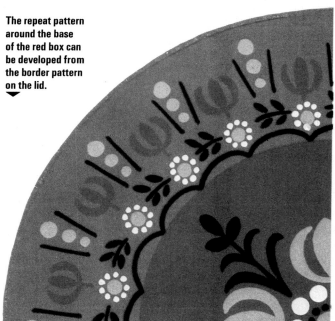

Three folk designs to trace

Before transferring the design, paint the box in the base colour with acrylic or poster paint. Light colours which do not cover well should have two coats.

The designs for the boxes in the top photograph on the left-hand page are given here. They can be transferred onto the box tops as follows: Place tracing paper over the designs and trace them in pencil very carefully.

To position the pattern correctly, divide the box top into halves or quarters, marking it lightly with a soft pencil. Then transfer the design onto the box. Transfer the design with carbon paper, going over the lines of the design with a pencil. Half the floral pattern is given; to transfer the other half, turn the tracing paper over. A quarter of the other two designs is given, so transfer this quarter four times, reversing the tracing paper as required.

If possible, go over the lines of the pattern with a felt-tip pen in the relevant colours of the sections. In this way, the boundaries will be neater than those made with a soft paint brush.

Now paint the design with the acrylic or poster paint, using a soft brush. Finally, varnish the box to give it a glossy appearance and to make it easier to dust.

The geometric patterns shown at the beginning of the chapter can be drawn straight onto the box top after practising on a piece of paper. Use a soft pencil which will not scratch the base paint and can be rubbed out if you make a mistake.

1 This tobacco box is simple, but effective. The only decorations are the letters and stripes, two at the lid edge and one around the base. Make or buy a stencil for the letters and work out the spacing carefully.

2 Geometric patterns often look much more complicated than they actually are. Try this one out first on paper. Divide the circle into eight parts. Connect the end of each line to the ends of the other lines. Paint in shades of one colour.

3 The design on this box is also basically simple. Divide the circle into four parts, then each part into eight sections. Mark the zigzag line around the edge. Paint alternately light green and dark green with a black background.

4 To make the star motif, divide the circle into eight parts. Divide each line in half, then draw a square so that two corners touch the end and half-line mark and the other two touch the next squares.

Summer flowers for a winter bouquet

*M*ake elegant arrangements or
informal bouquets with plastic
flowers painted in soft colours and dried
grasses or evergreen leaves.

Painting plastic flowers

1 Assemble the materials above. Use enamel paint.

2 These and many other plastic flowers are available from large stores. The more varieties you use, the lovelier the bouquet will be.

3 Cut off all the leaves along the stem. Leave the sepals.

4 Each bloom needs a stem. Add wire stems if necessary.

5 Trim any ragged edges of the petals with scissors.

6 Take composite flowers apart and paint each part singly.

7 Mix the colours on the plate. Pastel shades are made with large amounts of white. Paint the stems and sepals green.

Gay and practical for the kitchen

Hot stuff!

Here is a bright
idea for bringing
a splash of colour
to your kitchen.
Quick to sew from
the simple pattern,
they are lined
with wadding
or batting to save
burnt fingers.

Materials Required:

Remnants of printed fabric
from stores or your scrap
bag measuring approximately 0.15 cm ($\frac{1}{4}$ yd),
90 cm (36") wide (for one
mitt). Wadding or batting
to same size.

Making the mitts

Begin by tracing off the
three separate pattern
pieces from the actual-size
pattern opposite and then
cut out carefully. Cut out
wadding or batting with a
seam allowance of 0.5 cm

($\frac{1}{4}$") and then cut out the
fabric in the same way,
cutting each piece twice.
Place the wadding or batting
under the fabric piece and
pin in position. Sew long
basting stitches along the
seamlines to prevent the
pieces shifting. Stitch the
hand and thumb parts together, right sides facing,
from point a to b. Stitch the
other side in the same way.
Fasten the ends of the thread
securely in each case.
Now pin the centre piece
in place with right sides
facing. Stitch, beginning at
point c and then following
curve around to the corner
on the other side. Now
stitch the other curve. Finish
seam allowances together.
Make a lining in the same
way and insert it into the
mitt, wrong sides facing. To
finish the wrist, stitch a
decorative strip of another
printed or plain fabric across
the top of the mitt. Cut a
strip of fabric measuring

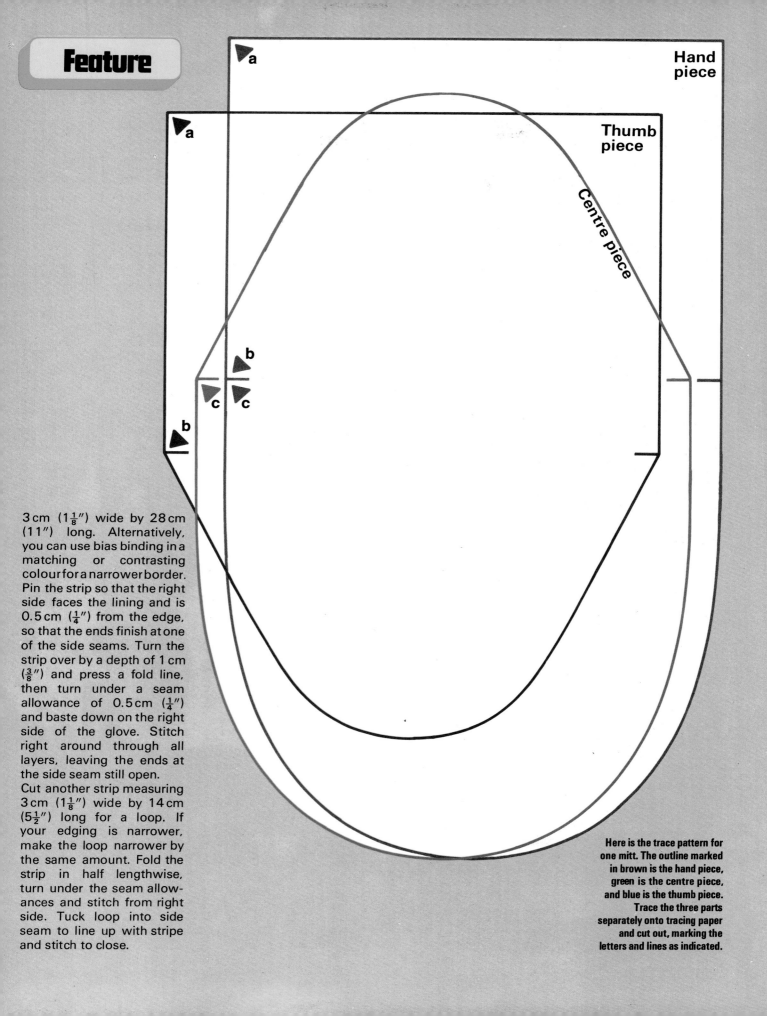

Hand piece

Thumb piece

Centre piece

a

a

b

c   c

b

3 cm (1⅛") wide by 28 cm (11") long. Alternatively, you can use bias binding in a matching or contrasting colour for a narrower border. Pin the strip so that the right side faces the lining and is 0.5 cm (¼") from the edge, so that the ends finish at one of the side seams. Turn the strip over by a depth of 1 cm (⅜") and press a fold line, then turn under a seam allowance of 0.5 cm (¼") and baste down on the right side of the glove. Stitch right around through all layers, leaving the ends at the side seam still open.

Cut another strip measuring 3 cm (1⅛") wide by 14 cm (5½") long for a loop. If your edging is narrower, make the loop narrower by the same amount. Fold the strip in half lengthwise, turn under the seam allowances and stitch from right side. Tuck loop into side seam to line up with stripe and stitch to close.

Here is the trace pattern for one mitt. The outline marked in brown is the hand piece, green is the centre piece, and blue is the thumb piece. Trace the three parts separately onto tracing paper and cut out, marking the letters and lines as indicated.

Begin the day in a cheerful mood with these beautiful, handmade, and embroidered towels. They make wonderful presents for your friends and why not treat yourself and your family to a set, too? Each set consists of a bath towel, a hand towel, a guest towel, and a face cloth, all made from terry towelling bound with braid. The motifs are transferred onto organza, which is then basted to the towelling. They are embroidered in satin stitch and the organza carefully removed thread by thread.

1

2

Embroidery on towelling
Bathing beauty

1 This chain pattern is pleasing in its simplicity. It forms a border to the larger towels, while the small ones have just one motif.

2 A dark red rose designed for those who love romantic designs. The scalloped edges add an extra feminine touch to this set.

3 The intriguing, intertwined pattern of the arabesques will please the whole family and is especially appropriate for gift sets.

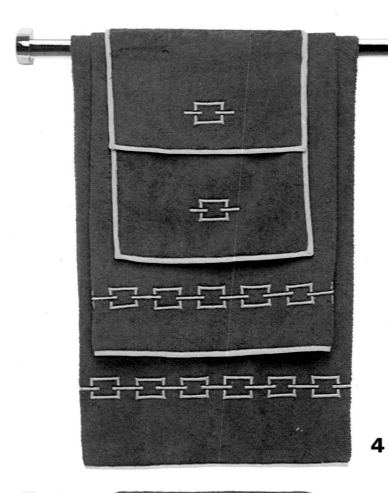

4

5

For 1 link of the chain, you will need $\frac{1}{3}$ skein of stranded cotton, for 12 links 4 skeins. A small rose takes $\frac{1}{3}$ skein, a large rose 2 skeins. A small arabesque takes 1 skein, a double one 3 skeins.

6

Making the towels
Sizes: Bath towel is 140 cm x 80 cm (55″ x 31½″), hand towel 100 cm x 50 cm (39½″ x 19½″), guest towel 50 cm x 30 cm (19½″ x 12″), face cloth 30 cm (12″) square.

Materials Required:
(for one set) Towelling: 2.50 m (2¾ yds), 90 cm (36″) wide. Cotton braid: 11 m (12 yds).

Cutting out: Cut the towels to the correct size without a seam allowance. Make a template for the scallops and rounded corners. Keep the curves fairly flat, as the gentler they are, the easier it is to sew the braid around the edges.

Attaching the braid: The towels are bound all around with braid. Press the braid in half lengthways, just off-centre, so that it is 0.2 cm (⅛″) wider on one side than on the other. Make sure that it does not stretch as it is pressed. With narrow side of braid on the right side of fabric, push the fabric right up into the fold and pin around edge. Baste carefully through all layers. At the corners, where the braid puckers, fold it over to form a mitre and sew down by hand after stitching.

On the scalloped edge, ease the braid around the curves, gathering it in or stretching it slightly as required.

To finish off the end of the braid neatly, turn it under 1 cm (⅜″) and overlap the beginning of the braid. With the narrow side of the braid facing, machine-stitch around the towel through all the layers.

Working the embroidery
Materials Required:

Stranded cotton in the following colours.

Set 1 = olive green
Set 2 = dark red
Set 3 = dark blue
Set 4 = light green
Set 5 = pink
Set 6 = light blue

For the small single motifs you will need 1 skein, for the larger single motifs 2–3 skeins, for the continuous borders 3–4 skeins. White organza. Small round embroidery frame.

Basic Stitch: Satin stitch with 3 strands of cotton.

Embroidering the motifs:
Trace the motifs and transfer onto the organza with dressmaker's carbon paper. Cut around the motif, leaving enough organza to fit into the frame. Baste the organza onto the towelling (as shown in the top photograph on the right), positioning motifs as follows:

Sets 1 and 4: From lower edge, face cloth 5 cm (2″), guest towel 7 cm (2¾″), hand towel 8 cm (3″), bath towel 12 cm (4¾″). On face cloth and guest towel, work 1 motif equidistant from the sides; for hand and bath towels, work across whole width of fabric. Use satin stitch.

Sets 2 and 5: From lower edge, face cloth 5 cm (2″), guest towel 5 cm (2″), hand towel 10 cm (4″), bath towel 14 cm (5½″), equidistant from the sides. Stems, leaves, and flowers are worked in satin stitch.

Sets 3 and 6: From lower edge, face cloth 4 cm (1½″), guest towel 5 cm (2″), hand towel 9 cm (3½″), bath towel 13 cm (5″), equidistant from the sides. Embroider the motif in satin stitch.

When the embroidery is complete, cut the organza away about 2 cm (¾″) from the motif, snipping inside the design if necessary. Remove organza threads with tweezers.

Satin stitch on towelling

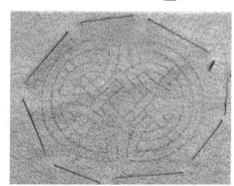

Trace the motif and transfer onto organza with dressmaker's carbon paper. When cutting around motif, remember to allow enough organza to fit into the frame. Baste the organza to the towelling around the motif.

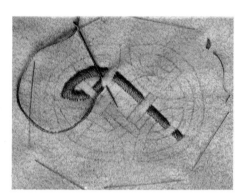

Follow the lines of the motif with straight or diagonal satin stitch, using three strands of cotton in the needle.

When the work is complete, cut around and, if necessary, inside the motif, then draw out all the threads with tweezers.

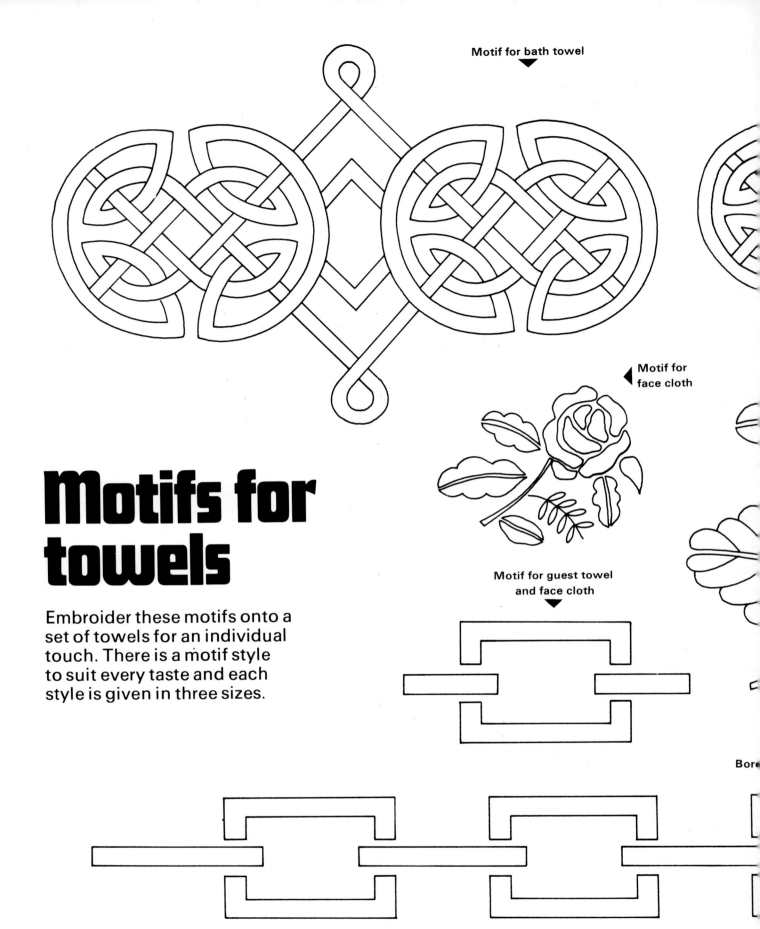

Motif for bath towel

Motif for face cloth

Motifs for towels

Embroider these motifs onto a set of towels for an individual touch. There is a motif style to suit every taste and each style is given in three sizes.

Motif for guest towel and face cloth

Bor

Motif for guest towel
and face cloth
▼

Motif for hand towel
▼

Motif for hand towel
and bath towel
▼

Motif for guest towel
▼

hand towel and bath towel
▼

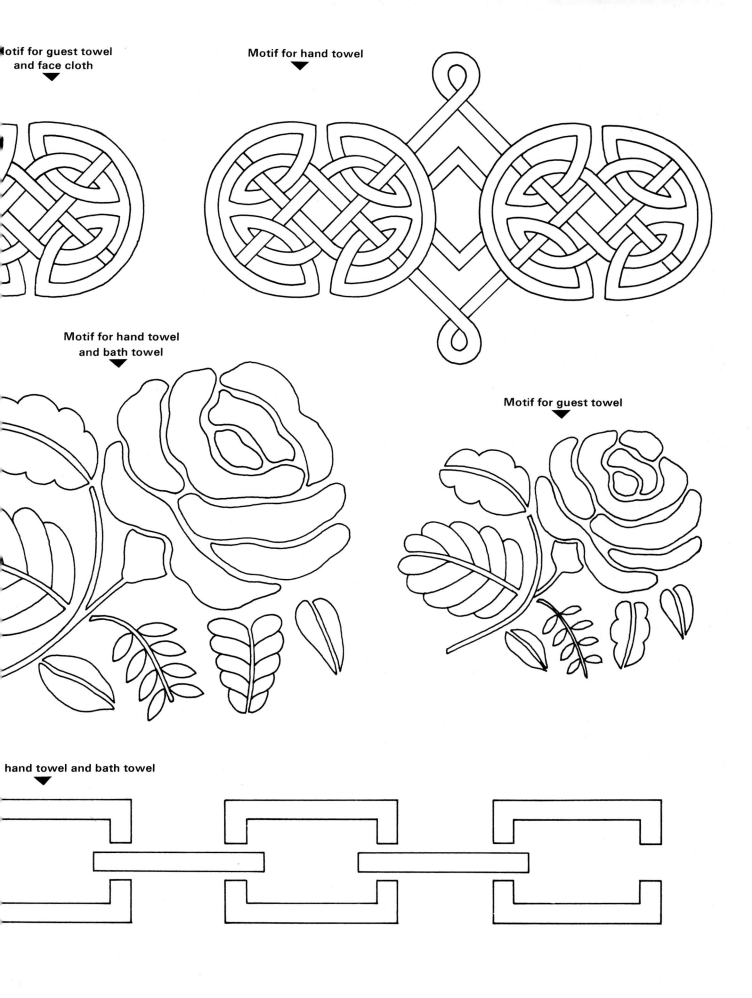

ABCDEFGHIJ
TUVWXYZ
abcdefghijklmnopqrstuvwxyz

MARIE

MARIE

MARIELLE

1 2 3 4 5   6 7 8 9 0

abcdefghijklmn
opqrstuvwxyz

Especially for Children

Toys and games

Here are some toys and games
for super-mums to make — and some for
clever children to make too.
New kinds of soft toys, an exciting
cardboard train, bead jewellery
and a wonderful puppet theatre
complete with puppets and costumes
— all in this section.

Quick and easy toymaking

From Mother, with love

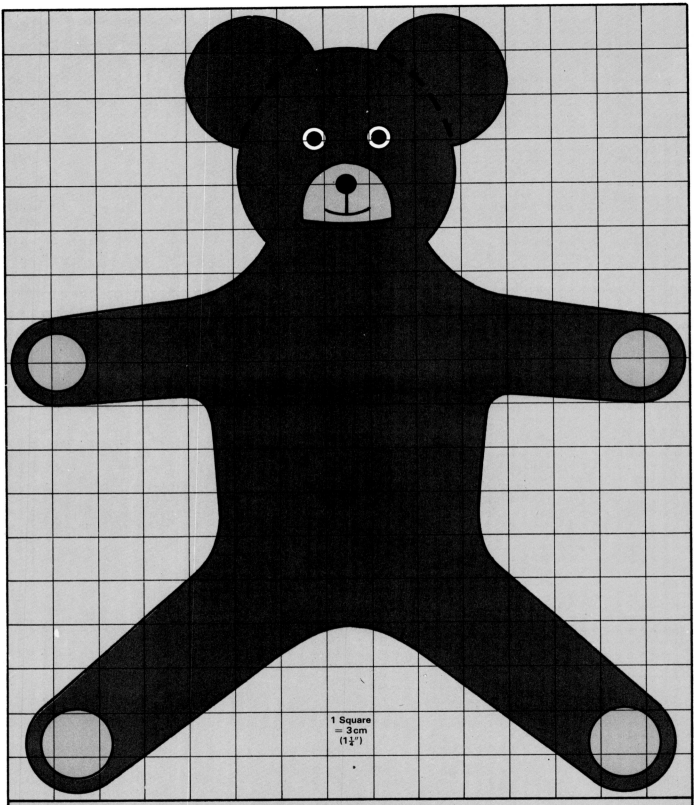

1 Square
= 3 cm
(1¼")

Enlarging a graph pattern

A graph pattern is simply a plan from which you draw your own paper pattern. The scale of the pattern here is 1 square = 3 cm (1¼"). To make a pattern for the bear, draw an area 45 cm x 54 cm (18¾" x 22½") on a piece of paper and mark it off into 3 cm (1¼") squares. Make dots where the bear outline touches the lines of the graph. Connect the dots and your pattern is ready to use. Any pattern can be enlarged by putting a grid over it and redrawing it on larger squares.

Size: 53 cm (21″) tall.
Materials Required:
Teddy Bear: Brown fake-fur fabric 70 cm x 140 cm wide (27″ x 54″ wide). Lightweight brown corduroy 10 cm x 45 cm (4″ x 18″). Small pieces of white and black felt. 2 stuffed-toy eyes. 1 small black dome button. Brown sewing thread. Foam pieces for stuffing. **Panda:** White fake-fur fabric 70 cm x 140 cm wide (27″ x 54″ wide). Black fake-fur fabric 23 cm x 90 cm (9″ x 36″). Lightweight black corduroy 10 cm x 36 cm (4″ x 14″). 2 stuffed-toy eyes. White and black sewing thread. Foam pieces for stuffing.

Making the teddy bear

Both the teddy bear and panda are made from a graph pattern. Follow enlarging instructions under graph to make the pattern.
1. Fold fabric in half, right sides together, making sure pile runs downward on both halves. Pin pattern in place and trace outline onto the fabric with tailor's chalk.
2. Baste fabric together so pieces won't shift. Cut out, adding 2 cm ($\frac{3}{4}$″) seam allowance around edge. Stitch on chalked line, leaving 10 cm (4″) open at crotch for stuffing. (If sewing by hand, use backstitch on all seams.)
3. Trim seam allowance to 1 cm ($\frac{3}{8}$″). Clip all corners and curves to stitching. Turn teddy bear to the right side.
4. Stuff with foam. Turn edges of opening to inside and slip-stitch closed.
Paws: Cut paw pads from pattern. Trace onto wrong side of corduroy. Cut out, adding 1 cm ($\frac{3}{8}$″) seam allowance. Work small running stitches on chalked line. Clip seam allowance to stitching and turn to wrong side on thread outline. Baste seam allowance in place. Sew paw pads to legs.
Face: Cut muzzle from pattern and trace onto wrong side of corduroy, adding

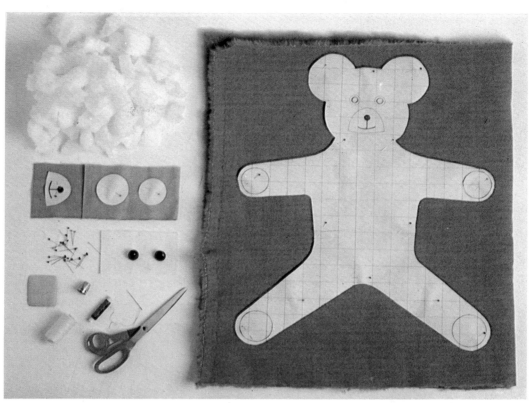

1. Fold fabric, right sides together. Pin pattern to the fabric and mark outline with tailor's chalk. Mark pads and muzzle.

2. Remove the pattern. Baste fabric together. Stitch on chalked outlines.

3. Cut out bear. Clip seam allowance to the stitching line along curves.

4. Stuff bear, making sure the ears and legs are well filled and joints are loose.

seam allowance as for pads. Cut mouth from black felt; stitch to muzzle. Sew on nose button. Make muzzle in same manner as paw pads and sew to face, leaving bottom open for stuffing. Stuff and sew opening closed. Cut two outer eye circles from white felt and secure in place with eyes.

Making the panda

Mark pattern on white fake-fur fabric as for teddy bear, but omit the ears. Mark and cut ears from black fake-fur fabric, adding 1 cm ($\frac{3}{8}$″) seam allowance. Baste body pieces together, but leave head unbasted. Stitch two ears to each head piece, right sides together. Fold up ears, baste head, and complete as for teddy bear. Make paw pads from corduroy and muzzle from fake-fur fabric. Mouth and nose are omitted. Secure eyes, but omit felt.

Running Stitch: Pass the needle over and under the fabric to make a line of stitches. The stitches are usually an even length.

189

Children love their toys, but they do have to stand up to a lot of rough handling! These cuddly animals are designed to be hugged, sat on, thrown around — and still be friends! We also recommend them for tiny tots because they are warm, soft, and safe. You'll find them a creative way to use up scraps of fabric.

Fun to throw — comfortable to sit on. Beetle is 23 x 37.5 cm (9″ x 14¾″).

Sturdy toys to make in an hour

Soft toys for hard play

The bright butterfly in fake-fur fabric measures 30 x 35.5cm (11¾" x 14"). The happy fish is a favourite in blue felt. He is 25 x 38cm (10" x 15").

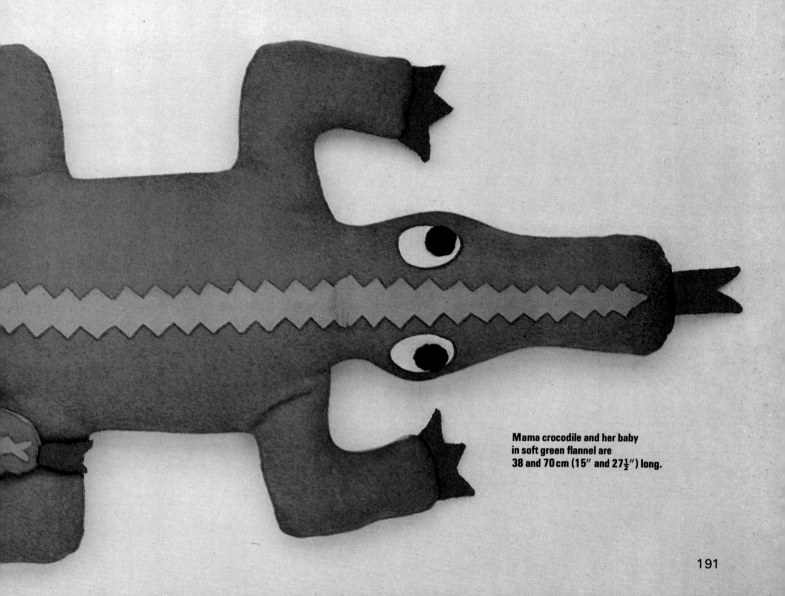

Mama crocodile and her baby
in soft green flannel are
38 and 70 cm (15" and 27½") long.

Materials Required: Remnants of fabric: cotton, wool, fake-fur, felt, etc. Matching sewing thread. Foam pieces or kapok for stuffing. Make eyes from felt or pompons.

DIRECTIONS

Draw paper patterns from the graph pattern. One square of the graph = 3 cm ($1\frac{1}{4}$"). The baby crocodile is same size and can be traced from the page. Mama crocodile is made from the enlarged graph pattern. Add 1 cm ($\frac{3}{8}$") seam allowance all around each pattern piece except eyes, mouths, body circles, and fish fin. Fold fabric, right sides together. Pin patterns to fabric, and cut out pieces. Place body pieces right sides together and stitch, leaving sufficient opening for turning and stuffing. Turn to right side and stuff loosely. Sew the opening closed. Further directions are given below.

Fish: Cut fins and stitch to body pieces, then make body. Make tail and sew to body. Cut out mouth and eyes. Slip-stitch in place.

Butterfly: Make body and a pair of wings separately. Sew wings securely to body. Sew two felt strips to head for antennae. Sew on the wing circles with slip stitch. Sew on the eyes.

Beetle: Stitch three sections together to make top body piece. Make body. Sew on body circles with slip stitch. Make antennae from tightly rolled tubes of fabric.

Crocodiles: Place claws and tongue on the right side of one body piece, with seam lines matching and pieces lying inward on the body. (They will be facing outward when the body is stitched and turned to the right side). Make body. Cut back stripes and eyes. Sew in place with slip stitch.

192

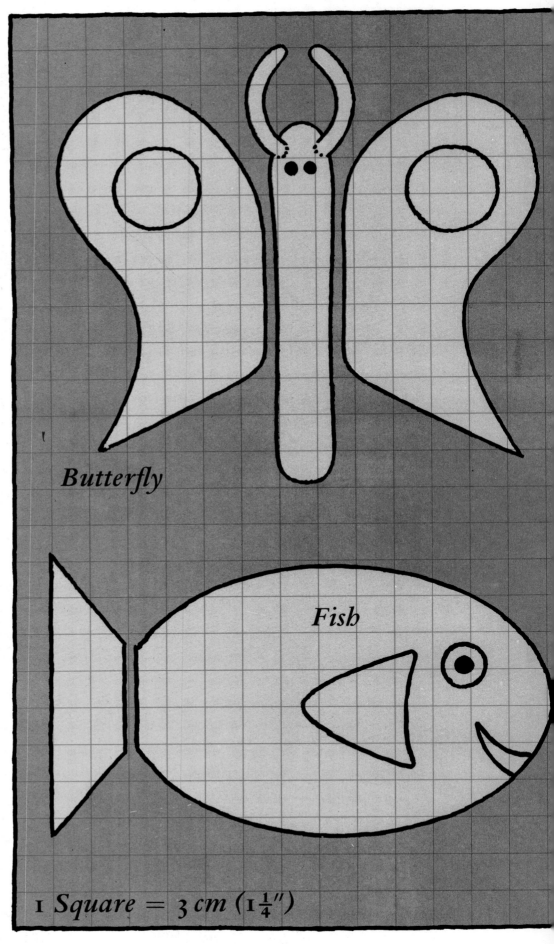

Butterfly

Fish

ɪ *Square* = ₃ *cm* (ɪ¼″)

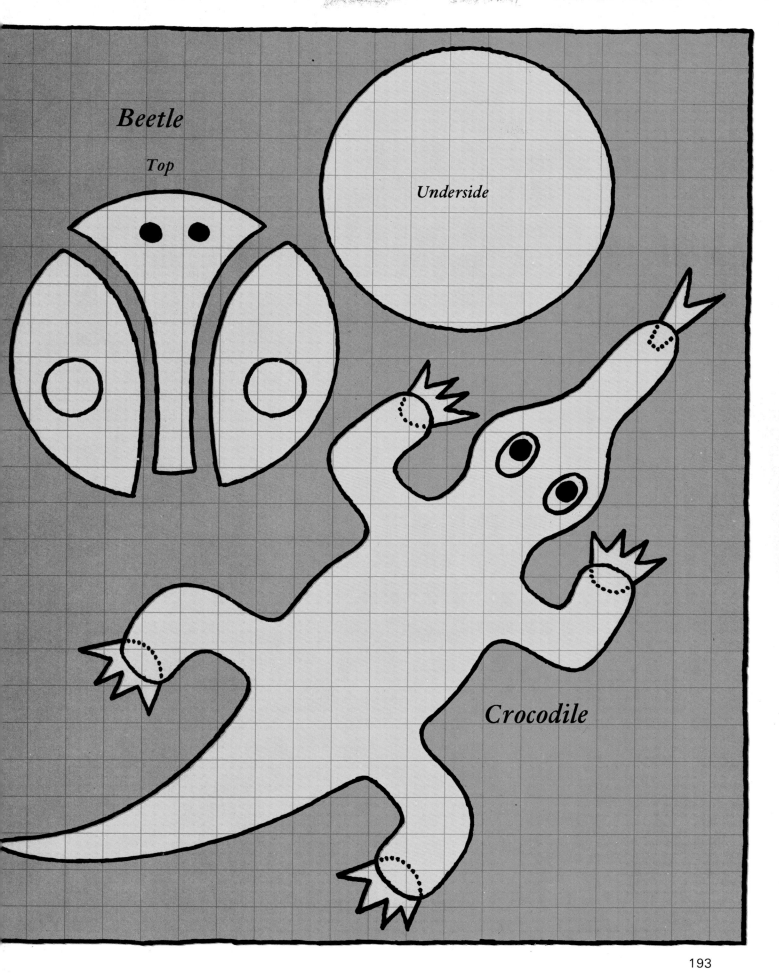

Beetle

Top

Underside

Crocodile

Romantic dolls
of yesteryear

If you have ever admired the beautiful china dolls of the Victorian age, you will love their modern cousins, with their pale, delicate faces and their romantic clothes. They measure 38 cm (15") from the tip of their boots to their hair ribbons and have a fabric body stuffed with kapok so that they can sit up. The limbs and head are white air-setting clay which can be painted and varnished for a smooth, porcelain-like finish.

All four are made in the same way but with different clothes and hair.

Making the dolls

Materials Required: White, air-drying modelling clay. Bottle of modelling glaze. Paintbox colours. Kapok for stuffing. Small amounts of fabric, narrow elastic, lace, and yarn. 2 paint brushes (medium and fine). Wooden board. Rolling pin. Small kitchen knife.

*

1 Warm the modelling clay slightly between your hands. For the lower arm, make a sausage 6 cm ($2\frac{1}{2}$") long (2 cm [$\frac{3}{4}$"] diameter at top, 1 cm [$\frac{3}{8}$"] at bottom). Smooth into shape with the fingers, wetting the clay slightly if it gets too dry. Wetting it also gives a smoother finish. At the upper end, make a bulge all around to hold it in the fabric upper arm.

2 The legs are worked in the same way. In place of feet, shape small boots. For the tops of the boots and laces, roll thin pieces of clay and press them on.

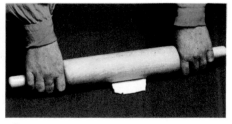

3 For the shoulder part, roll out a piece 5 cm x 8 cm (2" x 3") and about 7 mm ($\frac{1}{4}$") thick with the rolling pin. Round off corners and edges.

4 With the end of the paintbrush, make holes in the 4 corners.

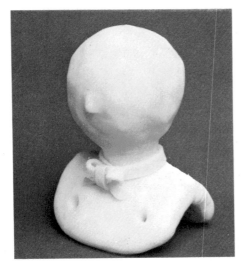

5 Make the neck 1 cm ($\frac{3}{8}''$) high and 2 cm ($\frac{3}{4}''$) in diameter and press onto the shoulder part. The head is then worked onto it. Make a ball about 5 cm (2") diameter and press onto the neck. Then with knife and fingers, model the nose and smooth over the join with the neck. Try to make the head and neck as even as possible. The neckband is a thin strip of clay formed into a bow.

Finally, bend the shoulder section around to a curve.

6 Place the shaped parts on one side and leave them to set. The clay is air-setting and becomes rock-hard with a marble-like finish.

7 Now paint the various parts — the boots with laces or buttons, the hands with gloves or nails, the bow at the neck. The features on the face can be sketched in first with a pencil. If it is not right the first time, you can wipe it off again. Glaze when dry. (Glaze becomes transparent as it dries.)

9 Stuff all 5 body parts firmly with kapok. Sew the upper arms and legs to the body where indicated. Push the bulges of the clay legs and arms into the fabric legs and arms. Draw narrow tapes through the casings and knot tightly. The head-shoulder part is sewn onto the body through the 4 holes with buttonhole thread.

Cut hair from wool yarn and stick onto the head with glue; trim into shape.

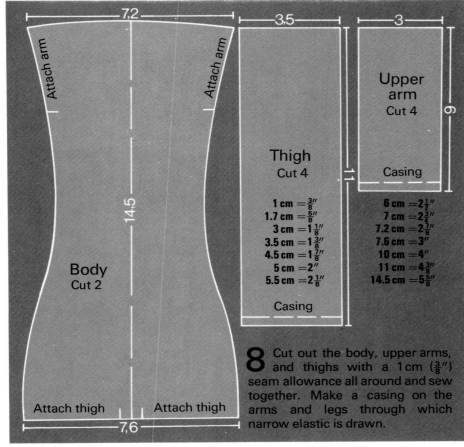

Body
Cut 2

Attach arm   Attach arm

7.2

14.5

Attach thigh   Attach thigh

7.6

Thigh
Cut 4

3.5

Upper
arm
Cut 4

3

9

11

Casing

1 cm = $\frac{3}{8}''$	6 cm = $2\frac{1}{2}''$
1.7 cm = $\frac{5}{8}''$	7 cm = $2\frac{3}{4}''$
3 cm = $1\frac{1}{8}''$	7.2 cm = $2\frac{7}{8}''$
3.5 cm = $1\frac{3}{8}''$	7.6 cm = 3''
4.5 cm = $1\frac{7}{8}''$	10 cm = 4''
5 cm = 2''	11 cm = $4\frac{3}{8}''$
5.5 cm = $2\frac{1}{8}''$	14.5 cm = $5\frac{5}{8}''$

Casing

8 Cut out the body, upper arms, and thighs with a 1 cm ($\frac{3}{8}''$) seam allowance all around and sew together. Make a casing on the arms and legs through which narrow elastic is drawn.

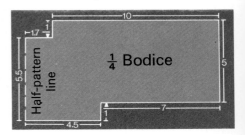

10

1.7   1

5.5   Half-pattern line

$\frac{1}{4}$ Bodice

5

4.5   1   7   1

10 Cut out the bodice of the dress twice with 1 cm ($\frac{3}{8}''$) seam allowance (it is open at the back). Join the shoulder, sleeve, and side seams. Turn in the edges of the sleeves and neck. Then cut out the skirt to measure 40 cm x 20 cm ($15\frac{3}{4}''$ x 8") plus seam allowance and join to a circle along the narrow sides. Gather one edge and sew to the bodice; hem the other edge. This is the basic shape for all the dress variations. You can now trim the dress with lace and braid. The outfit can be completed with a little apron and a wide sash, or the dress can be made from several fabrics, as illustrated on previous pages.

Pull the dress over the doll and sew up invisibly at the back by hand.

Introducing a new friend.....

May I introduce myself: I'm Floppy, the softest, furriest, and friendliest polar bear in the whole world and I can't wait to meet you. I'm always ready for a game, so please cuddle me, carry me, sit on me, or play with me — I never get tired of having fun. My coat is fake-fur fabric and my soft stuffing makes me nice to hold and hug. Let's be playmates!

Materials Required: White fake-fur fabric: 1.10 m (1¼ yd), 140 cm (54") wide. Remnant of black fake-fur fabric or felt for paws and nose. Kapok for stuffing: about 600 gm (22 oz). 2 eyes.

Cutting out: Enlarge the pattern pieces from the graph onto large sheets of tissue paper, adding seam allowances of 1 cm (⅜") on all pieces. Place the pieces on wrong side of single fabric and cut out. Half of front body is given; cut out the whole shape in one piece. Cut out the back body, side head, side snout, tail, and paws twice. Cut the ears 4 times. The remaining pieces are cut out once. Remember to cut the nose and paws from black fabric.

Sewing: Stroke the pile away from the seam before pinning and stitching so that it does not get caught up in the stitching.

Body: Stitch the darts in the 2 back pieces. Pin, baste, and stitch the 2 back pieces together, right sides facing, from point **b** to point **j**.

Stitch the tail pieces together around the curved edge, right sides facing. Turn and stuff. Pin the tail to the right side of the front body where indicated; stitch it along seamline. Now pin front and back body pieces together, right sides facing, leaving openings at paws and neck. Catch in the tail in stitching. Snip into the seam allowance at the corners and curves. Turn to the right side.

Head: Pin and stitch the upper head pieces together, right sides facing, matching points **c**; stitch the lower head pieces, matching points **d**. Stitch the upper head section to the side pieces, matching points **e**; then stitch the lower head section to the side pieces, matching points **f**.

Now join the snout pieces together, matching all markings. Stitch the snout to the head, matching points **i** and working from each corner to the next separately and finishing the thread off securely every time. Snip diagonally into the seam allowance at the corner of each side head piece. With double buttonhole thread, sew a line of running stitches right around the snout/head seamline. This thread is used later for shaping the head. Stitch the ears together around the curved edge, right sides facing. Turn to the right side and sew the straight edge by hand.

197

Our young model has played
with Floppy for hours.
After all, you can make up
so many games with him –
and use him as a pillow
when you're tired !

Here is the graph pattern for the pieces to make the cuddly polar bear in the photograph:
1 Body front. **2** Body back. **3** Side of head. **4** Upper head 1. **5** Upper head 2. **6** Lower head 1. **7** Lower head 2. **8** Snout side. **9** Upper snout. **10** Lower snout. **11** Ear. **12** Nose. **13** Back paw. **14** Front paw. **15** Tail.

Sew the ears to the side head at the positions marked.

The head is now ready to stitch to the body. The slit marked on the body front must be cut open to enable the pieces to be pinned together right sides facing. Distribute the ease evenly and stitch. Now pull the head back to the right side.

Cut the fur pile short on the snout and inside the ears. Attach the eyes firmly on the snout seamline. Stuff the head and legs firmly, shaping the snout slightly by pulling up the buttonhole thread.

Sew a few crossed threads loosely across head and leg openings to prevent the stuffing falling back into the body. Now stuff the body loosely so that it retains a soft, floppy shape. After stuffing, sew up the slit firmly by hand.

Finally, sew on the nose and paws, turning under the seam allowance. If using fur fabric, cut the pile short on the nose and paws in the same way as on the snout and ears.

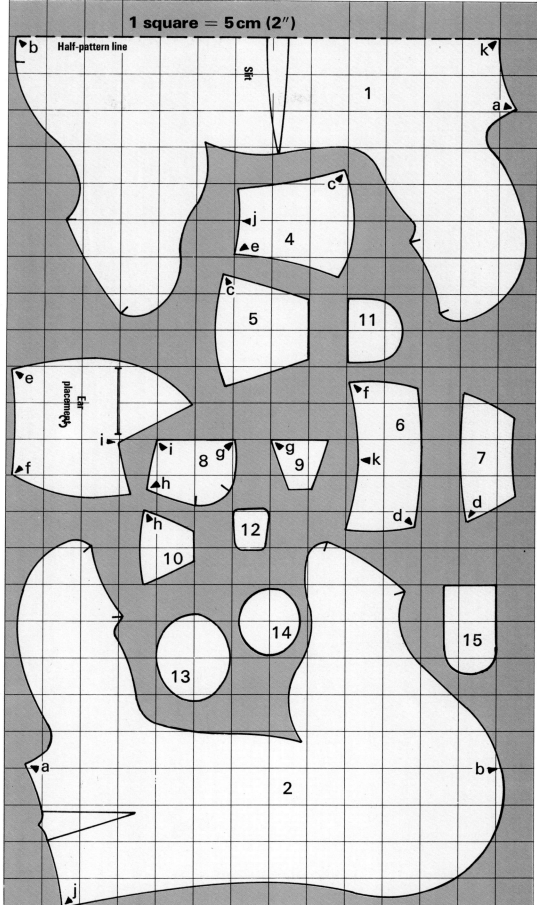

1 square = 5 cm (2″)

Half-pattern line

Small presents in beadwork

It's easy to make up your own beadwork patterns. Coloured beads, nylon thread, a fine needle, and a little imagination are all you need. You can arrange the beads on a slightly adhesive surface or a piece of felt so that they don't roll away.

Materials Required:
Beads in a variety of colours. Fine nylon thread. Embroidery or beading needle.

Threading the beads
Napkin rings: Fasten the thread by winding it twice round the 1st bead and knotting it, then pick up 7 more beads. To begin the 2nd row, pick up the 9th bead and insert the needle back through the 7th bead (Diagram 1).

The 9th bead now lies directly above the 8th bead. Next, pick up the 10th bead and insert the needle through the 5th bead. Continue in this way to the end of the row. The beads in one row lie in the spaces between the beads in the previous row (Diagram 2). Continue to work row after

Follow the illustrations to make these three colourful coasters.

row in this way until the work measures 10 cm (4"), ending with a row which fits into the first row.

To close the ring: Take the thread through the beads of each row (Diagram 3). Knot the beginning and end threads together firmly with a double knot. Use a double knot, also, if you have to change threads while working. Run the ends through several rows.

Four-sided coasters: The mat on the left measures 14 cm (5½") x 15 cm (6"), the one on the right 14 cm (5½") square. Begin with 26 beads and work a flat piece as for napkin rings.

Six-sided coasters: Start with 1 bead and add 1 bead on each end of every row until the mat is 13 cm (5⅛") wide. Work straight for 8 cm (3⅛"), then decrease 1 bead on each end of every row until 1 remains.

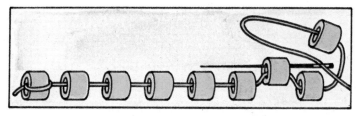

1. Leave small spaces between each of the beads when threading the first row.

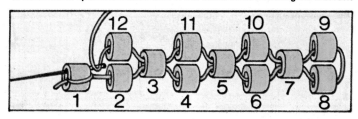

2. The beads in adjacent rows always fit together in a staggered formation.

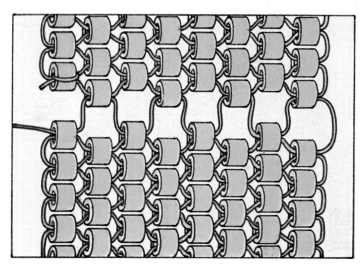

3. Draw the thread through the first and last rows of the piece to form a ring.

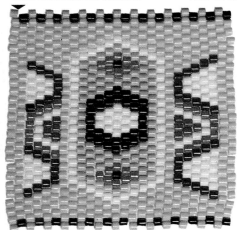

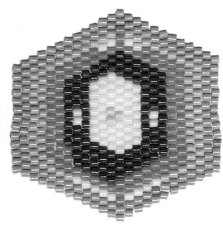

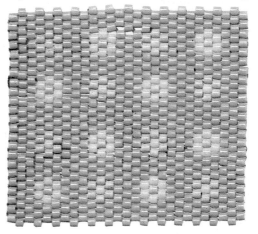

Sweet wagon   Stick wagon   Lollipop wagon

What an ambush!
A train-load
of delicious
sweets!

A party train in cardboard

Ambush on the Candy Express!

Partytime is time to have fun and to eat lots of brightly-coloured sweets. What better way of delivering the goodies than on the Candy Express with its sturdy locomotive and gay wagons full to the brim of tantalizing treats! It's simple to make from strong cardboard and will stand up to a lot of wear and tear on the day of the party. The children can each take home a wagon filled with booty, and when all the sweets have been eaten, the wagons can become boxes for storing small treasures.

Materials Required: Heavy cardboard. Craft knife. Poster paints. Quick-setting glue. Clear varnish.

Making the train
The parts of the locomotive and wagons are given on the graph overleaf. Enlarge them on a grid drawn directly onto the cardboard. Four of the wagons are exactly the same size; the only way they differ is in the cutting out of the sides and the painting. The exception is the stick wagon, which has only two low sides and no back or front.
When the outlines have been drawn on the cardboard, cut along the outlines with the craft knife held against a metal ruler to ensure a straight edge. Uneven edges can be smoothed with fine sandpaper.
After cutting out all the parts of the train, paint them in the colours and patterns shown on the graph.
Wagons: When the paint is dry, glue the sides of each wagon to the edges of the base (not on top of it). Then stick the front and back to the base between the side pieces. Add the strips along the top edge of the sides.

Bonbon wagon **Licorice wagon** **Locomotive**

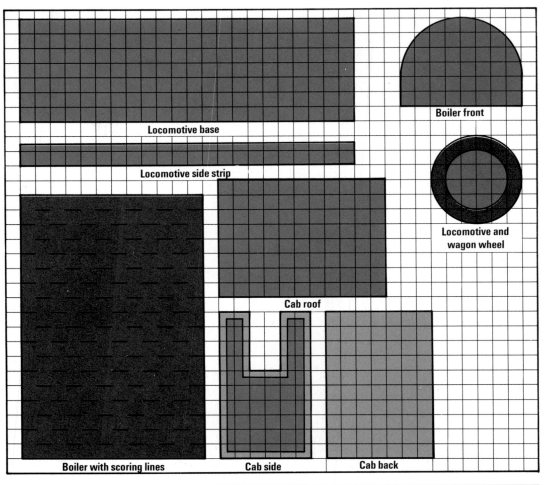

Locomotive base

Boiler front

Locomotive side strip

Locomotive and wagon wheel

Cab roof

Boiler with scoring lines

Cab side

Cab back

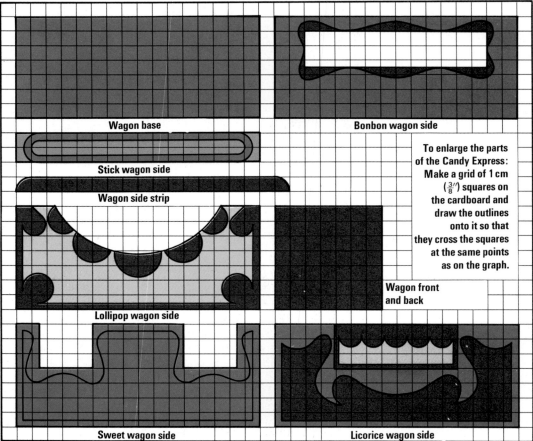

Wagon base

Bonbon wagon side

Stick wagon side

Wagon side strip

To enlarge the parts of the Candy Express: Make a grid of 1 cm ($\frac{3}{8}''$) squares on the cardboard and draw the outlines onto it so that they cross the squares at the same points as on the graph.

Lollipop wagon side

Wagon front and back

Sweet wagon side

Licorice wagon side

If you want the wheels to turn, pin them on with glass-headed pins; otherwise, glue them to the sides.

Finally, coat the wagons with clear varnish to make the surface smooth.

Locomotive: The locomotive is slightly more complicated to make. First glue the narrow side strips to the long edges of the base. Score the boiler along the lines marked on the graph pattern, bend it around to a cylindrical shape, and glue it to the top edges of the side strips, 2 cm ($\frac{3}{4}''$) from the front. Then glue on the front of the boiler, shaping it to fit with sandpaper.

Glue the sides of the driver's cab immediately behind the boiler, then add the back of the cab between the sides. Stick on the roof so that it protrudes 2 cm ($\frac{3}{4}''$) over the boiler in the front. Position the wheels as follows: The back ones go directly under the centre of the cab, the others are placed at 6 cm ($2\frac{3}{8}''$) intervals.

Coat the locomotive with clear varnish as for the wagons.

If you wish to make couplings so that the locomotive will pull the wagons, cut out strips measuring 1 cm x 6 cm ($\frac{3}{8}''$ x $2\frac{1}{4}''$) and fasten them with short pins to the underside of the wagons and locomotive. The train is now ready for action!

Making a wooden train

For a more substantial toy, the train can also be made of plywood with firm axles for the wheels. Cut out the shapes with an ordinary tenon saw, and the windows in the wagons and the wheels with a fret saw. Glue the parts together; paint and varnish them as for the cardboard train (for extra strength, use wood glue).

Pretty things to make

For her and her dolls

This is a perfect pastime for children. It is easy to knit long cords in bright colours and fun to think up things to make with them. We give some ideas on the next page.

It's easy to shape the coils into circles and squares to use as cushion covers.

Knitting on a spool knitter

1 You will need a spool knitter, a fine knitting needle, and yarn. You can make a knitter with a thread spool and four nails.

2 To cast on, put the yarn through the knitter from top to bottom and wind it around the post as shown.

3 Continue to wind the yarn from right to left around each post. You are now ready to begin knitting the cord.

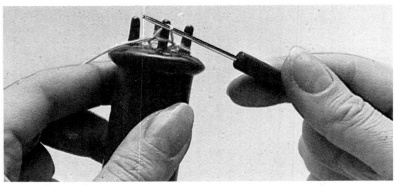

4 Bring the yarn past the first post so that it lies above the first loop. Put the needle into the loop and lift it over the yarn and the post. Turn the knitter to the next post and repeat. Continue to work in this manner until the cord is the required length.

5 From time to time, pull the cord down into the knitter. When you have knitted 1 cm ($\frac{1}{2}''$), the stitches form a spider web.

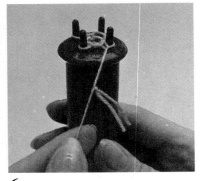

6 To join a new strand, tie the two pieces together and continue to knit. Stuff the ends into the centre of the cord.

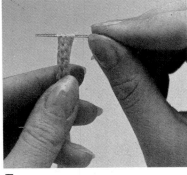

7 To end the cord, lift it from the knitter and thread the end of the yarn through the four loops. Pull the yarn tight.

8 Sew the coils together with overcasting on the wrong side, using yarn and a blunt-ended needle. Weave in the yarn ends.

These toy accessories and tiny mice are all made from knitted coils of yarn in different lengths and colours.

Wind a cord around a large cotton ball and sew the coils together loosely. Sew on felt ears, bead eyes, and yarn whiskers. Embroider the nose.

For a striped scarf, make several cords of different colours. Knot the ends and sew the cords together with matching yarn.

Take two long cords and begin in the middle with a knot. From there, wind and stitch the two cords in parallel coils around the doll's head until the cap is large enough. Turn in the two ends at the back of the cap and secure them on the wrong side.

Hold three cords side by side and form them into a spiral. Sew them in place. Make a loop at the end. Make the back from a scrap of cotton fabric.

Start winding from the feet of the baby doll, and stitching the coils together invisibly. For the head-piece, coil the cords in a circle.

Make a braid. Take it back over right shoulder, then around tummy. Make a loop at back and bring end over left shoulder to front. Stitch in place.

207

Here are all the characters together. Poor Gretel has fainted in fright at the sight of the wicked witch. But the Princess, with her beautiful blonde hair and golden crown, remains quite calm.

The wicked witch is up to her tricks here. She is driving away the worthy policeman with her broom stick as he comes to rescue Hansel and Gretel from her spells.

Take your seats for the best show in town! What could be more fun for the children than their very own puppet theatre which you have made for them yourself. All the much-loved fairy tale characters are here — Hansel and Gretel and the wicked witch, plus a charming and beautiful Princess, a crafty robber, and a brave policeman. The scenery, too, can easily be made at home with leftover paint, cardboard, scissors, and glue.

Now the brave policeman has got the situation under control. He has grabbed the witch's accomplice, the robber, and is about to haul him rather unceremoniously off to prison.

Gretel is still very frightened, but has managed to outwit the wicked witch who, in a towering rage makes her escape on her broomstick and vanishes into the distance.

Making the basic puppet

Materials Required: Wooden balls: one 6 cm ($2\frac{1}{2}$") diam., one 1.5 cm ($\frac{5}{8}$") diam., and two of 3 cm ($1\frac{1}{8}$") diam. Wood strips: 1.5 cm x 4 cm x 9 cm long ($\frac{5}{8}$" x $1\frac{1}{2}$" x $3\frac{1}{2}$" long), 2 cm x 2 cm x 22 cm long ($\frac{3}{4}$" x $\frac{3}{4}$" x 9" long), and 1 cm x 1 cm x 29 cm long ($\frac{3}{8}$" x $\frac{3}{8}$" x $11\frac{1}{2}$" long). Scraps of fabric, felt, and wool. Glossy paint for faces, socks, and shoes. Fine string. Needle and thread. Tacks. Small screw hooks. Hammer. Glue. Small saw. Gimlet. Sandpaper.

Here you can see all the wooden parts which make up the puppet. Head: Saw off 7 cm ($2\frac{3}{4}$") of the 1 cm x 1 cm ($\frac{3}{8}$" x $\frac{3}{8}$") strip and nail it to the large (head) ball. Sketch the face in pencil and paint it. The small (nose) ball is painted separately, then flattened a little on one side with sandpaper and glued on. Finally, insert a hook into the head to hold the string.

Legs and feet: Saw the 2 cm x 2 cm ($\frac{3}{4}$" x $\frac{3}{4}$") strip into two 6 cm ($2\frac{1}{2}$") and two 5 cm (2") lengths. Sand the corners and glue the two different lengths together for legs and shoes. Round off the toes with sandpaper. Paint shoes and socks in appropriate colours (see colours in the pictures).

Hands: Bore through the two 3 cm ($1\frac{1}{8}$") diameter balls with the gimlet.

Next, join the parts of the body together. First glue the head with the strip onto the wide (body) strip. Push the legs into the trousers, securing at the sides with tacks. Then nail the trousers to the body, folding in the width. Sew the hand balls to the sleeves through the bored holes. The top is left open at the back so that the puppet can be dressed and sewn up afterward. Fasten top to the wooden body with a tack at front and back. For the hair, wrap wool around a piece of cardboard to the required length and stitch at the centre with backstitches. Glue onto the head with the hook still protruding. Cut the hair open and trim as required.

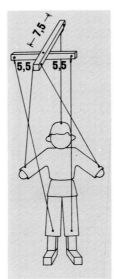

Finally, fasten the strings. Cut two 11 cm ($4\frac{3}{8}$") long strips from 1 cm ($\frac{3}{8}$") square piece. Nail them together at centre of one strip and 7.5 cm ($2\frac{7}{8}$") from one end of the other. Bore a hole at each of the four ends and thread the string through as shown. First the head string, about 50 cm ($19\frac{1}{2}$") long, then the leg strings, which must be long enough for the puppet to stand up straight when the cross is held horizontally. Sew the leg strings to the trouser fabric. Finally, the arm string is sewn to one sleeve, drawn through the front hole, then sewn to the other sleeve. Cut the arm string long so that the arms are raised.

Puppets' clothes: Numbers are centimetres; inch equivalents are: 2 cm = $\frac{3}{4}$", 2.5 cm = 1", 5 cm = 2", 5.5 cm = $2\frac{1}{4}$", 4.5 cm = $1\frac{3}{4}$", 7 cm = $2\frac{3}{4}$", 7.5 cm = $2\frac{7}{8}$", 9 cm = $3\frac{1}{2}$", 10 cm = 4", 12 cm = $4\frac{3}{4}$", 14 cm = $5\frac{1}{2}$", 15.5 cm = 6", 18 cm = 7".

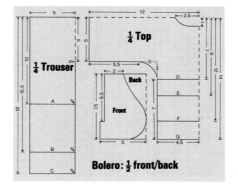

Bolero: $\frac{1}{2}$ front/back

Making the puppet clothes

Hansel

First stitch the top (length E), dress the puppet, and nail to the body. Cut the trousers in one piece (length A): fold the sides to the centre, stitch closely around line **a–b,** and cut open. Turn. Cut 2 straps and 2 hearts. Sew on straps with buttons and glue on the red hearts. Nail the trousers at the back; at the front, sew them to the shirt under the straps. The hair is 7 cm ($2\frac{3}{4}$") long at sides and 4 cm ($1\frac{1}{2}$") at front.

Princess

First stitch a pair of long white pantaloons (length C) as for Hansel's trousers, trim with white lace, dress the puppet and nail to the body. Then make the top (length F) and nail on. For the skirt, cut out a piece of fabric measuring 52 cm x 22 cm ($20\frac{1}{2}$" x 9"), join and hem it, then gather it to the waist measurement. Sew on a sash; add gold braid around the waist, hem, and neck. Sew the skirt to the top. The leg strings are drawn through the skirt and fastened to the pantaloons. The hair is 20 cm (8") long; the crown is made of stiff gold paper decorated with pearl buttons.

Policeman

First make the trousers (length C) as for Hansel and nail to the body. Then make the top (length F), sewing on small buttons. Dress and nail to the body. Sew a white belt over the tunic. For the cap, cut a circle 4.5 cm ($1\frac{3}{4}$") in diameter, a strip 20 cm x 2.5 cm (8" x 1"), and a small peak to go around $\frac{1}{3}$ of the circle. Sew them all together by hand. Above the peak, sew on a strand of white yarn with a knot at each end. Draw the head string through the top of the cap. The policeman's hair is 6–7 cm ($2\frac{1}{2}$–$2\frac{3}{4}$") long. For the truncheon, use a matchstick with a felt loop attached to it.

Gretel

First make the white top (length E), then the pantaloons (length A) as for Hansel's trousers. Trim both with lace and nail to the body. Cut out a strip for the skirt measuring 38 cm x 8 cm (14½" x 3"), join, hem, gather, and sew on floral braid at the hem and waistband. Sew to the blouse. Cut out the bolero as on the diagram and stitch. Embroider flowers on the front in lazy daisy stitch and put over the blouse. For the thick braids, the length of the hair must be at least 20 cm (8").

Witch

Stitch the white pantaloons (length C) as for Hansel's trousers and edge with lace, then make the black top (length F) and nail both to the body. Cut out a strip for the skirt measuring 50 cm x 18 cm (19½" x 7"), join, hem, and gather. For the apron, cut out a piece of fabric 16 cm (6¼") square. Hem on 3 sides, gather the 4th side and sew to the skirt. Put on the skirt and sew to the top. Sew a band around the waist. The hair is about 12 cm (4¾") long, and is made from untwisted string. The head-scarf is frayed. Draw the head string through it. Make the broom by tying small twigs around a stick.

Robber

Make the trousers (length B) as for Hansel and fray the ends. Nail to the body. Then make the top (length G) and fray all outer edges. Nail it over the trousers and wrap parcel string around the waist over the tacks. Wind the hair slightly longer than the policeman's and cut it unevenly. For the hat, use a piece of felt measuring 20 cm (8") square. Wet it, stretch it over a head ball and tie together underneath. Leave it to dry thoroughly, then untie it and trim to a round brim. Secure onto the robber's head and draw the head string through the top of the hat. Stitch a patch onto one of the trouser legs.

211

Scenery for the puppet theatre

To give your puppet play the right atmosphere, it is worth building a simple stage with scenery. The little theatre shown here is made of lightweight white cardboard. Enlarge the houses and trees straight onto the cardboard, being sure to leave enough cardboard for the sky above the houses. Paint the houses and trees with poster paints. Cut out the scenery with a mat or craft knife.

Under each tree is a corresponding base. A slit is cut in the centre to fit the size of the trunk, so that it can slot in and be held firm.

The row of houses is held up at the back with triangular supports stuck on with adhesive tape for easy folding. The stage front is also made from lightweight cardboard supported by triangles. The overall size is optional, but the opening measures 50 cm x 70 cm (19½″ x 27½″). To finish off the stage front, attach a little velvet curtain at either side of the opening.

Here you can see the whole stage. Place the large trees at the front, the row of houses at the back and, in between, the smaller trees. This arrangement gives the stage more depth.

To enlarge the scenery:
Draw a grid very lightly onto the cardboard, so that each square measures 5 cm x 5 cm (2″ x 2″). Redraw the outlines from the graph pattern onto the new grid.

Clothes and accessories

Here is a whole range
of things you can make for children
– clothes to sew and crochet,
bright ideas for children's rooms
and for the garden.

Crochet a playsuit in cheerful colours

Size: 6–9 months.
Materials Required:

100 gm or 4 oz each blue, yellow, red, and green. Crochet hook size 2.50. Zipper: 55 cm or 22" long.
Basic Stitch: Treble stitch with 3 ch for turning.
Tension: 27 sts and 13 R = 10 cm or 4".
Abbreviations: St(s) = stitch(es). R = row(s). Ch = chain. Tr = treble stitch.

DIRECTIONS

The Back and Fronts are worked in strips. **Strip Pattern:** Make 17 ch and work 1 tr into 4th ch from hook and in each ch across. Work straight in tr to 20 cm or 8", then decrease 1 tr at beginning of next R, then decrease 1 tr alternately at end, then beginning of every 9th R 3 times. Continue straight on 11 sts to 41 cm or 16¼".
Back: (Worked from right to left.) **Strip 1:** Work in blue to 41 cm or 16¼", then alternate 4 R green, 4 R blue to 53 cm or 21". Fasten off.
Strip 2: Work in yellow to 41 cm or 16¼", then alternate 4 R red, 4 R yellow to 65 cm or 25½". Fasten off.
Strip 3: Work in green to 41 cm or 16¼", then alternate 4 R blue, 4 R green to 65 cm or 25½". Fasten off.
Strip 4: Work in red to 41 cm or 16¼", then alternate 4 R yellow, 4 R red to 65 cm or 25½". Fasten off.
Strip 5: Repeat Strip 1, but work to 65 cm or 25½".
Strips 6 and 7: Repeat Strips 2 and 3.
Strip 8: Repeat Strip 4, but work to 53 cm or 21".
Left Front: Make Strips 1 and 2 as for Back Strips 1 and 2.
Strip 3: Repeat Back Strip 3, but 7 R from the end, decrease 1 tr at end of next R and every 3rd R 2 times. Fasten off.
Strip 4: Repeat Back Strip 4, omitting the last 7 R. Fasten off.
Right Front: Work to match Left Front for shape, and colour sequence.

Sleeves: Make 39 ch. Tr in 4th ch from hook and each ch across. Work on 37 tr in 2 R blue, 2 R red, 2 R green, and 2 R yellow, increasing 1 st each end of 2nd R and then alternately every 3rd and 2nd R 10 times. Work on the 59 tr to 25 cm or 9¾". Fasten off.
Hood: Make 111 ch and work in tr in stripes as for Sleeves for 17 cm or 6¾". Fasten off.
Finishing: Join strips in order, right sides facing, with backstitch. Join seams. Sew on hood, easing lower edge to fit neck. Work 1 R double crochet along front edges. Join lower edges. Sew in zipper beginning from lower edge.

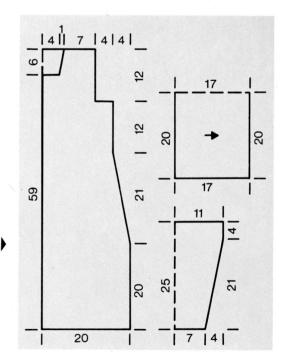

Half-pattern for baby playsuit. The measurements are in centimetres; inches are given in the directions.

215

Bright bonnet for baby

A warm head covering is an important item in every baby's wardrobe. This colourful little striped bonnet will keep your baby well protected during his outings. Crochet it in a variety of bright colours for a change, rather than the usual pink or blue.

*

Size: For a baby 6 months to 1 year.

Materials Required:

Leftover yarn in various colors. Crochet hook 3.50.

Basic Stitch: Treble stitch and chain 3 for turning. Every row begins in the 2nd stitch and ends in the turning chain.

Tension: 22 sts and 10 R = 10 cm or 4".

Abbreviations: St(s) = stitch(es). R = row(s). Tr = treble stitch. Dc = double crochet.

DIRECTIONS

Front: Chain 36 in any colour. Tr in the 4th chain from the hook and in each chain across, chain 3, turn. Work straight in Basic Stitch for 32 R or until piece is 32 cm or 12⅝". Work every R in a different colour and join each new colour in the 1st st of the turning chain.

Back: Chain 22 in any colour. Tr in the 4th chain from hook and in each chain across, chain 3, turn. Continue in Basic Stitch, working a new colour in every R as before. At 7 cm or 2¾", begin to decrease 1 st at each end of every 2nd R 3 times—14 sts at 13 cm or 5".

Finishing: Sew the Front to the Back. Using 2 strands of yarn, work 1 R of dc around the edges of the bonnet. For the ties, use 3 strands of yarn in the same colour as the edging. Make 2 chains, each 40 cm or 15¾" long. Sew 1 tie to each corner of the bonnet. For each tassel, cut a piece of yarn about 12 cm or 4¾" long in each colour. Make 2 bundles and tie each in the middle with yarn in the same colour as the ties. Fold the bundles in half and wrap the yarn around the tassels to form a knob. Tie securely. Sew the tassels to the ties.

A crocheted bonnet can be made very quickly – this one was made in a single afternoon.

The pieces are worked in treble stitch, using a different colour in every row. Make a random colour pattern or try alternating stripes.

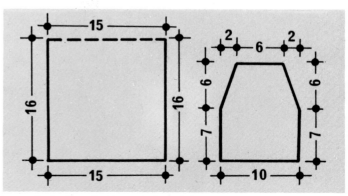

Pattern for back and half-pattern for top. Measurements are in centimetres.

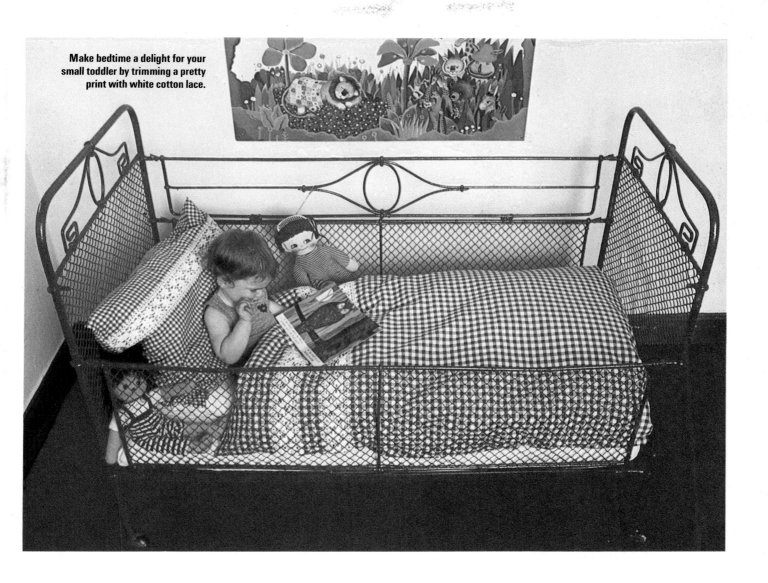

Make bedtime a delight for your small toddler by trimming a pretty print with white cotton lace.

More ideas for the home in easy-care fabrics

One way to sleep pretty...

Duvets or Continental quilts are becoming increasingly popular with young and old alike. Making a bed is so much quicker and easier and suddenly blankets seem very old-fashioned. Here are some ideas for quilt covers and pillows. Note that the open side is closed with ties to make life even simpler.

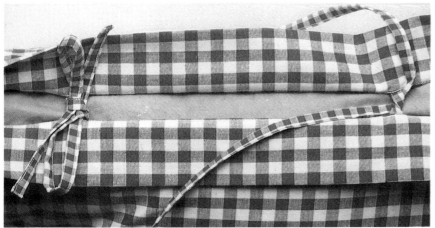

The open edge is closed with ties. Note that a wide hem hides the bows when they are tied.

Size: Pillowcase: 48 cm x 76 cm (19″ x 30″). <u>Child's Quilt Cover</u>: 100 cm x 135 cm (39½″ x 53″). <u>Single Bed Quilt Cover</u>: 135 cm x 200 cm (53″ x 79″).

Tie closing: The ties are arranged in pairs under the hems — three pairs at the end of the child's cover, and six along the side of the single bed cover. For each tie cut a strip 2.5 cm x 20 cm (1″ x 8″). Fold in half lengthwise, turn in raw edges, top-stitch. Attach ties when stitching hems.

CHILD'S BED
Materials Required:
Sheeting: 178 cm (70″) wide. Pillowcase: 0.6 m (⅝ yd). Cover: 2.2 m (2⅜ yds). Cotton lace: 3 m (3¼ yds).

Pillowcase: Cut two pieces 48 cm x 76 cm (19″ x 30″) plus 1 cm (⅜″) seam allowance on three sides and 5 cm (2″) hem on one short side. Stitch lace to one piece 8 cm (3¼″) from one long edge. With right sides facing, stitch case on three sides. Turn to right side; hem fourth side.

Cover: The opening is at the foot end of the cover. Cut two pieces, 100 cm x 135 cm (39½″ x 53″) plus 1 cm (⅜″) seam allowance on three sides and 5 cm (2″) hem on one short side. Stitch lace to one piece 18 cm (7″) from top short end and second row 6 cm (2½″) below. With right sides facing, stitch cover on three sides. Turn, and hem fourth side.

GREEN BED
Materials Required:
Sheeting: 178 cm (70″) wide. Pillowcase: 0.6 m (⅝ yd). Cover: 3.5 m (3⅞ yds). <u>False turn-back and ruffle</u>: 0.9 m (1 yd) (contrasting colour).

Pillowcase: Cut two pieces 48 cm x 76 cm (19″ x 30″) plus 1 cm (⅜″) seam allowance on three sides and 5 cm (2″) hem on one short side. With right sides facing, stitch three sides. Turn to right side and hem fourth side.

Cover: Cut one piece 135 cm x 200 cm (53″ x 79″) plus 1 cm (⅜″) seam allowance on three sides and 5 cm (2″) hem on one long side. Cut one piece 130 cm x 135 cm (51¼″ x 53″) plus seam allowance.

For the false turn-back, cut one piece 70 cm x 135 cm (27½″ x 53¼″) plus 1 cm (⅜″) seam allowance on three sides and 5 cm (2″) hem on one short side. For the ruffle, cut one strip 178 cm (70″) and one 100 cm (40″) long, both 6 cm (2½″) wide plus 1 cm (⅜″) seam allowance on all sides. Join to make one long strip Finish seam allowances together, then hem one long edge. Gather the other edge to 135 cm (53″). With right sides facing, and the ruffle in between, stitch turn-back to one 135 cm (53″) edge of the shorter cover piece. Open out to make one large piece. Right sides facing, stitch pieces together on 3 sides. Turn. Hem opening.

RED BED
Materials Required:
Sheeting: 4.9 m (5⅜ yds), 178 cm (70″) wide.

Pillowcase: Cut two pieces 48 cm x 76 cm (19″ x 30″) plus 1 cm (⅜″) seam allowance on three sides and 5 cm (2″) hem on one short side. For ruffle, cut two strips 178 cm (70″) long, 8 cm (3″) wide, plus 1 cm (⅜″). Join into a circle. Finish seam allowances, then hem one long edge. Right sides facing, pin ruffle in small pleats around one pillow piece, pinning it to hem line on fourth side. Baste second piece on top, right sides facing, and stitch around three sides through all layers. Turn to right side. Hem fourth side. Stitch ruffle to upper piece.

Cover: Cut two pieces 135 cm x 200 cm (53″ x 79″) plus 1 cm (⅜″) seam allowance on three sides and 5 cm (2″) hem on one long side. With right sides facing, stitch the cover pieces on three sides. Turn to right side and hem fourth side.

YELLOW BED
Materials Required:
Sheeting: 178 cm (70″) wide. Checked fabric: 4.3 m (4¾ yds). Striped fabric: 0.9 m (1 yd).

Pillowcase: Cut two pieces in checked fabric 48 x 76 cm (19″ x 30″) plus 1 cm (⅜″) seam allowance on three sides and 5 cm (2″) hem on one short side. Cut four right-angled triangles of striped fabric with two

sides measuring 30 cm (11¾″) and long side 44 cm (17⅜″), plus 1 cm (⅜″) seam allowances. Stitch triangles to top piece of pillowcase before assembling as for Green Bed.

Cover: From checked fabric, cut one piece 135 cm x 200 cm (53″ x 79″) and one piece 135 cm x 150 cm (53″ x 60″) plus 1 cm (⅜″) seam allowance on three sides and 5 cm (2″) hem on one long side. From striped fabric, cut a piece 50 cm x 135 cm (20″ x 53″) plus 1 cm (⅜″) seam allowance on three sides and 5 cm (2″) hem on one short side. With right sides facing, stitch striped piece to smaller checked piece. Assemble cover as for Green Bed.

BLUE BED
Materials Required:
Sheeting: 4.8 m (5¼ yds), 178 cm (70″) wide. Cotton edging: 4.1 m (4½ yds).

Pillowcase: Cut two pieces 48 cm x 76 cm (19″ x 30″) plus 1 cm (⅜″) seam allowance on three sides and 5 cm (2″) hem on one short side. With right sides facing, pin edging around one pillow piece, matching raw edge to raw edge, mitring corners and pinning to hem line on fourth side. Assemble as for Red Bed.

Cover: Cut two pieces 135 cm x 200 cm (53″ x 79″) plus 1 cm (⅜″) seam allowance on three sides and 5 cm (2″) hem on one long side. Stitch edging 45 cm (17¾″) from top. Assemble as for Red Bed.

Just cut out and iron on...

Appliqué these fabric motifs with bonding net and save yourself all the sewing! The motifs will add a touch of whimsy to jeans and jackets or decorative scatter cushions and covers. Use the motifs in more delicate fabrics to decorate tablecloths, mats and runners for festive occasions. The motifs can be traced actual size but the shapes are simple enough to be enlarged easily. All kinds and weights of fabric can be used to give more unusual effects.

Appliqué is great fun, and with bonding net it's no trouble at all. The bonding net binds two fabrics together securely so that you do not need a needle and thread.

Making the motifs

Trace the motif and transfer onto the paper side of the bonding net with dressmaker's carbon paper. Place the adhesive side of the bonding net onto the wrong side of the motif fabric and press firmly down for 2–4 seconds with an iron at the heat setting for wool. The bonding net will adhere to the fabric and the motif can be cut out with a sharp pair of scissors. Allow it to cool for about 1 minute, then lift the paper backing from the bonding net and press the motif temporarily onto the background fabric—cushion, tablecloth, blouse, etc. Complete the process by pressing the motif firmly with a damp cloth for about 10 seconds. Let the piece lie flat for at least 10 minutes before testing that it has adhered properly. The motif should now be fixed firmly in place.

This is all you have to do to give new life to all kinds of dull household items and clothes.

Hint: A quick festive idea for Christmas — make a circular cloth decorated with little apples, Father Christmas figures, bright birds, or fir trees to put under the Christmas tree. For special presents, wrap them in fabric decorated with colorful iron-on motifs.

For Easter, improvise with coloured eggs, spring flowers, or birds on a dainty tablecloth.

222

Children will love this fanciful little bird. Iron it onto curtains or cushions to brighten the nursery.

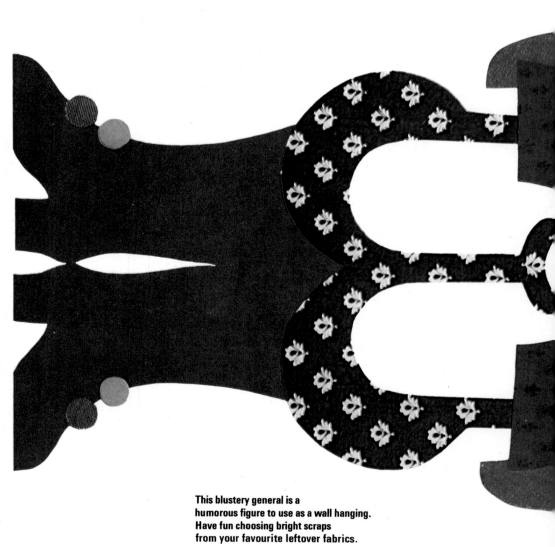

This blustery general is a humorous figure to use as a wall hanging. Have fun choosing bright scraps from your favourite leftover fabrics.

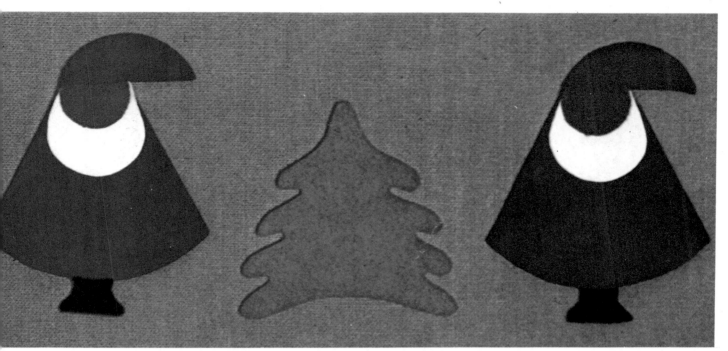

Jolly Father Christmas figures and Christmas trees will be family favourites year after year. They are decorative, quick to make, and look very festive.

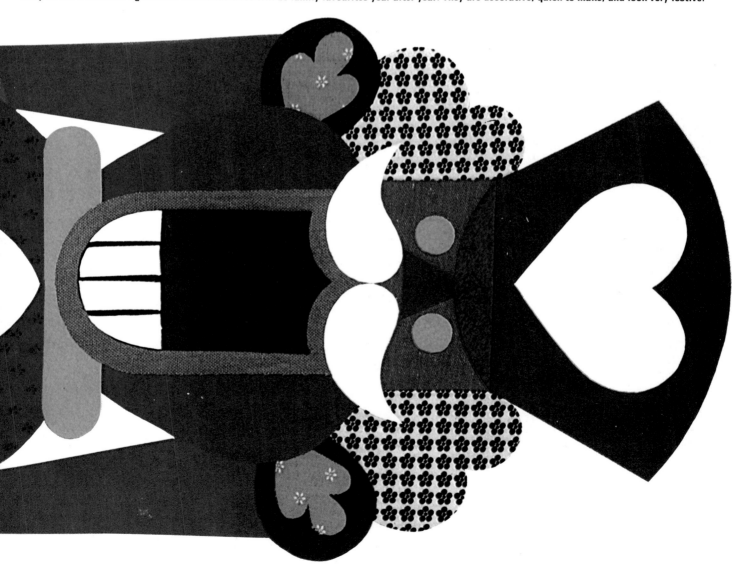

So easy to make

For young swingers

Here's a hammock specially designed for younger children. It's perfect for those long summer days and rolls up compactly to take on picnics. Made of heavy, unbleached cotton it's tough enough to withstand any amount of swinging, and is very quick and simple to construct.

Here you can see one of the long sides of the hammock. A length of cord is drawn through a casing and the fabric is gathered up along it.

Materials Required:

Be sure you use strong materials which will stand up to a lot of wear and tear. Heavy unbleached cotton: 3.10 m ($3\frac{3}{8}$ yds), 90 cm (36") wide. 2 wooden strips: 60 cm ($23\frac{3}{4}$") long, 5 cm (2") wide, and 2 cm ($\frac{3}{4}$") thick. Thick cord: 1.60 m ($1\frac{3}{4}$ yds). Strong rope, such as a washing line. (Use plenty of rope to enable you to hang the hammock on higher or wider-spaced trees if necessary.)

Making the hammock

Cut the 3.10 m ($3\frac{1}{2}$ yds) length of fabric widthwise into 2 pieces [i.e., each piece measures 1.55 m ($1\frac{3}{4}$ yds)]. With right sides facing, stitch the 2 pieces together along both long edges, close to the selvages. Turn to the right side, then make a 1.5 cm ($\frac{5}{8}$") hem along each long side, thus forming a casing for the cord. Cut the cord in half and pull through the casing on each side. Gather up the fabric to measure 76 cm (30") and pin firmly to the cord to hold the ends in place.

The wooden strips at each short side have a notch cut into each end. The rope is fastened so that it rests in the notch and cannot slip out.

On the short sides, make casings for the wooden strips. Turn under raw edges 1 cm ($\frac{3}{8}$"), then 10 cm (4"). Stitch down twice, catching in the ends of the cord. (If the cord is too thick for the sewing machine, sew it securely by hand).

Make a notch at each end of the wooden strips, 3 cm ($1\frac{1}{4}$") away from the edge. Push the strips through the 2 wide casings and gather up the fabric until the notches are exposed.

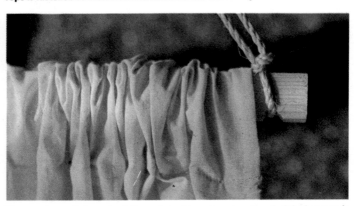

The wooden strip is pushed through a wide casing at each end of the hammock and the fabric is gathered up to expose the notches at either end.

Knot a length of rope into each notch so that it cannot slip out. Then at each end of the hammock, knot the lengths of rope together at a point equidistant from the notches (see large photograph). The hammock is now ready to hang.

It is very important to fix the rope for hanging securely to a tree or hook. Make a suitably strong knot which cannot slip or work undone.

There will be sweet dreams for baby
with these whimsical dozing sheep
on the sheets and pillowcase.
With such enchanting companions,
you'll have no more trouble
getting the children to bed!

Sleepy-time sheep

A row of lovable woolly sheep make a delightful decoration for a child's sheets. The large sheep on the pillow even sports a monogram — an idea which will appeal to adults, too! You can also embroider these motifs onto clothes or other nursery furnishings.

Materials Required: Stranded cotton in pale pink, deep pink, pale blue, dark blue, and white. For the large motif: 1 skein pale blue, ½ skein each of the other colours. For the border: the same quantities.

Basic Stitch: Satin stitch worked with only 2 of the 6 strands in the needle.

Working the embroidery

Trace the motifs from the pattern and transfer to the fabric with dressmaker's carbon paper. Work the sheep in pale blue with white hooves; work ears and face in pale pink. Work the ground in pale pink. The flowers have pale pink and deep pink petals; the leaves and stems are 2 shades of blue.

Trace the required letters for your own monogram onto the fabric and embroider each letter in deep pink with a white border.

Sheep motifs for bed linen

Embroider these whimsical motifs onto your child's sheets or anywhere else in the nursery. Add initials for fun.

For relaxing out-of-doors

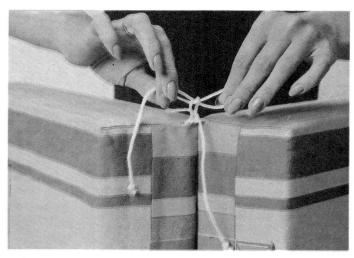

▲ Nylon cords join the cushions into a mattress. Catch the ties in at the corners so that the cushions lie flat against one another when packed away.

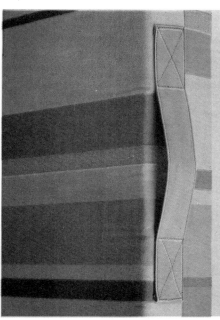

◀ Two of the cushions have handles which are stitched on off-centre so that they lie close together for carrying purposes.

If you wish to prop up the cushions as a chair, connect the back 2 sections with a strip of fabric and 2 buttons at either side to hold them firm.
▼

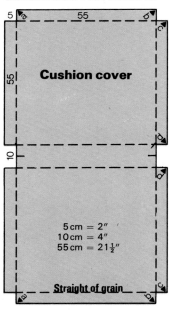

Size: 55 cm x 55 cm x 10 cm (21½″ x 21½″ x 4″).

Materials Required: Canvas: 2.10 m (2¼ yds), 140 cm (54″) wide *or* 4 m (4⅜ yds), 90 cm (36″) wide. Buttonhole thread. 3 foam rubber pads: 55 cm x 55 cm x 10 cm (21½″ x 21½″ x 4″). Nylon cord: 2.40 m (2⅝ yds). Heavyweight sewing machine needle. 4 buttons.

Cutting out: Cut out each cover, plus 1 cm (⅜″) seam allowance all around. For handles and connecting strips: Cut 2 strips for each, measuring 7 cm (2¾″) wide by 32 cm (12½″) and 45 cm (17¾″) long respectively plus seam allowance. Cut 8 cords, each 30 cm (11¾″).

Sewing: Join the seams as follows: First stitch along **a–b**, then **c–d**, including the seam allowance at either end. At the remaining open side, stitch 6 cm (2½″) at each end. Stitch corners, catching in cords (see photograph). For handles, turn in seam allowance, fold lengthwise, top-stitch all around. Stitch to sides with a decorative cross. Insert cushions; slip-stitch openings. Make connecting strips as for handles, plus buttonholes. Add buttons.

Cushion cover

5 cm = 2″
10 cm = 4″
55 cm = 21½″

Straight of grain

Cut out the cushions according to measurements on the diagram.

Easy enough to make in a weekend!

The five bright motifs are ironed onto
the felt with bonding net,
so the only stitching is around the pockets.
This is quick and fun appliqué!

Materials Required: Felt: 0.6 m x 160 cm wide and 1.1 m x 90 cm wide ($\frac{5}{8}$ yd x 60" wide and 1$\frac{1}{4}$ yds x 36" wide) for background and pockets. Pieces of felt for motifs. Iron-on interfacing: 48 x 82 cm (19" x 32$\frac{1}{4}$"). Packet of bonding net. 2 wooden rods for hanging.

Making the calendar
Cut out the background piece to measure 54 x 88 cm (21" x 34$\frac{1}{2}$"). As felt shrinks, it is wise to iron it with a damp cloth before cutting out. Iron the interfacing onto the back of the felt, leaving a 3 cm (1$\frac{1}{4}$") border all around.

Pockets: Cut 4 strips 8 x 45 cm (3$\frac{1}{8}$" x 17$\frac{1}{2}$"), 3 pieces 8 x 9 cm (3$\frac{1}{8}$" x 3$\frac{1}{2}$"), 1 piece 20 x 23 cm (7$\frac{7}{8}$" x 9"). Mark off the strips at 9 cm (3$\frac{1}{2}$") intervals. Appliqué a motif on each pocket. Stitch on the pockets: the top centre pocket is 14 cm (5$\frac{1}{2}$") from the top edge and 23 cm (9") from each side. Stitch 1 pocket side close to the pocket edge. The pocket is pleated, so push the excess to the centre and stitch the other side. At the

base, make a $\frac{1}{2}$ cm ($\frac{1}{4}$") pleat on each side and stitch across. Attach the strips in the same way, beginning 7 cm (3") from the side edges. Add the 2 small pockets and 1 large pocket at the bottom. Turn the 3 cm (1$\frac{1}{4}$") seam allowance to the back and stitch it down with bonding net. Turn under 6 cm (2$\frac{1}{2}$") at top and bottom of the felt. Iron down 3 cm (1$\frac{1}{4}$") at the outer edge with bonding net, leaving room to insert the rods. The calendar is now ready to hang on the wall. Fill pockets with gifts for each day up to Christmas Eve.

All the motifs are given actual size so that they are easy to trace.

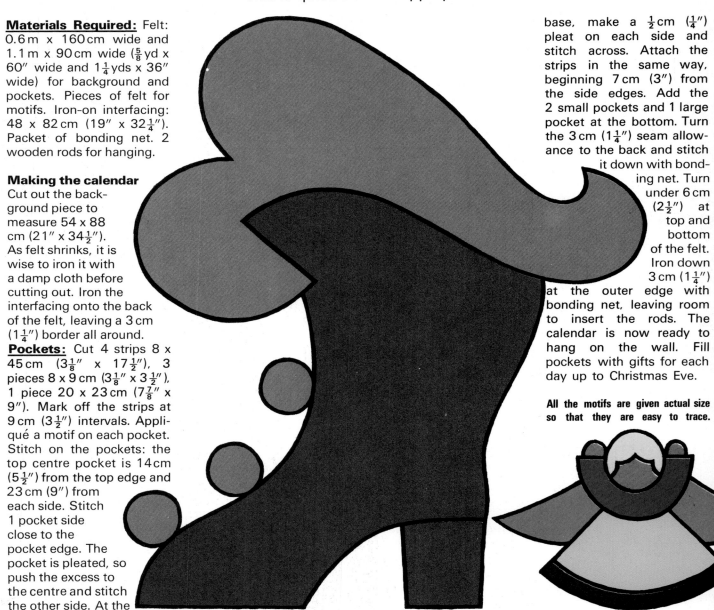

Appliqué- with bonding net

Adhesive iron-on bonding net sticks two pieces of fabric together so that sewing becomes superfluous. It is backed by a special paper on which you can draw or trace the appliqué motifs.

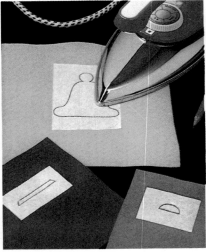

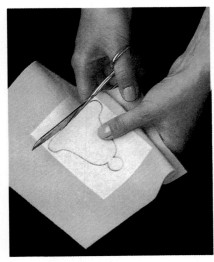

1 Draw the motif on the paper side and cut out roughly. Place the adhesive side on the wrong side of fabric and press for 2–4 seconds.

2 Cut out the motif with a pair of sharp scissors. Take great care to cut around the curves and corners as accurately as possible.

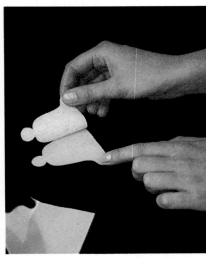

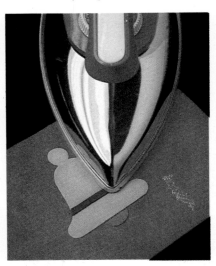

3 Allow to cool completely for about 1 minute, then peel off the paper carefully. A film of adhesive will be left on the fabric.

4 Press the motif onto the background, then press with a damp cloth on the wrong side for 10 seconds. Test after 10 minutes.

234

Colourful appliqué in cotton
Picture book landscape

Size: 2.1 m (2$\frac{1}{4}$ yds) long by 1.75 m (1$\frac{7}{8}$ yds) wide.

Materials Required:
Lining fabric: 4.2 m (4$\frac{3}{4}$ yds), 90 cm (36") wide. Blue cotton: 2.15 m (2$\frac{1}{2}$ yds), 90 cm (36") wide. Green cotton: 2.15 m (2$\frac{1}{2}$ yds), 90 cm (36") wide. Floral cotton: 2.15 m (2$\frac{1}{2}$ yds), 90 cm (36") wide. Remnants of plain and patterned cottons.

DIRECTIONS
Begin by enlarging the pattern given on the graph overleaf. Add 4 squares to the top of the sky and draw the top of the clouds, then make templates of the various pieces. The smaller pieces are appliquéd directly onto the fabric with a close zigzag stitch so seam allowances are not required on these pieces. However, add 1 cm ($\frac{3}{8}$") on the edges of the three large pattern pieces — the meadow, sky, and hill — and 10 cm (4") on the lower edges of the sky and hill. Mark the outlines of the hills on the sky. Turn under the seam allowance of the hills, clip the curves, baste in place. Stitch with small, close zigzag stitches, following the marked outline precisely. Position and stitch the meadow the same way.
The smaller motifs are then appliquéd in position. Start at the right with the railway carriages, then apply the wheels on top of them. Stitch the tree trunks, then the tops. For the house, stitch the path first, then pin all the house pieces in place and stitch, finishing off firmly. Cut the lining fabric in half and join along two long edges to make one large piece. Baste to the front, right sides facing. Cut off the corners diagonally and turn to the right side. Top-stitch all round the four sides and press lightly.

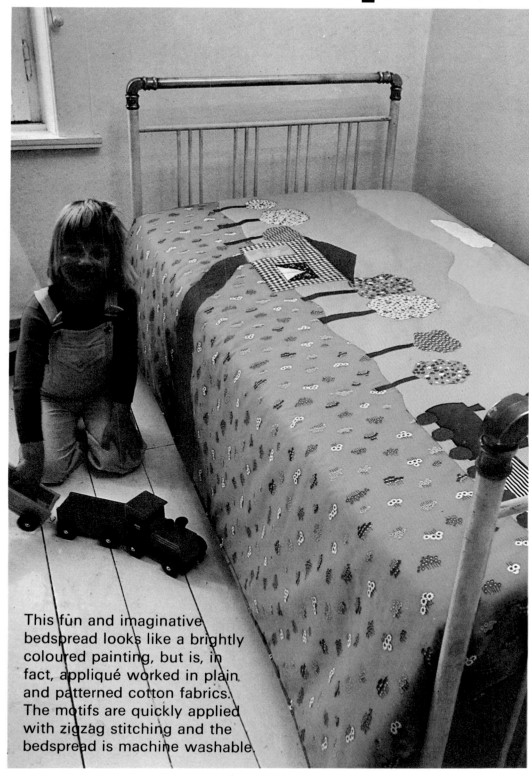

This fun and imaginative bedspread looks like a brightly coloured painting, but is, in fact, appliqué worked in plain and patterned cotton fabrics. The motifs are quickly applied with zigzag stitching and the bedspread is machine washable.

Enlarge the pattern
for the bedspread
from this graph. Draw
a grid of 10 cm (4″)
squares, then transfer the
design onto your
enlarged grid. You
should make templates
for the pattern pieces.

Each square = 10 cm (4″)

Wind screen or play tent

When you're relaxing on the beach, catch the sun and keep out the wind with our versatile canvas wind screen. It doubles as a tent for the children, too. Just add a roof and they can play happily, rain or shine. The construction is very simple — there are four sections and five poles which can be placed in a straight line, a semi-circle or closed into a square as you wish. The roof ties on to the top separately. There's also a zippered ''door'' and useful pockets inside to keep the sand and insects out of your belongings. The screen is held up by guy ropes and tent pegs.

Materials Required :

Canvas: 6.15 m (6¾ yds), 120 cm (48″) wide. Zipper: 60 cm (24″) long (an open-ended one can be used). Dowelling: 5 lengths measuring about 1.40 m (1½ yds). 5 screw eyes, 5 metal eyelets to punch in, 2 metal rings, all 2 cm (¾″) diameter. Strong cord, eg. washing line: about 15 m (16¼ yds). Tent pegs.

Sewing: Cut the 4-section wind screen to measure 120 cm (48″) wide by 4.6 m (5 yds) long plus

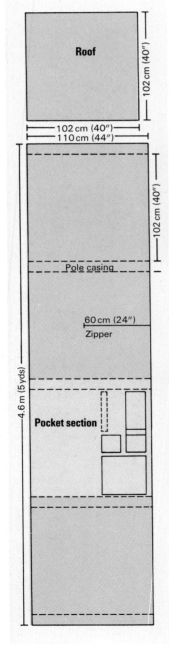

1 cm (⅜″) seam allowance at each short end. Make a 5 cm (2″) hem along both long edges (the height of the wind screen is thus 110 cm (44″). Sew the casings for the dowelling as follows: At the 2 ends, turn in first the seam allowance, then another 10 cm (4″) and stitch down close to the edge. For the 3 inner casings, mark off the 10 cm (4″) divisions as in the diagram. Stitch the fabric together along these lines, thus forming 3 casings for the poles. The width of each section of the wind screen is 102 cm (40″) (see diagram). At the top of each casing, stitch across the fabric to prevent it from slipping down when the poles are inserted. Leave just enough open to fasten a screw eye into each pole.

The guy ropes and the roof are fastened onto the screw eyes with the strong cord. Make sure that the screw eyes are fixed securely into the poles to take the strain.

The poles are sharpened to a point at the lower end, so that they can be pushed into the ground more easily. Before inserting the poles, stitch the various pockets and the zipper into the middle 2 sections of the screen (see the diagram on the right). First stitch

In the diagram on the right, you can see the pocket sizes and how they are positioned on the fabric. Add 1 cm (⅜″) for seams and 5 cm (2″) for the pocket tops.

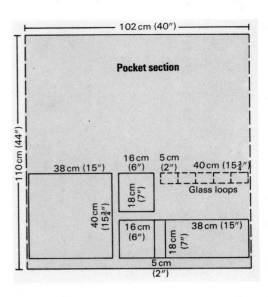

the 5 cm (2″) hems at the pocket top edges. Then press the other seam allowances to the inside and stitch on the pockets. On the long lower pocket, stitch further divisions of 16 cm (6″), 5 cm (2″), and 38 cm (15″).

Make the loops for the glasses to fit your own glasses. Cut the strip for the loops 10 cm (4″) wide plus seam allowance. Stitch together lengthwise and turn, then stitch to the screen at regular intervals. For the zipper, cut a facing strip 63 cm (24¾″) long and 11 cm (4½″) wide plus seam allowances. Press under the seam allowances and stitch the strip over the slit mark around 3 sides. Leave the lower narrow side open. Then cut a 60 cm (24″) slit through both layers of fabric and snip in diagonally 1 cm (⅜″) toward the corners. Turn each edge under 1 cm (⅜″) and baste. Place the zipper in between the layers and stitch in.

Finish the lower edges together with the zipper ends. Punch a metal eyelet to the left and right of the zipper.

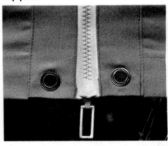

Sew a metal ring to the outside of the fabric at the pole edges on either side of "door" section. The flaps can be fastened with cord to keep the "door" open.

For the tent roof, cut out a 102 cm (40″) square of fabric plus 5 cm (2″) all around for the hem. Stitch the hem, mitring the corners, and then punch an eyelet into each of the corners. The roof can easily be fastened to the tent.

To secure the roof, the 4 corners are fastened to the screw eyes with cord.

Children's bathrobes
Towel togas

These bathrobes
are such a
simple design
that even a
beginner can
make them.

These bathrobes are really roomy so that children will not only find them very comfortable, but will also not outgrow them too quickly.

Size: Two sizes are given: size U, height 122 cm (48″) and chest 64 cm (25¼″); size W, height 134 cm (53″) and chest 68 cm (26¾″).

Fabric Required: 90 cm (36″) wide fabric is used. In 2 colours: Size U, 1.8 m (2 yds) for robe, 1.4 m (1⅝ yds) for trim. Size W, 1.9 m (2⅛ yds) for robe,
1.5, (1¾ yds) for trim. In 1 color: For both sizes, 2.1 m (2⅜ yds).

CUTTING OUT

Before cutting into the fabric, wash it carefully in case of shrinkage. The Back and Front are cut in one piece. Place the centre back along the fold of the fabric
so that the front edge lies 1 cm (⅜″) inside the fold line. At the front edge, cut along the fold line and around the neck, leaving a 1 cm (⅜″) seam allowance. Add 2 cm (¾″) on the side and sleeve seams and 6 cm (2¾″) on the hem and lower edge of the sleeve. Cut two belt loops measuring 3 cm
(1¼″) wide for a finished width of 1.5 cm (⅝″) and 7 cm (2¾″) long, plus seam allowance. Cut the pocket with a seam allowance of 1.5 cm (⅝″). Cut the Front band and tie belt from contrasting fabric, allowing 1 cm (⅜″) seam allowance.

SEWING

Join the side seams with flat-fell seams; with the wrong sides of the fabric facing, stitch only as far as the armhole markings. The seam allowances are now on the outside. Snip diagonally into the seam allowances, downward from the top, close to the stitching line. Then, trim the back seam allowance to 0.5 cm (³⁄₁₆″). Turn under the front seam allowance and top-stitch close to the edge. Join the sleeve seams with flat-fell seams; insert at marks. Turn under the hem of the robe and the sleeves twice and top-stitch close to the edge. Work zigzag stitch on one side of the front band and stitch the other side, right sides facing, to the front edge of the garment. Press the seam allowances toward the band. Fold the band in half, then turn in the seam allowance at band hem and slip-stitch together by hand. On the right side, stitch along the seam, catching in the zigzag-stitched edge underneath. Top-stitch all around. Pocket: Work zigzag stitch all round the edges. Turn under the seam allowance on the top edge, baste in position, and top-stitch once close to the edge, and again 3 cm (1¼″) from edge. Tie belt: Turn in the seam allowances and fold in half lengthwise, wrong sides facing. Top-stitch all around. Loops: Turn in the seam allowances on the long edges. Fold in half and top-stitch. Turn under the seam allowances on the short edges and stitch to the side seams at the waist.

242

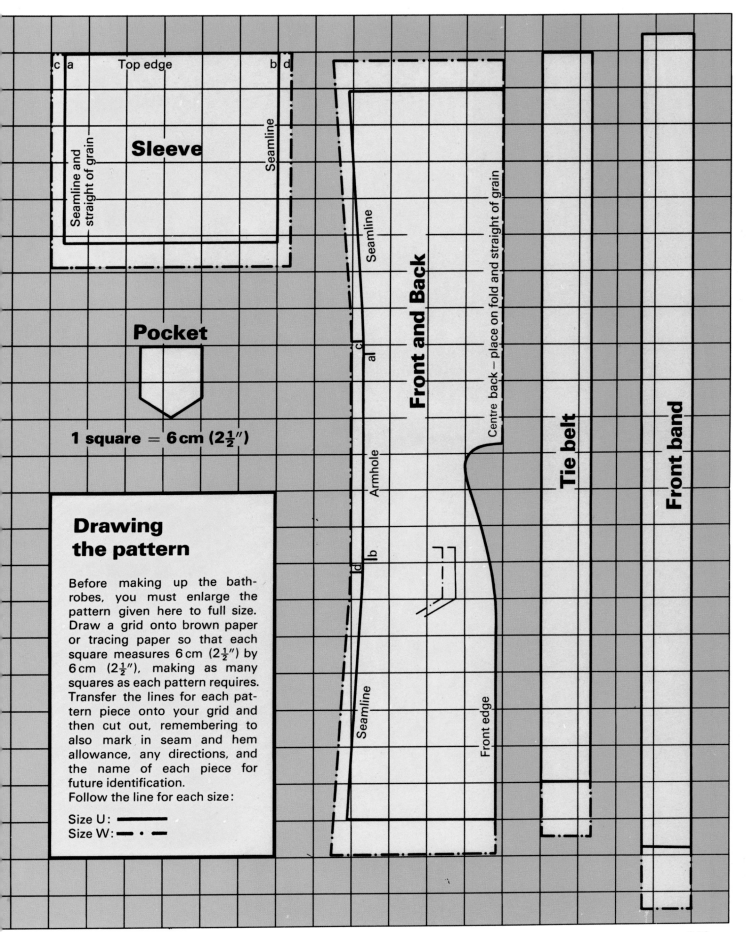

Sleeve

c a — Top edge — b d

Seamline and straight of grain

Seamline

Pocket

1 square = 6 cm (2½″)

Drawing the pattern

Before making up the bathrobes, you must enlarge the pattern given here to full size. Draw a grid onto brown paper or tracing paper so that each square measures 6 cm (2½″) by 6 cm (2½″), making as many squares as each pattern requires. Transfer the lines for each pattern piece onto your grid and then cut out, remembering to also mark in seam and hem allowance, any directions, and the name of each piece for future identification.

Follow the line for each size:

Size U: ———————
Size W: —— • ——

Front and Back

Seamline

a l

c

Armhole

d l b

Centre back – place on fold and straight of grain

Seamline

Front edge

Tie belt

Front band

These plain plates have been painted with a black rim, a coloured circle in the centre, and a bee motif which can be seen actual size, opposite.

244

Paint a set of mugs and a jug with a cloud motif and a variety of stylized fruit. The fruit motifs are shown actual size overleaf. The paints are just as effective on dark china as on white.

Here is one way to brighten a child's day when a cold or flu means that she can't play.

Funny faces painted onto little pitchers will be sure to make the children laugh. The faces can be given different expressions quite easily by changing the features.

Bon appetit!

Children love to have their own special mugs and plates, and would be delighted with this gaily-painted china. All you need is plain china and enamel paints. Let the children choose a few simple motifs such as flowers and animals or use the ideas given here. You don't have to be a great artist to reproduce bold designs such as the ones illustrated. Overleaf are a few tips for using the paint.

245

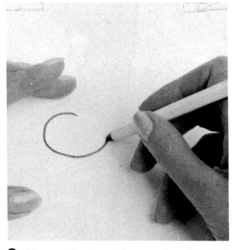

1 On the mug, paint the cloud shape first as a base. You can easily do this freehand as the shape is very simple and can be corrected without difficulty if you do make a mistake.

2 If you don't wish to paint the fruit motif freehand, make a stencil to help you. Trace the shape at the bottom of the page onto thin cardboard and cut it out accurately.

Painting on china is easy

Here are a few tips for painting your china.

Enamel paints are suitable for glass, plastics, ceramics, pottery, and china as well as other solid materials. Before you begin, make sure that the article to be painted is clean and free of dust and greasy fingerprints. Stir the paint well before applying it.

Use a soft brush to achieve even coverage. The thinner the paint, the quicker it will dry. After about 4 hours, the surface paint will have dried; after about 60 hours, the paint will be completely dry.

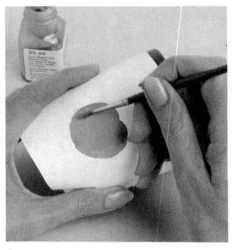

3 When the white paint of the cloud is dry, place the stencil over the mug and fill in the apple shape in green paint. Make sure the stencil is positioned correctly and hold it very still.

4 Paint the leaf on the apple with or without a stencil. Leave the paint to dry again. Finally, outline the apple and the leaf with fine brush strokes in black.

It can be hardened further on glass, pottery, and china articles by "baking" them in the oven at least one day after the last application of paint. Place the articles in a cold oven and heat it up to 120°C to 150°C (250°F to 300°F). Turn the oven off after 30–40 minutes, leaving the china to cool. Heating the paint in this way has the advantage of making the colours more scratch-proof and water-resistant. In fact, the paint has excellent durability and washability, but, all the same, it is not advisable to paint areas on which knives or other sharp implements will be used.

Here are the fruit motifs on the jug and the set of mugs shown actual size. Use the same method for painting the orange, lemon, and strawberry as described above for the apple.

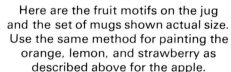

Patchwork cover

Feather your nest with colour

This gay bedcover is made
from pieces of patterned fabric and lined
for comfort and warmth.
Use it on a cradle or bed or as a play sheet
on the floor or in a play pen.

Make a patchwork bedcover

Size: The patches are each 8 cm (3¼") square. The directions are for a cover 100 cm (40") square. It is made up of eleven strips, each eleven patches long, with a 12 cm (5") plain border all around.

Materials Required: Fabric 90 cm (36") wide: 0.7 m (¾ yd) each of plaids and prints, 2.2 m (2½ yds) plain. Batting or wadding for interlining. Sewing thread in colours to match.

Cutting patches

The pieces will be easier to sew together if straight edges are cut with the straight grain of the fabric. Be careful to make all pieces exactly the same size so that they will form continuous lines when sewn together. Cut a card-board template 10 cm (4") square. Place the template on the fabric and trace around it with chalk. The three photographs in the centre of the page show how a template can be placed on a plaid fabric to produce three different pattern effects. Plan the patches carefully. Cut out the patches.

Sort the patches and then arrange them in a random pattern to produce a varied, but balanced effect.

Making the coverlet

Stitch the patches together in strips, making 1 cm (⅜") seams. Stitch the strips. Cut interlining and backing to size. With interlining in between, place patchwork on backing with the wrong sides together. Stitch the three layers together 1 cm (⅜") from the edge.

For the borders, cut 4 strips 14 cm (5¾") wide by the length of the sides plus 12 cm (4¾") at each end of each strip for the corners. With right sides together

and allowing excess to extend at each end, stitch the borders to the back, stitching just beyond the seamline. Stitch the corners as illustrated above. Turn the border to the front, turn in the seam allowance, and top-stitch on seamline.

Brushed-fabric jacket

I like it!

A small child will love this soft and fuzzy little jacket.

Size: Pattern is for a child 104 cm (41″) tall with a 58 cm (23″) chest.

Materials Required: Brushed fabric: 75 cm ($\frac{7}{8}$ yd), 140–160 cm ($55\frac{1}{8}$–63″) wide. Cotton braid: 3 m ($2\frac{3}{4}$ yds), 3 cm ($1\frac{1}{4}$″) wide. 3 large hooks and eyes (fur hooks preferably). Sewing thread to match.

Drawing the pattern

Draw a grid of squares on large sheets of paper, each square measuring 4 x 4 cm ($1\frac{5}{8}$ x $1\frac{5}{8}$″). Make dots where the contours of the pattern pieces cross the lines and squares. Join all the dots and you have an actual-size paper pattern. Transfer all marks, arrows, etc. Trace separate pocket pattern piece and then cut out all pattern pieces. Keep pattern for future use.

Cutting the pieces

Cut this type of fabric from single rather than double layers, so make a complete pattern for the back. For the sleeves and fronts, make two pattern pieces so that you don't accidentally have two right or two left pieces.

Add a 1.5 cm ($\frac{5}{8}$″) seam allowance on shoulder, side, armhole, and sleeve seams. The remaining edges of the front, back, and sleeves do not require seam allowances as they are to be bound with braid (see the photograph at left). The pocket and collar should have a 2 cm ($\frac{3}{4}$″) seam allowance. Cut all

◀ Bind the edges with a brightly coloured braid which contrasts with the fabric. Close the front with fur hooks and eyes.

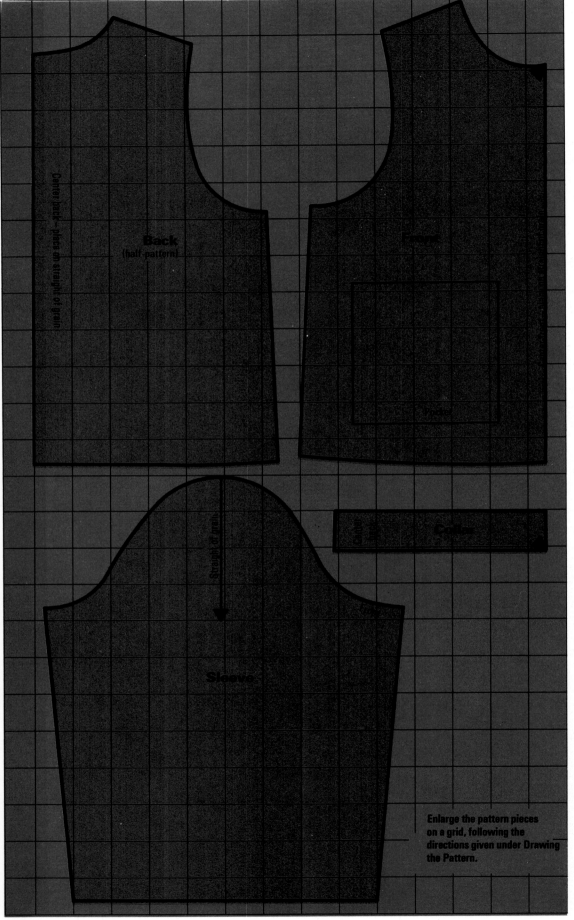

Back
(half-pattern)

Center back—place on straight of grain

Front

Collar

Sleeve

straight of grain

Enlarge the pattern pieces on a grid, following the directions given under Drawing the Pattern.

the pieces with the pile running in the same direction (from top to bottom). Cut two pockets. Place the pattern piece for the stand-up collar onto a fold of fabric and cut one.

Sewing the jacket
First baste all the seams, as this type of fabric tends to shift position easily while stitching.

Join the shoulder and side seams, then trim and finish the seam allowances. Stitch the collar to the neck edge, finish the seam allowance, and press it up toward the collar. Join the sleeve seams, and insert the sleeves into the armholes, matching the grain line of the sleeve to the shoulder seam and the sleeve seam to the side seam. Finish raw edges.

Bind the edges with braid as follows: Pin and baste one edge of the braid 0.5 cm ($\frac{1}{4}$″) from the fabric edge on the wrong side. Stitch 1 cm ($\frac{3}{8}$″) from the edge. Turn the braid over the fabric edge neatly, fold it under, and baste to the stitching line before sewing neatly in place by hand. On corners, fold the braid over and hand-sew together neatly and firmly. At the sleeve edges, cut the braid to the correct length and join into a circle before stitching as described above. Stitch braid to the top edge of the pockets and then turn under and baste the other edges. Pin the pockets to the marked lines on the fronts and sew in place by hand. Sew on hooks and eyes so that they are approximately 0.2 cm ($\frac{1}{8}$″) inside each edge.

YARN LISTS FOR KNITTING AND CROCHET

CHRISTMAS
STYLE

CHRISTMAS STYLE

Debi Staron and Bob Pranga

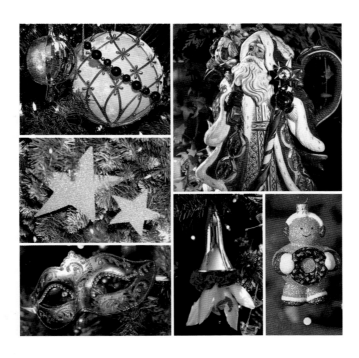

Photography by David Mager

DK Publishing, Inc.

LONDON, NEW YORK, MELBOURNE
MUNICH, DELHI

Senior Editor Barbara Berger
Assistant Managing Art Editor Michelle Baxter
Editorial Assistant John Searcy
Additional Design Tai Blanche, Melissa Chung,
Susan St. Louis, Stephanie Sumulong, and Miesha Tate
DTP Coordinator Milos Orlovic
Production Manager Chris Avgherinos
Jacket Design Dirk Kaufman
Project Director Sharon Lucas
Creative Director Tina Vaughan
Publisher Chuck Lang

Photography David Mager
Photographic Assistants Monica Morant,
Beth Coller, Charchi Stinson

First published in Great Britain in 2004 by
Dorling Kindersley Limited
80 Strand, London
WC2R 0RL

A Penguin company

2 4 6 8 10 9 7 5 3 1

A CIP catalogue record for this book is available from
The British Library

ISBN: 1–4053–0702–1

Colour reproduction by Colourscan, Singapore
Printed and bound by Toppan Printing Co. (Shenzhen) Ltd.

Discover more at
www.dk.com

CONTENTS

FOREWORD

IT'S LIKE A BIG CRESCENDO of emotions, that's what the holiday season is. We spend so much time building the notes higher, and higher, and higher, and when we reach the top we want to try to hold those notes for as long as we possibly can. The memory of it is so powerful and so delicious that we try to recreate it year after year. Most of us try to capture at least part of the experience from our childhoods. I guess that's why I have come to rely on Bob and Debi—Dr. Christmas—to help orchestrate the holiday for me.

It's a delicate balance; a little bit of tradition, add some whimsy, heavy on meaning and substance; then bring in legacies and color. Finally, when all of those notes are ringing in complete harmony, make it work on time and on a budget! It's no wonder that, as the conductor of that orchestra, we're often frustrated and feel like failures.

I first met Bob when I was hosting and producing my talk show—he was a slam-dunk guest. Every time he came on, it was a self-produced masterpiece that really resonated with my viewers because he always found a way to make the holiday accessible and affordable. We all know, of course, in our heart of hearts, that the trimming and the glistening of ornaments, and the stockings, the centerpieces, the wreaths, and all the rest are merely window dressing for what is to most people a deeply religious season. But without it, it sure seems empty and lackluster—and that is *not* Bob Pranga.

I must confess to being a little nervous the first time Bob came over to my home with his little team of elves to transform my living room and dining room. But now, after many years of depending upon his skill and taste, I can't image the holiday without him. Bob and Debi manage to consider whatever Christmas means to each client—celebrity or otherwise. No matter how big the star, there is always a young child behind all those accomplishments wanting to recapture that excitement of the holiday.

Bob took ornaments that my kids had made in grade school—popsicle sticks and yarn held together by Elmer's glue and topped with a handful of glitter—and somehow managed to make them coexist beautifully with handmade, mouth-blown, one-of-a-kind ornaments. If I tell him a picture is important, he finds a way to showcase it. If I want some of the kids' toys and keepsakes to mix in with the fine china and candles, voilà, there they are.

I will never forget returning from Palm Springs one weekend after Bob and Debi had done their magic—

▲ **Heavenly table** A detail of the "dense forest of birch trees . . . set among the clouds, ready for a peace banquet," created by Dr. Christmas for Leeza Gibbons.

I opened the door, and chill bumps—there it was—that feeling from my girlhood.

I think the thing that is most amazing about a Dr. Christmas holiday is the care that goes into every decision. While they make it appear effortless, Debi and Bob obsess over every detail. They love to share their passion with others, easily chatting about everything from the right lighting, to proper placement of the tree, to the color scheme.

One year, I was providing a report to air on *Extra* about celebrity trees. Debi was passing on the art of weaving ribbon throughout the branches of the tree. Of course, I needed the sound bite in about 30 seconds, so she went into "warp speed" to explain the kind of ribbon to use, how to place it on the tree, and how to economize if you needed to! Bob is always the emotional glue, providing punctuation for Debi's practical tips.

On these pages you'll see how versatile and talented these two really are. You'll understand why many stars depend on them and why most don't even question the process. They just say "do it" and trust that it will be the perfect representation of individuality and taste.

This year, I just decided to "trust the process" and turned over my home to the Dr. Christmas team for a couple of days. Who knew my dining room would vanish? It was replaced by a dense forest of birch trees and a heavenly table set among the clouds, ready for a peace banquet. Twinkling lights and illuminated snowbanks made the whole scene look like something out of an adult's holiday dream. I cried when I saw it and then made all my friends come over and experience a bit of the magic. That's when you know you got it right—when someone can stand at the entry and behold this magnificent vision so powerful it can only provoke a deeply felt "Ahhh." There are no words. Well, maybe two: Dr. Christmas.

Leeza Gibbons

LEEZA GIBBONS

AUTHORS' PREFACE

Hello, everyone. We are Dr. Christmas—Debi Staron and Bob Pranga. We're not a medical corporation. We *are* specialists of Christmas and have decorating ideas and tips to share, and the holidays are fast approaching. But before getting started, we'd like to take this opportunity to tell you about our approach to decorating, and to introduce you to some of the people who have contributed to this book, and influenced and enhanced our lives.

...from Debi

Debi and her dad, Ted

*M*y earliest memories of Christmas are of sitting in Santa's lap in the local shopping mall and of helping my dad, the "Master" of outdoor Christmas decorating, as he strung lights from antenna tip to basement window. My dad did the best Christmas decorations. People drove for miles around to see his display. I still remember the look on his face as he watched the faces of the neighbors, who marveled at his creative expertise. Having developed a similar passion for decorating, I consider it an honor to carry on the fine tradition of Christmas decorating, on a "slightly" grander scale. To him, my inspiration, my teacher, and my Christmas guide, I dedicate this book.

I would also like to thank Dr. Howard Maize, D.C., client and healer, for helping to keep me "upright" so I'm able to do what I do, and for his kind words: "Finally, a book that depicts, even if just a sampling, the magic that is Dr. Christmas. After having the unique experience of actually watching Deborah set up my office for the past several Christmases, I have been in awe of her innate ability to set just the right, the exact mood for our needs. Her flair, her expertise, elan, panache . . . are a sight to behold!"

...from Bob,

*W*hen one is presented with a great opportunity, it's easy to settle into the mindset of "It's about time". . . I have to admit to being guilty as charged. When asked about my dedication for this book, I had to get real about how I got here. It's amazing how much the "I" is not a part of the equation. I dedicate this book as follows:

To my family, especially my parents, who passed their love of Christmas on to me. To my mentors and other "moms," Judy Andruss, Connie

Bob and his friend Ben McCormick

Pentek, and Patricia Strang, for your faith, tenacity, and life experiences. To Kathy Hilton, whose belief in my abilities opened the doors. To Julia Finlay and Judy Merrell, your influences I still carry with me. To my coach, Rick Tamlyn, for changing my life. To Chuck Lioi, for giving the world the big "scoop" about us. To Susan Ranta, my friend and muse. To Molly Lewis, who keeps me laughing. To Dayna Jackson, for keeping me clear. To my Los Angeles family, thank you for being part of the journey. And to Ben McCormick, my friend and fellow dreamer. One dream down, more to follow.

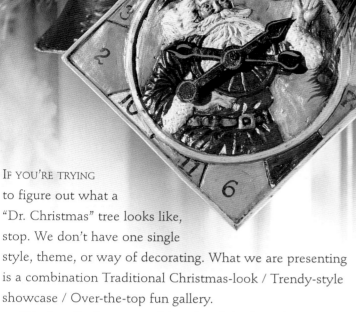

IF YOU'RE TRYING to figure out what a "Dr. Christmas" tree looks like, stop. We don't have one single style, theme, or way of decorating. What we are presenting is a combination Traditional Christmas-look / Trendy-style showcase / Over-the-top fun gallery.

We describe how we achieved each look so that you can recreate it in your own home. And we explain in more detail how to tackle certain projects, with accompanying step-by-step, easy-to-follow photos.

If you've always wanted to turn your tree into something more than a green, bushy holder for your ornament collection, we'll show you how. Over the years, we've learned that with tree decorating, anything goes—we've wired the most amazing assortment of things into trees: diamond tiaras, sports equipment, mannequins, framed celebrity pictures, toys, curtain rods, train sets, furniture, and even a wedding dress!

You can put just about anything you want into your tree, as long as the tree can support the weight. Don't limit yourself to traditional themes—break loose and experiment.

Okay, we have said "Hello" and explained the Dr. Christmas philosophy; now for the introductions. First, meet Donald Clay. We brought Donald on board

Donald Clay

because of his expertise in floral design. He was excited to conjure up the decorated trees based on the ideas we had for the floral chapter. Donald's use of flowers and fruit was incredibly innovative and exceeded our expectations. For that we thank him.

Now meet chef Richard Rocha. All of the scrumptious desserts and pastries featured throughout the book may be credited to him. We provided him with the themes and moods we wished to achieve and he delivered the appropriate fare. Kudos.

Chef Richard Rocha

Finally, our able and overworked helpers, the Elves: Garry Kubel, Jay Krich, Lynn Klein, Gail Jorden, Brent Braun, and Brent Bateman (who is missing from the photograph below).

The Elves, from the left: Garry Kubel, Jay Krich, Lynn Klein, Gail Jorden, Brent Braun

They are the backbone of Dr. Christmas. Without them, we're nothing. The same is true for all of the fantastic people who we call our clients. These are the folks who have allowed us time and time again to "play" in their beautiful homes and show them off to the world. Bette and Scott Milne, Barron and Marilyn Hilton, Carrie Fisher, Candice Bergen, Teri Garr, Marion and David Dennis, Ilene Graham, Richard Bronson, Edie Baskin-Bronson, Larry and Dee Dee Gordon, Martin and Wen Mull, Jillian Barberie, Kevin Bailey and James Mellon, Tracy Thompson, Karen, and our angel, Leeza Gibbons.

Debi Staron

Bob Pranga

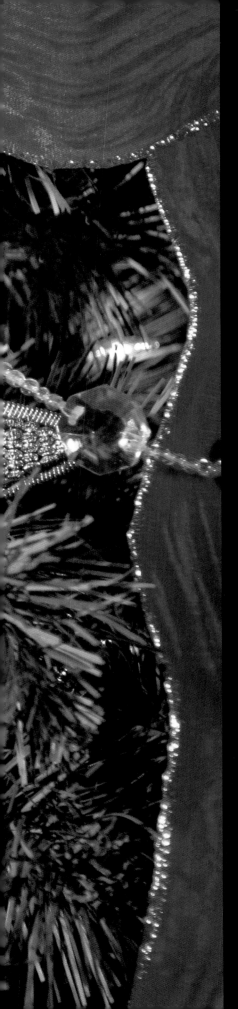

1

THE ART OF HOLIDAY DESIGN

*O*nce, decorating for Christmas meant picking out a tree, stringing several lights, and hanging a few balls and garlands. But no more. Christmas has now become a spectacular art form. The broad array of quality decorations in many assorted colors now rival those exhibited in couture fashion. In fact, in recent years, Christmas trends have begun to follow fashion trends. Christmas is no longer limited to just red and green, but is now all about artistic expression. Enjoy!

Traditional

STYLES OF DECORATING that have been around for many years, and trimmings in colors and shapes of seemingly timeless appeal—these are elements of what is known as "Traditional" Christmas design. Examples of popular traditional tone-setters include both the classic color combinations of primary red and green with round or bell-shaped ornaments; and Victorian burgundy, forest green, and mauve with feminine ornaments, angels, and Father Christmas motifs. The following pages feature examples of traditional design created for today's home.

TRADITIONAL LUXURY

TAILORED, COLOR-COORDINATED, AND CRISP describe Upscale Traditional design. Red is a color featured in most traditional Christmas displays—make your design upscale by mixing red with silver and gold instead of other primary colors, and replace cotton and paper with higher-quality materials like silk, brocade, and velvet.

Here, we used custom-made velvet ribbon to create large, full bows that were placed on everything from mirror garlands to alcoves

to stairways and trees—carrying the luxurious theme throughout. The ornament selection included mouth-blown one-of-a-kind pieces rather than mass-produced decorations.

When decorating in Upscale-Traditional style, think clean lines and sophisticated luxury. The end result: an impressive, decor-enhancing Christmas showcase.

▲ **Decorative alcove** This nook, which is adjacent to the entrance, was outlined with a garland and decorated to match the hallway in order to continue the clean line of the overall design.

▶ **Meet and greet** These two large brass deer serve as holiday greeters at the front entrance. To dress these everyday reindeer for the season, red ribbon collars and jingle bells were fitted around their necks.

◀ **Framing potential** The traditional color palette of red and green enhances an already-grand entry hall. The red ribbon, greenery, and twinkling lights lead you on a journey down the long hall to the main attraction, the elegant family tree in the drawing room, where the window makes a natural frame.

MAJESTIC STATEMENT

This magnificent tree rises twelve feet from floor to ceiling. It serves several functions during the holiday season for the family who lives in this mansion: it acts as the center of attention for family parties, it is the glamorous backdrop for the annual family Christmas card, and, of course, it is the exciting place where everyone gathers on Christmas morning to open their fabulous presents.

Every year, the tree goes up on December 1 and is taken down after New Year's Day—because a live tree would lose its luster long before Christmas, and since the tree sits in direct sunlight, a prelit artificial tree is used. Clear lights create an upscale look. Red-velvet ribbon continues the statement begun in the entrance hallway, and a red-velvet tree skirt provides an inviting stage on which gifts will be displayed.

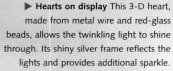

▶ **Hearts on display** This 3-D heart, made from metal wire and red-glass beads, allows the twinkling light to shine through. Its shiny silver frame reflects the lights and provides additional sparkle.

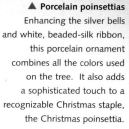

▲ **Porcelain poinsettias** Enhancing the silver bells and white, beaded-silk ribbon, this porcelain ornament combines all the colors used on the tree. It also adds a sophisticated touch to a recognizable Christmas staple, the Christmas poinsettia.

▶ **Treasures of Egypt** Handcrafted Egyptian glass adds upscale Middle-Eastern flair to the tree. The 18-carat gold that has been applied to the etched glass counterbalances the silver metallic wire of the red-beaded heart. Its unusual shape is eye-catching.

◀ **Silver bells** This lovely collectible silver wedding bell sits amid a swirl of beaded-silk ribbon. Several bells were placed throughout the tree. These bells and the white ribbon are complementary elements that set off the large red bows, the principal statement pieces.

▶ **Center of attention** Framed in this dramatic window setting, all eyes are immediately drawn to this fabulous spectacle of Egyptian glass, 18-carat-gold-and-crystal ornaments, designer porcelains, and crystal-bead garlands. Gold icicles add vertical lines, encouraging the eye to travel up and down the height of the tree.

STUNNING SPIRAL

When you arrive at this house, upon entering the grand hallway, two choices present themselves: a right turn will take you to the drawing room with its twelve-foot-tall tree. A left turn, however, will bring you here, to this spiral staircase and beautiful crystal chandelier.

Therefore, we decided to place a smaller version of the drawing-room tree next to this stairway. The red-velvet ribbon continues the "through-line" (a decorating term referring to a fabric, color, or ornament that is repeated in a design to tie the look together) to this end of the house. Since the stairway, the grand hallway, and the drawing room can all be seen at the same time, it was important to create uniformity. By doing so, one long, continuous flow of red, silver, and gold was achieved.

The hand-carved wooden stairway designed by renowned Los Angeles architect Paul Revere Williams demanded special attention, so it was draped with several pieces of lush garland, matching that used in the hall. Red bows, twinkling lights, and crystal ornaments help lead the eye up the stairs.

▶ **Golden orb** The only one of its kind on the tree, this piece was chosen for its simple elegance. The gold is in keeping with the theme colors chosen, but the unique shape stands out.

▶ **Ornate beading** In place of the white beaded ribbon used on the main family tree, these custom-crafted silk-and-glass-bead ornaments were hung on the staircase tree. This gave the tree a feeling similar to that of its larger counterpart, but a unique style.

◀ **View from above** Looking down from the second-floor landing, the eye is treated to a different perspective. When you peek down through the crystal chandelier to the polished marble floor, the tree is seen as the major focal point, which is intimately wrapped up in this famous stairway.

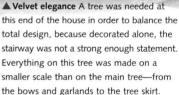

▲ **Velvet elegance** A tree was needed at this end of the house in order to balance the total design, because decorated alone, the stairway was not a strong enough statement. Everything on this tree was made on a smaller scale than on the main tree—from the bows and garlands to the tree skirt.

▼ **Beaded star** This beaded treetop star is a companion piece to the beaded ornaments. Normally found at the top of the tree, here it shares the spotlight with the true stars of the tree, the dramatic red ribbons and bows.

VICTORIAN INFLUENCE

VICTORIAN DESIGN IS UNIQUE—it is the only Christmas look named after a historical era. Although Christmas trees were introduced to Britain by Victoria's grandmother, Queen Charlotte, it was Queen Victoria's consort, Albert—a German prince—who popularized the custom of decorating trees. Victoria and Albert decorated their trees with glass ornaments imported from Germany, alongside candies, wax dolls, fruit and nuts, and candles for illumination. Other elements used in Victorian Christmas-tree design included small toys, paper ornaments, and ribbon, and the colors were dark jewel tones. When this look came to America, it was softened by the addition of pinks and mauves, giving Victorian Christmas a more feminine feel.

◀ Pastels in paper The pink hydrangeas on the tree were introduced in order to create floral highlights. The "vases" —paper Victorian-motif cones—could also be used to hold candies and other sweets.

◀ A royal dining experience Traditional Victorian Christmas tables served up boar, roast beef, and mince-meat pie. Set here at a flower-laden modern table with Victorian influence, bone china and lace placemats stand ready to present a more contemporary meal. A small floral-themed tree nestles in a garlanded bay window; live plants grace the chandelier, and a dried wreath hangs on a side door.

▲ Victorian rose Designer-silk chair wraps were used to disguise the homeowners' chairs, which were not suited to the Victorian style. The rosette tied on the back is in keeping with the room's floral theme.

◀ Village charm This Victorian church and tavern are parts of an illuminated snow village that adds charm to the sideboard. Victorians often created tableaux on their Christmas tables; now they can be an upscale way of displaying your collectible villages.

REGAL HOLIDAY BANQUET

Color was the motivation for selecting the decorative pieces displayed in the dining room. Instead of using the traditional Victorian dark jewel tones, lighter colors such as pink, cream, fuchsia, and mint green were used to soften the dark, heavy wood. Silks, brocades, velvets, porcelains, ceramics, and glass were blended with paper, tin, and live flowers to create a delicate and romantic feeling.

This room was dressed for an elaborate holiday party, so every surface in the room was decorated, including pedestals and door arches—even the food platters were embellished. A gourmet pastry chef was commissioned to make beautiful, elegant desserts that were appropriate for the theme.

The windows, buffets, and pedestals were all festooned in artificial greenery lit with clear, twinkling lights. Burgundy and emerald-green velvet bows provide a regal accent.

▶ **Sugared teacakes** A silver serving dish garnished with leaves and crystal twigs gives these cakes special distinction. They were designed to look like miniature presents, right down to the narrow ribbons and tiny bows.

▲ **Christmas-tree confection** "Sugarcoated" with glitter so that it looks good enough to eat, this stunning glass piece is whimsically colorful, with pastel green, red, pink, and purple flowers, bows, and sashes.

▶ **Hearts and flowers** Romance is embodied in this delicate glass heart, hand-painted with leaves and flowers. During the romantic Victorian era, hearts were a popular motif.

▶ **Victoriana on stage** (far right) The main buffet needed a strong dramatic statement. A miniature stage with bright-red curtains and gold trim was a perfect set for an angelic Victorian vision.

▶ **Old-world charm** (top left) This Father Christmas earthenware figurine is a cleverly sculpted teapot.
▶ **Merry minstrel** (top right) Green velvet bows top a decorative pedestal wrapped in a thick garland with twinkling clear lights.
▶ **Rich brocade** (bottom left) A feminine fabric ornament helps soften the darkness of the tree.
▶ **Porcelain in pink** (bottom right) Two finely crafted porcelain drops hang side by side. The delicate floral motif echoes the romantic theme.

VICTORIAN INNOCENCE

Toys were common decorations on Victorian Christmas trees. Our model for this tree was a giant dollhouse, so the vision for this design was simple: Start with one special collectible, feature her prominently at the top of the tree, and surround her with doll friends and a collection of red hats so they can play dress-up. Since all of the dolls were dressed in their winter finery, we chose a frosted artificial tree that looked as if it was dusted with snow.

White faux fur is a common element on the dolls' costumes, the fabric ornaments, and the oversized matching tree skirt. (When outfitting a large tree, it is important to use a skirt big enough to extend beyond the bottommost branches of the tree to balance the design.)

In order to share this Victorian vision with neighbors, we opened the curtains and tied them back with maroon crushed-velvet ribbon. Intricately carved Bavarian wood pieces depicting Christmas scenes brighten the dark windows.

▶ **Father Christmas** A rosy-cheeked glass Saint Nicholas ornament carries a tiny tree and gold-wrapped present.

◀ **Toyland** Bay windows are excellent tree locations, allowing you to to create a tableau, away from the flow of traffic. Because dolls are the principal focal points on this tree, miniature pieces of doll furniture—satin lamps and velvet chairs—were added to support the theme. Pink and maroon bead garlands tie in to the Victorian colors used in the dining room (previous pages).

▶ **White fur** The faux-fur trimming on this ornament mimics the fluffy collars on the dolls' dresses, while the winter-red fabric stands out against the frosty branches. An airy top bow contrasts with the heavier brocade.

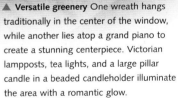

▲ **Versatile greenery** One wreath hangs traditionally in the center of the window, while another lies atop a grand piano to create a stunning centerpiece. Victorian lampposts, tea lights, and a large pillar candle in a beaded candleholder illuminate the area with a romantic glow.

◀ **Fringed footwear** A collection of miniature Victorian-style floral shoe ornaments continues the "dolly dress-up" motif.

▲ **Victorian bonnet** Doll-size hats—little girls' playthings—adorn the tree. Like Victorian hats, they are decorated with a mix of ribbon, lace, flowers, or feathers.

ANGELIC TABLEAU

A decorated stairway can become a background that adds interest to your tree display. Matching the staircase trimming to the tree gives your design area a coordinated look. As this is the entry hall, a rich Victorian tableau was created to set the theme for the entire home.

Hunter green and burgundy are traditional Victorian tones. Angels, velvet ribbons, paper ornaments, and miniature flowerpots complete the theme. The bright-red angel gives this rather dark corner a dramatic lift. If this tree were truly from Victorian times, candles would have been used as illumination. Although they cast a romantic glow, candles are a fire hazard and are not recommended.

▲ **Framed portrait** It was common practice to use colorful pictures and postcards as decorative flourishes in Victorian times. This antique postcard has a period feel.

▶ **Celestial movement**
These angels were designed with movable joints, allowing you to change their positions and place them in a variety of poses.

▶ **Heavenly angels**
Angels have traditionally been used only as treetoppers. However, flying several of them throughout the tree—and even in the garland—lends an illusion of movement, while Santa in his sleigh keeps the tree grounded.

▲ **First look** The front door is the first thing your guests will see. By placing a decorative wreath out front, you give them a prelude to the grand overture waiting inside. This wreath features a maroon crushed-velvet bow made of ribbon, which is used throughout the interior design.

▲ **Lamplight** For a party—on a clear night—try tying a simple bow on existing exterior light fixtures. Here, alongside a stone garden cherub, nothing more was needed but a sprinkling of clear lights in the background, which created a lovely starlight effect.

Celebrations

THE WINTER MONTHS are a popular time of the year for grand celebrations in many different cultures around the world: some are religious festivals, some celebrate bounteous gifts, and some are remembrances of ancient miracles. All of them share common bonds—they are times of loving, sharing, and giving thanks with family and friends. Here we celebrate these special moments.

COMBINED TRADITIONS

IMAGINE THAT SOMEWHERE DEEP in a winter forest sits a magical table covered in snow, illuminated by candles, and dressed for a feast, in anticipation of the day when the world's great cultures unite in peace. Here, we created a whimsical and elegant "winter wonderland" dining room with crystal accents, where Christmas, Hanukkah, and Kwanzaa—and other winter holidays such as Id-ul-Fitr, celebrated at the end of the Islamic month of Ramadan, or Bodhi Day, the anniversary of Buddha's enlightenment—can be celebrated together.

One way to decorate your home for an interfaith or intercultural holiday celebration that respects different religions, communities, and customs is to use a neutral color like white as a unifying theme. White can also serve as a backdrop for the introduction of other colors associated with these various holiday traditions, such as blue for Hanukkah; or red, black, and green for Kwanzaa.

◄ **Celebrating together** Family members and friends of all faiths can break bread together in this fantasy setting. The illusion of a forest was created with birch trees trimmed in crystal-and-white ornaments and clear lights, surrounding a table and chairs covered in faux-fur fabric and flocked with cotton "snow" batting.

▼ **Mixing symbols** In keeping with the theme of unity, neutral crystal was chosen for the centerpiece elements: a dreidel for Hanukkah, a Kwanzaa cup, and a Christian nativity scene, all arranged together on a layer of artificial snow.

ELEGANT ICE

No one does it better than Mother Nature when it comes to winter design. Pure white snow and the sparkle of ice crystals put even the most spectacular diamond to shame. It's a hard act to follow, but it can be done using the right blend of acrylics, porcelain, and crystal glass. Remember, nature isn't perfect, so try to use ornaments, garlands, and decorative pieces that have unique textures, shapes, and sizes. Incorporating elements of nature such as live tree branches, pine cones, and winter berries will enhance your display. Try using several mirrors in your design: mirrored ornaments and wall mirrors that hang or lean near your display not only reflect the sparkle of lights and crystal, they can also add depth and dimension. Lastly, a thick blanket of snow provides the finishing touch to any winter wonderland. Here, we used pieces of rolled-cotton batting, rounded their edges, and added a fine dusting of artificial snow.

▲ **Winter star** This majestic acrylic star makes a dramatic statement with its size and shape. Its straight, crisp, distinct lines and pointed rays stand out against the naturally irregular branches. When using large heavy decorations on thin branches, make sure the trees can support the weight, and never place them directly over the heads of your guests.

▶ **Frosty fashion** We added high-end elegance to the display with the help of this fabric-covered ornament. The highly detailed piece combines silk and satin ribbons, beaded tassels, silver braiding, and a sophisticated pattern.

▲ **A hint of blue** This acrylic snowflake introduces a subtle daub of color to the white canvas and increases the wintry feeling. Its color also represents Hanukkah; honor different holidays by adding decorations in traditional colors.

◀ **Graceful porcelain** Delicate designs cover this collectible porcelain ornament. Its unusual urn shape conveys an element of grace to the overall design, so several pieces were hung throughout the display.

▶ **Snowy glen** A forest of crystal and snow rests atop this elegant buffet. Three white candles sit nestled in a wreath of ice crystals. Pearl garlands strung randomly from tree branches create an elegant necklace for this winter wonderland.

CHRISTMAS

It all started with a baby in a manger. Everything that is Christmas began with one special moment in time—the birth of Christ in Bethlehem more than two thousand years ago. The grandeur of Christmas is showcased in this dramatic living room, which we decorated with Christian religious symbols and icons associated with the Holy Family and the Nativity.

The tree was decorated to match the room's color scheme, which supported traditional spiritual tones: royal purple, midnight blue, matte gold, and creamy white. To give the design a warm, earthy feel, we selected a live tree. This tree was too full to allow us to adequately display many of the large pieces we chose to showcase, so we added live manzanita branches in several locations to provide needed display space and to break up the natural line of the tree. To complete the look, we framed the windows behind the tree with lit garlands that were left undecorated, so they would not pull focus from the tree itself.

◀ **Glorious angel** In the tree, angels of different ethnicities symbolize universal acceptance. The theme was tied together with gold satin, emulating the angels' robes.

▶ **Ship of the desert** Carrying the nativity theme from tabletop to tree, this molded-glass camel presents an interesting shape.

▼ **Away in a manger** The Nativity scene is the most well-known Christmas religious symbol. This large Nativity set was placed on a table near the tree.

▲ **Cross** Although the empty cross is actually an Easter symbol, symbolizing Jesus's resurrection, the jewel colors on this ornament perfectly accent the tree.

◀ **The Magi** The Gospels tell of three wise men who rode camels from eastern lands, following a star to Bethlehem to see the baby Jesus. The scene is hand-painted on this gold glass ornament, fitting the Nativity theme well in both color and subject matter.

▼ **Heralding angel** This molded-glass, handpainted piece was suspended from a branch to give the appearance of flight.

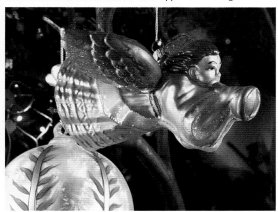

HANUKKAH

In Hebrew, "Hanukkah" means dedication, and its celebration commemorates the rededication of the Temple in Jerusalem more than two thousand years ago, after it was destroyed by foreign invaders. The legend of Hanukkah, known as the Festival of Lights, tells of how a small army of Jews led by Judah Maccabee won back the temple, only to find one day's supply of oil left to light the gold menorah (a Jewish religious candelabra); miraculously it burned for eight days. Today, candles are used instead of oil.

Blue is the primary color associated with Hanukkah (it is considered a holy, royal color in Judaism), and it is typically mixed with silver, gold, or white. Here, we combined the symbols of Hanukkah—the menorah, the dreidel (a spinning top), and the Star of David—into a striking display for a Hanukkah party. A shiny silver tree with crystal-drop accents was added to give height to the display and provide a unique "Festival of Lights."

▲ **Star of David** A delicate glass Star of David hangs proudly. The six-pointed star, an ancient symbol believed to have magical properties, was not officially adopted as a symbol of Judaism until the 1700s.

◄ **Menorah** An elegant silver menorah is a stunning decoration for this holiday table. On each of the eight nights of Hanukkah, an extra candle is lit. The center candle is used to light the others.

◄ **Temple** This electrically lit porcelain building is a modern part of the decorating scheme. It is a model of New York Central Synagogue (c. 1839), the oldest Jewish house of worship in continuous use in New York City and a magnificent example of American synagogue architecture.

▶ **Festive table** Twinkling candlelight casts a glow on this decorative table created for an intimate Hanukkah gathering. To honor the holiday's roots, the large candle featured on the table is actually an oil candle, filled with decorative foliage in tones of silver and blue.

▲ **Dreidel and gelt** This crystal dreidel adds sparkle to the table amid a sea of chocolate gelt ("money" used in the dreidel game). The dreidel is engraved with Hebrew letters meaning "A miracle happened here." The game dates back to the Maccabees.

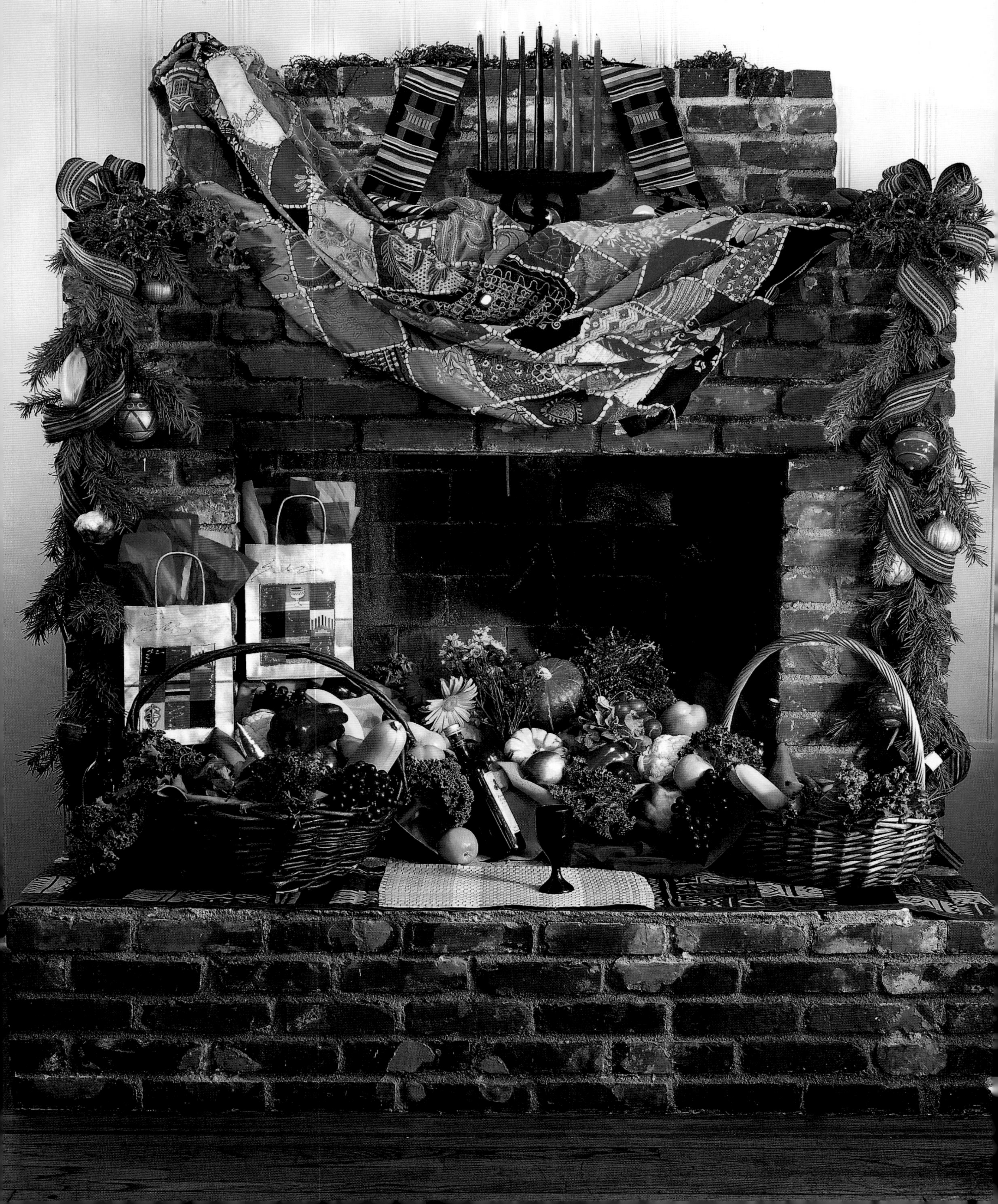

KWANZAA

The African-American and Pan-African holiday of Kwanzaa, which celebrates the reaffirmation of family, community, and culture, was founded in 1966. The name "Kwanzaa" is from the Swahili phrase *matunda ya kwanza,* meaning "first fruits," and Kwanzaa's origins are rooted in celebrations of the harvest that have been practiced by African peoples since the time of Ancient Egypt and Nubia.

When designing this room for a Kwanzaa gathering, we wanted to emphasize the warm feeling of celebrating one's community. It seemed appropriate to beautify this home's living-room fireplace, the heart of the house. The rustic, brick fireplace signifies warmth and lends itself to displaying traditional Kwanzaa elements, such as a cornucopia, a candle-holder, and a Unity Cup. The colors of Kwanzaa—red, black, and green—flow beautifully against the red stone background.

▶ **Unity Cup** This wooden goblet, called the *Kikombe cha Umoja,* symbolizes the principle of unity. It is placed front and center on a mat called a *Mkeka,* which represents the foundation of African cultural history.

◀ **Harvest hearth** Putting a new spin on fireplace decorations, colorful African fabrics and red and green ribbons were incorporated into the design.

▼ **First fruit** These fruits and vegetables represent the bounty of the harvest. Glass vegetable ornaments were interspersed with the real ones, to add glitter to the display.

▲ **Ornamental accent** Picking up two of the traditional colors of Kwanzaa, this holiday ball nestles in the artificial pine garland and an African-textile-patterned ribbon.

◀ **Candles** The Kwanzaa candleholder is known as a *Kinara.* A symbol of ancestral Africa, it holds seven candles that stand for the seven principles of Kwanzaa: unity, self-determination, collective work and responsibility, cooperative economics, purpose, creativity, and faith. Red represents the struggle for freedom, black represents the people, and green represents both the harvest and hope for the future.

All That Glitters

ALL THAT GLITTERS is gold—and much more. Metallic hues—from silver, platinum, copper, and brass to every jewel-tone imaginable—sparkle and shimmer, mirroring the bright lights of the holiday season. The upscale quality of polished metal provides a spectacular, sumptuous display, rich in color and dramatic in design. Lights and candles play an important role in glittery decor, providing extra points of light that dance beautifully off the many reflective surfaces.

GOLDEN OPULENCE

GOLD, ACCENTED WITH OTHER METALLIC COLORS—platinum, silver, and copper—brings this design to life. A one-color scheme would have flattened the overall look of the white tree, but the combination of two or more colored metals gives the tree depth and "pop" against its mostly white surroundings.

Drama is the key element for a metallic look. Choose shiny, bright, and glittered or sequined pieces—anything that will reflect light. The beauty of designing with gold is its versatility. Adding an accent color creates a different mood, and you can vary colors from year to year. The addition of black, as seen in the tree on the next page, can be quite dramatic and adds richness.

◀ **Silver and gold trimmings** Handmade fabric ornaments and handpainted glass pieces hang on the blank canvas of a white tree, while countless twinkling lights are reflected in the polished marble floor of this classical room setting. Matching sleigh, tree skirt, and garlanded pillars add to the sparkle.

◀ **Matte softness** The matte finish and polished veneer of this white-and-gold ornament works well to balance the more striking metallic elements on the tree. Topped with a gold ribbon, it gives the tree a soft shine and adds depth.

▲ **Striking the right chord** A faux-jewel-accented gold harp is in perfect harmony with the angelic surroundings. Relating decorations to one another, such as placing this harp next to a neighboring angel, lets you tell a story within your decorating scheme.

◀ **Perfect placement** This angel stands in the center of a wreath on an entry-way table, instead of on the treetop. An angel, a figurine—or even a pretty bowl of ornaments—can be set in a table wreath to create a festive centerpiece.

DECADENT DESIGN

Individually, black, gold, silver, and pearls are colors and jewels associated with wealth and stature. However, when combined, as in this room, all of these elements not only state those themes, but push the envelope as they become an exciting treasure chest of excess.

We didn't want to lose the opulent feeling created by the tree, and we felt that the room demanded that the decorations flow from tree to mantle to fireplace and from tabletop to the three French doors. The dark furniture and gold walls made the perfect backdrop for a tree with the look of such great wealth and beauty.

While this house easily supports such a lavish use of black, the color is not so easily incorporated into every home's decor. If you do opt to decorate with black, it is important to have elements in your home to support it; otherwise the look will be jarring and the effect will be uneven and overpowering. But when done correctly, black is simply divine.

▶ **A Hollywood spectacle** Sitting in the living room of a 1920s mansion, this tree shimmers in black, gold, and pearl, and is meant to evoke star style in the early days of silent-screen pictures.

◀ **Garlanded hearth** The dramatic potential of black is given full rein with this magnificent fireplace. Here, a decorative garland was designed to embellish the home's architecture. Lit candles and milk-colored ceramic light bulbs provide a soft glow, reflecting off the golden walls and hearth.

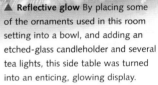

▲ **Reflective glow** By placing some of the ornaments used in this room setting into a bowl, and adding an etched-glass candleholder and several tea lights, this side table was turned into an enticing, glowing display.

◀ **Matched set** The door garlands in this room were all matched to the fireplace, using small- and medium-sized ornaments and black-velvet bows. The garland was lifted in the center to allow the French doors to open easily.

▼ **Draped glamour** Taking advantage of the black metalwork extending down from the stair railing, layered garlands shimmer in the entryway. Ornaments hung from crystal hangers provide shapely, colorful drama.

ROYAL VELVET

Fit for a king and queen, this fifteen-foot-tall tree, set up in the corner of a spacious, ornate drawing room, blends gold with copper to create a medieval feel. Renaissance-inspired shapes and patterns mix with religious icons to evoke the grandeur of cathedrals and royal castles. The crushed-velvet ribbon cascades through the tree like a queen's sash. Matching velvet balls, miniature crowns, and rose-window ornaments produce layers of texture and color, while thin colored-glass icicles add vertical elements reminiscent of the elongated lines of Gothic architecture.

Ornaments of mouth-blown glass painted with eighteen-carat gold help reflect the twinkle of clear miniature lights that illuminate the tree. Under the color-coordinated presents, an oversized tree skirt flows around the tree, evoking a nobleman's cape. The tree's rich tones—traditional bright reds and greens were replaced with deep hunter greens and moody burgundies—add drama to this white, airy space, but may be too dark for a room painted in similarly dusky hues.

▲ **Natural wonder** The gold, silver, and platinum in this glitter-edged leafy drop offer metallic shine as well as fine craftsmanship, with precise detailing of the leaf veins.

▶ **Royal crown** Ruby beads gather on this inverted teardrop with a decorative gold crown. The ruby is echoed on the tree in other ornaments, and around the room in the velvet ribbons and bows.

▶ **Ornate array** (far right) A strand of dark beaded garland cuts across a grouping of a light fabric ornament and a ball of eighteen-carat gold and clear glass, making a luxurious tapestry of bright and dark, matte and shine.

▲ **Sumptuous garland** Burgundy and green are repeated in two-tone full-pom bows and beaded garlands in the same colors, accented with a gold cross ornament.

▶ **Velvet jewel box** This tree is a spectacle of velvet jewel-tones contrasted with the warmth and glitter of polished copper and gold.

JEWEL-TONE GLAMOUR

WHEN MOST PEOPLE THINK OF DECORATING for Christmas, they usually think in terms of traditional colors—primary red and green. Why not dip into other hues of the color palette for something more exotic and dramatic? Royal purple and blue—typically associated with royalty—are traditional colors associated with the Advent season observed by some Christians four weeks before Christmas.

In addition to their religious significance, purple and blue—when combined with vibrant fuchsia, hot orange, golden yellow, ruby red, emerald green, and metallic tones—create a luxurious, festive atmosphere that conjures up a mood of Carnivale, which is famously celebrated the Tuesday before Lent in Venice, Rio de Janeiro, and New Orleans (where it is called Mardi Gras).

Carry the theme throughout your tree with ornaments, bead garland, and ribbon. For a glamorous showstopper of a tree that positively glitters, jewel tones will brighten a dark room, add color to a neutral space, and provide an elegant, different look for a special party.

◀ **Elevated beauty** For a party, a miniature jewel-tone Christmas tree livens up the bar. The multihued ornaments selected for this tree seem even more jewel-like with the addition of color-contrasted glitter in swirl and dot designs. Placing a small tree on a table, bar, or buffet saves space.

▶ **It is best to use a variety** of ornament shapes on your tree—round, elongated, faceted, molded, and angular—and to hang different shapes next to each other whenever possible. Your eyes will be taken on an exciting visual journey. Using ornaments in only one shape creates a static-looking tree.

CROWN JEWEL

The main statement in any Christmas design is always the tree. Therefore, it is important that you choose themed trimmings that will enhance your star attraction. Here, bright Venetian carnival masks and an electric-pink tree skirt intensify the collection of myriad jewel-tone colors. Ribbon was kept to a minimum—just a few swirls of fuchsia-and-gold mesh—so that nothing would detract from the vivid impact of the ornaments. This tree sits in a library window, in front of gauzy burnt-orange curtains, surrounded by curved wooden shelves, leather-bound books, and rich upholstered furniture.

In keeping with the sophisticated surroundings, we used sculpted ornaments. Each ornament was handpainted with intricate designs: lines, arcs, and dots of glitter in contrasting colors. The end result was a lush jewel-like confection that embodied the spirit of Carnivale. Once established in the tree, the party theme was continued throughout the room.

▲ **Sparkling ornaments** Ornaments can be displayed in many ways. If you have ornaments to spare after trimming your tree—and they are beautiful jewels like these—try layering them in wide-rimmed glasses.

▶ **Hot-pink tree skirt** Here we chose a fuchsia tree skirt with faux-marabou feathers and gold-flecked satin; its intense color and material complements the window's burnt-orange satin curtains and the mood of the tree. You could also choose a tree skirt to match any of the other jewel-tones on the tree.

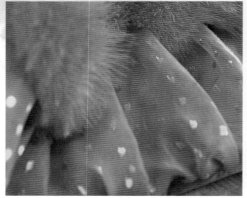

▶ **Etched cocktail glasses** For a party, continue the theme by serving drinks in jewel-colored glasses. Make it more festive with a decorated garland. Or, place a small candle inside each glass to create striking tea lights.

▲ **Statement piece** Present whimsical objects in an upscale way by choosing them in colors or styles that complement your tree. This green rhinestone mask instantly evokes a "Carnivale" feeling.

▶ **Frame your showpiece** A window can frame your main event. The architecture of a home often plays an important part in deciding the location for your tree. An arched doorway or a grand stairway are equally impressive alternatives. Wherever you put it, your tree should always be the center of attention.

A FEAST OF COLORS

Your tree theme can even be introduced into your party menu and buffet decorations. Here, the jewel-tone motif is evident in the dazzling display of rich colors, dramatic textures, fragrant candles, and a sideboard filled with beautiful "jeweled" desserts. The secret to a successful holiday party is to involve your guests. First, make them aware of the party theme. Then encourage them to dress accordingly. Finally, reward them by giving them visually stunning surroundings.

All that is needed to complete this party is atmosphere—a serenading string quartet (or an appropriate CD) to transport us to the romantic canals of Venice and to Carnivale.

◀ **Dining fantasy** (previous page) Glass-bead garlands hang from the chandelier to form the centerpiece of this lavish Venetian table. A gold tree glitters in the window. Lit entirely by candle-light, this room was transformed into an elegant enclave for a romantic dinner.

◀ **Decorative mantelpiece** Use multiple elements in similar hues to create a strong statement. A treetop finial, used as a mantel decoration, is combined with votives, an angel, a jeweled candelabra, and glass garland, all in ruby tones that complement the theme.

▶ **Jeweled desserts** Elegant glazed pears sit atop silver-candy beads, joined by sugared figs, sliced holiday nut rolls, and a sugar-dusted fruit torte: a brightly colored buffet of sumptuous desserts.

▲ **Feather tree** These brightly colored trees were placed on the table to provide dashes of strong color and a different level to the display. Their sparse, airy design helps showcase a few select ornaments.

▲ **Silverware cozy** Decorative handmade silverware holders provide interesting new twists at the dinner table. Their color-coordinated, luxurious gold design blends well with the overall jewel theme.

▲ **Beads and baubles** Added to the chandelier, multicolored glass beads and brilliant jewel-like ornaments of etched blown glass create additional sparkle as they reflect the gentle glow of candlelight.

Natural Christmas

Y OU CAN BRING THE BEAUTY OF NATURE into your holiday design, whether you live in the city or the country. Your trimmings can include flowers, pinecones and berries, handcrafted ornaments, home-baked goodies, or a combination of all of these; in natural decorating, individual style is key. This is probably the most personal of all decorating styles, since the elements include selecting your favorite flowers, stringing berries and popcorn, or baking from scratch. We have provided a range of design ideas, from pastoral to country chic, but the options are as limitless as nature.

COUNTRY WARMTH

"COUNTRY" IS AN AMBIGUOUS DESCRIPTIVE TERM, because design varies greatly from nation to nation. Whether English Country, American Country, French Country, or Bavarian Country, though, some common elements are shared. Country design has a warm, comfortable feel. Decorations are generally handmade with inexpensive materials found in and around the house. Most have a rural flavor and incorporate elements of nature such as birds, berries, pinecones, and food.

Upscale Country complements modern homes, and is best described as crisp, showcasing pieces like hand-carved wooden decorations made by fine craftspeople. Traditional Country—a natural for rustic homes—is more whimsical and childlike, and features homemade ornaments.

But there are no hard-and-fast rules—although the living room shown here is in a home that is more modern than rustic, we have combined Upscale and Traditional Country elements.

▼ **Bear in the air** This cute collectible hangs high above her fellow cubs, scampering in the tree. Alternating toys, bows, and other special pieces in the garland makes a unique statement.

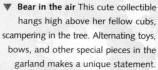

▲ **Starry night** Red and white balls with painted stars and home-crafted-looking bows add warmth to the tree and garlands. The star motif is echoed in papier-mâché ornaments and the tree lights reflected in the windows like hundreds of twinkling stars.

▶ **Child's play** We designed this display for a family with children. A jolly wooden Santa and snowman placed on either side of the tree fill the space and create a vignette. Clear lights keep the color palette simple. Points of red and green were added to the room with hand-stitched felt stockings and bags, brightly colored ribbon, and a mix of vivid glass ornaments.

COUNTRY CRAFTSMANSHIP

The decorations shown in this living room run the gamut from pieces found in nature to handcrafted decorations with a touch of whimsy to more sophisticated, upscale glass ornaments created by fine craftspeople.

This is not a country-style home, yet we were able to make the mix of country decorations work with the space. So, what do you do if you have a contemporary-looking home but want to decorate it in country style?

First, you remove all of the decidedly "un-country" elements—modern furniture and other pieces in nontraditional colors. For example, in this home, contemporary sculptures were put away for the holiday season. In their places are whimsical decorations in country Christmas colors of red and green, which complement the existing neutral rug and walls.

▶ **Golden pear** An upscale collectible glass piece works with this country setting because of the food motif; the oval shape adds interest and gives a "nod" to the country-fresh egg.

▲ **Snowy sweeper** This ornament also works as a freestanding statement piece. We added him to the fireplace garland to carry on the theme from the tree and to give the whole room a unified look. This decoration is old-fashioned in design and adds a touch of warmth and nostalgia so prominent in country style.

▶ **The "Christmas Pickle"** The glass gherkin hanging here is a tribute to an old German tradition, which dictated that parents were to hide a real pickle in the Christmas tree. The first child to discover the pickle then received an extra gift. This is a fun tradition which families all around the world have adopted and enjoy to this day.

▶ **Felt stocking** (top left) Adding to the homespun feel, this simple handcrafted stocking cheerily enhances the room.

▶ **Painted poinsettia** (top right) This bright green ball with its fiery red flower puts a fresh twist on a traditional image.

▶ **Country sweets** (bottom left) Although real sweets are often used in country Christmas decorating, these donuts, pastries, and stick candies— which appeal to the child in all of us—are glass.

▶ **Sentimental snowman** (bottom right) The use of decorations handed down in the family, like this fabric snowman, gives the tree its nostalgic heart.

◀ **Santa's helper** This cute, red, molded-glass reindeer sports glitter-covered antlers. He, along with other ornaments and felt bags, adds contrast to the brown bears.

▲ The power of three At the right end of the fireplace, we placed three different-sized slim-line trees at different heights to form a group that resembles one multilevel tree. Their staggered placement also gives the appearance of trees growing naturally on a hillside.

▲ Shimmering vegetables The vegetables hung on the fireplace trees are made of molded glass decorated with sparkly glitter, giving these familiar shapes a new slant. They are a fun look for kitchens and dining rooms.

◄ European country buffet (previous pages) This home, with its massive stone fireplace, provides a natural setting for a festive dessert buffet surrounded by hints of Europe. Nutcrackers, carved wooden pieces, and the gingerbread-house votive create an inviting atmosphere.

HOLIDAY HEARTH

This room provided interesting challenges. Since the fireplace is made of stone and its contemporary design didn't include a traditional mantelpiece, we were forced to take a different approach to the usual "mantelpiece-decorated-with-garland" look.

We decided to frame the fireplace with freestanding slim-line trees on either side. To create an asymmetrical look, we grouped three trees on one side and placed one large tree alone on the other side. Since the fireplace was not in use, we placed lit holiday greenery in the hearth to brighten the dark space.

▲ **Sugared maple leaves** These holiday "sugar cookie" ornaments bring the dessert theme from table to stairway.

This house sits in a warm climate, but we still wanted to bring the feeling of winter into the home, so we laid a snow blanket at the base of the trees to give them an Alpine flavor. This also echoed the snowy theme on the dining-room table and grounded the look.

▲ **Carved Claus** We attached this two-sided Santa plaque to the stairway banister as a statement piece. The muted colors and antique finish work well with the country theme.

▶ **Simple stairway** A decorative garland hung with statement pieces and stockings makes a nice backdrop to the collection of nutcrackers dressed as characters from *A Christmas Carol* displayed on an adjacent table.

◀ **Holiday harvest** Hung with an array of brightly colored fruits and vegetables and multicolored lights, the main fireplace tree creates a focal point of color in the corner of the dining room.

WINTER FROST

While this tree is perfectly suited to the beamed wood ceilings and inlaid stone floor found in this warm and charming retreat, it would be equally at home in a Swiss mountain chalet or a cozy log cabin. Nostalgic figurines represent images from early-1900s Christmastimes. Whimsical, collectible nutcrackers add Old World charm, while brightly colored cranberry balls and frosted apples and pomegranates give the tree its striking colorful appeal and provide a bright contrast against the frosty white-tipped branches.

Traditional plaid ribbon is woven through the tree, and when combined with pinecones, it makes a nice rustic statement. Ornamental woolen mittens drape over the tree branches as if some playful child just hung them there to dry. Following the line of the ceiling, a decorative garland features antique paper boots, game spinners, balls, and bows. This picturesque setting makes you want to settle into a comfortable chair and wait for the next snowfall while sipping a cup of hot cocoa.

▶ **Bûche de Noël** Originally from France, the *Bûche de Noël*, or yule-log cake, is a perennial holiday favorite that's perfect for a country Christmas. This version has white frosting and is accented with plastic red holly berries.

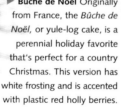

▲ **Frosted pomegranate** This fruit has long been treasured in the Mediterranean and India for its deep-colored flesh and delicious, winy flavor. This sparkly ruby pomegranate ornament is an excellent addition to country decor.

▶ **Little blue bugle boy** Young boys served as buglers and drummers in the military until the late 19th century, and the bugle-boy motif has persevered. Vintage-style buglers are still popular as ornaments and figurines, and this sweet example fits in perfectly with the rustic theme.

◀ **Santa spinner** Sometimes taking a simple child's toy and placing it in the greenery of the season can add a whimsical tone to the room. This colorful, resin game spinner has an old-time country appeal.

▶ **Snowy charm** Warm woolen mittens, vintage figurines, iced cranberry balls, plaid ribbon, and jeweled pomegranates adorn a sun-dappled, snow-kissed fir. Something this enchanting deserves a stunning finale—a burgundy silk tree skirt, hand-beaded with snowflakes and edged with delicate jingle bells.

AROUND THE FIRE

Who wouldn't want to gather around this warm, inviting hearth, decorated with elements of nature and vintage tableaux set with winter-sledding scenes? The large fireplace allowed for many decorations. In order for this look to work, each piece had to have the feel of both fine craftsmanship and aged beauty. This home is full of stylish yet comfortable furnishings, so we chose a relaxed design to complement the welcoming environment.

Plush stockings hang from the garland, and a wool tree skirt, embellished with hand-beaded snowflakes, lines the table to add an upscale touch of class to the woodsy room. The window is graced with a lit, red-berry wreath that matches the red-berry topiary and ball on the mantelpiece.

Needlepoint pillows with holiday themes accent the couches and the fireplace. A large wooden Santa, driving a reindeer, stands guard in front of a roaring fire, the perfect setting for a family gathering.

▶ **Nature in a jar** (above right) Both real and glass pinecones were used throughout this home; these oil candles filled with pinecones, berries, and evergreen branches brought an extra touch of the outdoors inside.

▶ **Sugared apples and berries** This ball of color works equally well as an ornament or highlight on the mantel of the stone fireplace. Nestled within the frosted branches of the tree, the sugared fruit contributes to the ice-and-snow effect.

▶ **Party on ice** A bevy of bisque-porcelain snow folk frolic on this handpainted votive music box. When it is wound up, a lone skater glides across the pond to the tune of "Jingle Bells."

◀ **Woodland fireplace** Draped from corner to corner with a garland accented with branch twigs and wrapped with patterned ribbon, the fireplace is a multilayered vignette surrounded by lit greenery, candles, and figurines.

▲ **Forest offerings** For a lovely country centerpiece, take a silver bowl, add several pinecone ornaments in muted colors, and highlight with a few autumn-colored glass balls. Place the ensemble in the center of a lit wreath, and surround it with a few decorative candles and figurines.

◀ **Cardinals rule** This brilliantly plumed songbird inhabits woodlands and gardens from eastern Canada to Mexico. The bright red male bird perched here is a common choice in country-Christmas decor because of his cheery appearance.

CHRISTMAS IN BLOOM

NATURE OFFERS A WONDROUS BOUNTY, a colorful array of fresh, fragrant, and visually explosive buds, blooms, and berries. This gorgeous flora, combined with delicate designer glass and a few special accents, bursts into brilliant bloom here as four different geographical areas of the United States are represented by regional floral Christmas trees.

Our design was greatly influenced by which flowers were available in each part of the country. Therefore, for these unique trees, we chose to decorate with flowers, fruits, and plants that were available and popular regionally, and to showcase these elements in ways not commonly envisioned—such as mixing ice twigs with orchids or limes with pinecones to create a dramatic artistic statement. The element common to all four designs was the artificial-tree base, yet each tree was given an individual personality by customizing the trimmings.

◀ **Radiant and vibrant** (clockwise from top left) Miniature New Zealand calla lilies adorn the Northeastern tree, coxcomb and hypericum berries populate the Midwestern tree, waxflowers and roses inhabit the Southern vignette, and eggplant, protea, and kale mingle in the Western display.

◀ **Rosy delight** Not wanting to detract from the floral theme, for the Southern tree we chose designer pieces with handpainted flowers instead of plain glass balls. A dainty rose dangles below this ball, enhancing the flowery mood.

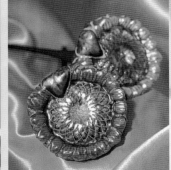

▲ **Stately sunflowers** An intricate seed pattern, framed by bold orange and lemony yellow rays, makes sunflowers a beautiful addition to floral displays. These glittery glass examples, used in the Western tree, stand out when mixed in with live flowers.

◀ **Romantic arrangement** Juniper and cedar branches, waxflowers, and roses spill forth from this distressed cast-iron urn from Paris. We included live flowers to add both intoxicating fragrance and natural beauty to the Southern tree.

NORTHEAST CHIC

The Northeast is represented with a dazzling display of orchids and roses that enhances this light-filled bedroom. The crowning touch is a spectacular treetop, created by Donald Clay, which merges live orchids with icy twigs made from crushed safety-glass attached to tree branches with glue (available at floral-supply stores). They make a nice contrast to each other, suggesting the crispness of winter and the promise of spring.

Green pears, arranged on the desk and inserted in the tree, create a through-line (a design element that ties a look together) in this room, and they echo the color of the orchids. Bright red was introduced to the tree sparingly by hanging glass balls that beautifully set off the green pears and orchids. To add to this tree's unique look, we included upside-down silver vases filled with floral accents.

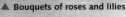

▲ **Bouquets of roses and lilies** An heirloom sterling-silver tea set lends classy support to the overall design. You can use everyday items found throughout the house as accent pieces.

◀ **Bedroom romance** Bright red rose petals scattered generously on the bedspread contrast with the deep greens of the tree and bed covering—and they also add a dramatic expression of passion.

▼ **Floral treasure** This glass piece is both an ornament and a "pick" (a decorative branch-tip accessory). It easily clips onto tree branches, garlands, and wreaths. Position it carefully so it stands up straight.

◀ **Cool and crisp** The tree is draped with acrylic "ice-chip" garlands and icy twigs interspersed with large crystal snowflake ornaments, recreating the icy feel of a Northeast winter's day.

▲ **Lilies on ice** The calla lily thrives in greenhouses all over the world. While most popular as an Easter decoration, it looks equally lovely at Christmas displayed in a clear vase filled with glass "ice."

MIDWEST HARVEST

Pinecones are the main feature of the Midwestern tree; we selected them for their traditional, homey feeling. This feeling was echoed in the cranberry and popcorn garlands that were meticulously handstrung, piece by piece. A tradition carried over from Victorian times, the craft of stringing fruits and other foods is time-consuming. There are prefabricated reproductions available on the market, but they cannot substitute for the fun of making garlands with friends and family.

Native Midwestern fruits and plants such as juniper, rosemary, and crabapples are clustered together throughout the tree and garland, making colorful statement pieces. Freshly sliced limes add a decorative twist. Fuchsia-colored coxcomb, with its fuzzy, textured surface, brings in warm luxury. The waxy-looking surface of the hypericum (also called coffee berry) provides a gentle reflection of light, and the delicate miniature yellow and red spray roses counterbalance the sharp-edged cedar and juniper branches. The finishing touch: large floral ornaments in traditional red and green.

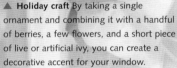

▲ Holiday craft By taking a single ornament and combining it with a handful of berries, a few flowers, and a short piece of live or artificial ivy, you can create a decorative accent for your window.

◄ Holly and ivy The contrast of the red berries, deep, dark green ivy, and the serrated edges of the holly stand out on this white egg-shaped ornament that echoes the clusters of fruit and leaves elsewhere on the tree.

▼ Santa's ride This tabletop floral arrangement, arranged tightly in a sleigh, contains all of the floral and fruity elements found on the tree. Its cheery countenance brightens the room and expands the theme.

► Nutcracker tassel This clever decoration was made by attaching the top half of a miniature carved wooden nutcracker to a bunch of colorful threads; the end result is a stylish tassel ornament.

◄ Harvest beauty Strings of popcorn and cranberries create irregular and eye-catching lines across this country-style tree. Clusters of sliced and whole fruit, inviting florals, and pinecones in various sizes—from small to enormous—convey an earthy heartland mood.

WESTERN CORNUCOPIA

The Western wilderness was the inspiration for this tree. We carefully placed branches and other elements in the tree to give an illusion of natural randomness. As in the other floral trees, roses played a part in our decorating scheme, providing many bright points of color in sharp contrast to the dark green of the tree and branches. They also softened the look.

A touch of the exotic was added by introducing bright orange birds of paradise (which grow freely throughout the Western states) and deep-crimson pomegranates. Sliced oranges contributed a fragrant citrus appeal. For novelty's sake, we replaced the traditional tree stand with an antique apple pail. Once again, glass ornaments were kept to a minimum, except for those that worked well with the Western floral theme in both color and design.

▶ **Red, red rose** Handpainted ornaments such as this rose ball help to continue the rose theme, prevalent in all four floral displays in this chapter. Roses are readily available in all parts of the country.

▲ **Exotic bouquet** This eclectic grouping of sliced citrus, pinecones, and assorted flowers creates an exciting cluster. Place bunches like this throughout your tree and on garlands, or use them to enhance tabletop topiaries.

▼ **Glittery florals** This unusual piece helps to bring a feeling of lightness and glitter to an otherwise dark and heavy tree. Its warm colors complement the tree and room tones.

◀ **Wild West** This wild tree looks perfectly at home in its cottage-like environment. The relaxed design was inspired by the informal gardens surrounding this home.

▲ **Bucket bouquet** To create a rough, rural country feeling, a rustic metal bucket was filled with colorful roses arranged around a red-and-green apple center.

SOUTHERN ELEGANCE

This tree personifies classic Southern romance. In creating it, we were inspired by imagery from the works of Southern authors such as Margaret Mitchell, Mark Twain, and Anne Rice. Fragrant magnolia blossoms, salmon-pink roses, and drippy Spanish moss conjured up visions of the old South and days of gracious living in simpler times. The Southern look works especially well in rooms that are decorated with casual floral patterns and painted in muted or neutral colors.

Traditional red and green Christmas elements just wouldn't work with this particular theme. Instead, we used a small number of handpainted, floral-themed ornaments in a variety of styles, shapes, and colors. Tree branches and mosses create interesting lines and textures. Roses and waxberries in pastel shades expand on the enchanting floral theme.

◀ **Matched set** A decorative glass handbag and shoe have feminine Southern charm and keep the tree dressed in style.

▶ **Summer breeze** This sultry, romantic tree entices; a gentle wind seems to waft through the branches, while the flowers bloom and release perfume into the air. Flowers fill different-sized urns and props placed at varying heights, creating a multilevel garden.

▼ **Pussywillows and poppies** Delicate depictions of flowers, in the form of glass ornaments with handpainted blossoms and branches, help to accentuate the "ladies-who-lunch" feel of the tree.

▲ **Flower garden** Framed by amaranthus to the left and magnolia leaves to the right, this gold, red, green, and white ornament brings all the colors found on the tree onto one glass canvas.

▶ **Lovers entwined** Passionate pink roses sit nestled in an aluminum watering can, in the embrace of a sturdy tree branch—a delicate dance between the masculine arms of the tree and the feminine softness of the roses.

Pop Culture

ECLECTIC, ALTERNATIVE, TRENDY, FUN: these styles all
allow for total freedom of expression. They follow no rules of
design. Whether you are looking back to your childhood for
inspiration, creating an amazing party surprise for your guests, or
just showcasing your collectibles, the bottom line is to cut loose . . .
anything goes! Use your imagination and "think outside the box."

RETRO WHIMSY

RETRO IS JUST ANOTHER WORD for nostalgia. In the 1950s, oversized, multicolored light bulbs (C-9s), tinsel icicles, and large, colorful glass ornaments defined the look of a Christmas tree. Before the advent of themed trees and designer ornaments, Christmas trees incorporated a variety of traditional elements representative of Christmas: Santas, elves, candy canes, train sets, and gift-wrapped packages stacked under the tree.

What once stood as the standard for Christmas is now just one of many choices in the broad spectrum of holiday themes and designs. Like Victorian, this design is specific to one particular era, but its appeal is timeless.

◀ **Gingerbread man** To make a cookie decoration, poke a hole into the cookie before it fully cools to prevent breakage. Once the cookie cools, ice it and thread a piece of floral wire through the hole and hang.

◀ **Helping-hands kitchen** Gingerbread cookies serve two purposes: they are tasty holiday treats as well as holiday decorations. A whimsical Christmas village built on a buffet adds to the warmth of the kitchen and pulls your eye toward the Christmas display in the adjacent room. A needlepoint potato-chip-canister Santa smiles in approval.

▲ **Jaunty cap** A novelty light cap in the shape of Santa's hat is perfect for a retro setting. The hat sits over a simple miniature bulb. Mix novelty light sets with plain lights to prevent your design from looking too busy.

◀ **Combined charm** This clever snow-globe plays music and has a built-in candle to light the way for Santa and his reindeer as they revolve around the base. In the background, his final destination: a quaint, snowy illuminated village.

A CHILD'S PARTY

Create a festive environment for your child (or the child in you) by removing all things adult and everyday. This clears your decorating space and allows you to build a Christmas fantasy land. In this particular home, it was the dining room that was transformed from an ordinary workspace into a place filled with wonder and visual excitement.

The goal was to design something fanciful, suitable for a child's Christmas lunch. We mixed primary colors with traditional Christmas reds and greens to achieve a bright, fun palette reminiscent of a box of crayons.

On the table, felt ornaments in shapes ranging from snowmen and Santas to angels and gift packages double as silverware pockets. Even the milk glasses got a holiday makeover: each base has its own slip-on "skirt" with decorative appliqués. Peppermint candles burn and scent the air with their gentle aroma, and small decorative items scattered about the table lend their charms.

▶ Fun with felt This perky snowman with his bright-red scarf and cheery smile has become a Christmas staple. He evokes memories of childhood arts-and-crafts projects created around the kitchen table.

▶ Bag of sweets This brightly colored felt bag hangs merrily on the tree. Inside, candy canes and assorted sweets await a child's eager hand on Christmas morning.

◀ Holiday hutch Deck out your dining-room furniture by removing everyday dishes and filling the nooks and crannies with everything Christmas. Turn an ordinary hutch into an exciting showcase for all your Christmas collectibles, dishes, and figurines.

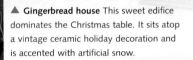
▲ Gingerbread house This sweet edifice dominates the Christmas table. It sits atop a vintage ceramic holiday decoration and is accented with artificial snow.

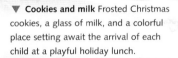
▼ Cookies and milk Frosted Christmas cookies, a glass of milk, and a colorful place setting await the arrival of each child at a playful holiday lunch.

AROUND THE TREE

This is where it all happens on Christmas morning, as colorful lights brighten the room and the sound of the train whistle cuts through the air. Children and adults alike descend on the piles of brightly wrapped presents, eagerly anticipating what's inside. The crowning moment when the wait is over has at last arrived—Christmas is finally here!

In order to create treasured memories like these, first make sure that your tree sits in an accessible location. If children are involved, include them by making decorations together and then hanging your decorations on the tree. The nostalgic look shown here is about family and remembering the past, and is inspired by Christmas days long gone.

Keeping family decorations and placing them on the tree from year to year helps to keep memories and traditions alive. You can buy collectible ornaments, but sometimes the ones that are the most valuable are those that you make yourself.

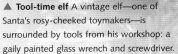

▲ **Tool-time elf** A vintage elf—one of Santa's rosy-cheeked toymakers—is surrounded by tools from his workshop: a gaily painted glass wrench and screwdriver.

◀ **Childhood memory** This tree is considered by many to be the definitive look of Christmas, with its brightly colored lights and fabulous tinsel icicles.

▶ **Fire engine** Many a child has wished for a shiny fire truck on Christmas. This glass ornament is a nod to those dreams.

▼ **Chugging along** Train sets bring back memories of hours spent playing in imaginary towns under the trees of our youth.

◀ **Stained-glass Santa** This crystal-like Kringle would normally be hung in a window to take advantage of direct sunlight. For something different, try incorporating window decorations into the tree.

▲ **Plucky ducky** This cheery pull-toy is right at home on this tree filled with childhood enchantments. Simple white buttons are the wheels on a cart, made to steer this yellow fellow about.

LOOKING IN

The retro style is known as much for the decorations displayed outside the home as for those inside. A classic retro home leaves no dark area untouched. Every single available space is filled with lit plastic figures, large multicolored ceramic light bulbs, decorative wreaths and garlands, animated pieces, and a candelabra in every window.

Homes are decked out from ground to roof. Santa, flying with his eight tiny reindeer, frequently takes a break from his hectic delivery schedule on Christmas Eve to stop by for a guest appearance and wave from the rooftop.

◀ **White magic** Multicolored bubble lights stand out dramatically against this white tree, sitting in front of a darkened window. Stained-glass holiday figures and decorative glass plates make fashionable accessories.

▶ **Berry wreath** Illuminated with tiny clear lights, this circle of berries makes for a warm welcome on the front door.

▲ **Snowy carolers** Lighting up to greet holiday visitors, snowman bulbs put on happy faces and help set the festive mood.

◀ **Debi's vintage Claus** This plastic Santa head has stood the test of time. It hung on Debi's childhood home in New Jersey, but migrated west to new California digs.

▼ **Bob's sentinels** Framed by strings of multi-colored lights and oversized novelty bulbs in front of the patio, two toy soldiers stand guard. They date back to Bob's youth; recently relocated from Michigan to Hollywood, they arrived in time for their big break.

SMALL QUARTERS

Decorating a more intimate space, such as a condo or cottage, works on the same principles as decorating a large house, just on a smaller scale. Living in an apartment should not diminish your holiday spirit. Since you have a smaller area to decorate, make your holiday display count. Select a few fine pieces and feature them prominently, rather than using many smaller, less impactful decorations.

You should always start your design with the largest element, which in most cases will be the Christmas tree. Depending on the space available, you may want to use a small tree and set it on a table to give the illusion of greater height, or try a slimline tree, which is tall and narrow.

Most apartments do not have working fireplaces, so if you like to use garland, you can drape it over large pieces of furniture, frame a mirror, outline a window, or run it along your holiday buffet.

▶ **Live retro** This tree mixes upscale glass ornaments with traditional vintage decorations. In lieu of a tree skirt, white cotton batting was placed at the base of the tree. On the coffee table, a train-depot vignette also sits on a bed of cotton "snow."

▶ **European angel** Surrounded by delicate gossamer strands of spun gold, this angel looks heavenly.

▲ **Red ball** This is an upscale reproduction of a classic retro design. With its intricate molded glass shape, including an additional ball at the bottom, lovely glitter pattern, and vibrant color, it stands out and makes a fine collectible.

▶ **Sock monkey** Hanging from a branch and clutching a banana, a cute glass monkey ornament provides comic relief. In true retro fashion, this tree combines sophisticated designer pieces with whimsical elements.

▲ **Snow angel** This brightly clad little boy has happily plopped down in the snow and eagerly waves his arms and legs to create the outline of an angel.

◀ **Roly-poly snowman** Another playful piece on this retro tree is the well-coordinated snowman here, outfitted in matching hat, scarf, and mittens and carrying a broom to help clear a path in the snow.

TROPICAL DELIGHT

WARM CLIMATES INSPIRE alternative holiday decorations. Located inside a poolside guesthouse, this tree can be used in some parts of the country year-round. It is the ultimate cool party prop.

In recent years, the tropical theme has island-hopped to the mainland and gained greater acceptance. Surfing Santas, tropical fruits, and exotic flowers have freed many decorators from what has long been considered the conventional and only correct way to decorate the home for Christmas.

This tropical tree is a classic example of decorating according to the style of the house. Eschewing the traditional treetop, we set aside the artificial tree's actual top and made use of this guesthouse living room's rattan palm-tree chandelier instead.

▶ **Exotic cocktails** Green-cactus glasses serve up freshly sliced limes along with an explosion of tropical glass ornaments—pineapples, sugared conch shells in pretty pastels, vivid bird-of-paradise blooms, and shy seahorses—turning a simple bar decoration into an island stunner.

◀ **Fruit medley** Keeping it light and fruity, this garland plays host to a variety of sweet, tropical delights. Fresh limes, blown-glass pineapples and watermelon slices, and paper strawberries and pears create a mouthwatering fruit salad.

▶ **Poolside party** This shows how you can take one simple, inexpensive, and offbeat element and turn it into an entire tree. Several hundred cocktail umbrellas serve as bright, tropical bursts of color on a tree grounded with lime-green packing peanuts! Hawaiian-themed designer ornaments add special island flavor.

ISLAND FLAVOR

Christmas ornaments shaped like rainbow-hued fish, unusual local flowers, and brightly plumed birds evoke daydreams of vacations on exotic islands around the world.

A tropical tree sets the scene for a party—in your house, at poolside, along the ocean, or in your own personal backyard paradise. Make your tree the life and soul of the party. This bright beacon of light and form can be used to provide unique and alternative lighting as your party changes from a sunny afternoon barbecue into a late-evening luau.

The placement of the tree is vitally important when used as a party prop. Decide whether you want to use it to draw guests into your soiree, to point the way to the bar or buffet or, as seen here, to stand alone—apart from the party—and merely cast a lovely reflection into the pool.

Remember: As with all things electrical, be sure to keep cords and lights well away from the water. Extension cords should be secured. (Safety should always be part of holiday festivities!)

▶ **Dazzling flier** A Native American myth tells how the first two hummingbirds were created from feathers left over from other birds. The sun cast rays on the pair, causing the male to glow with brilliant colors. This clip-on fellow is caught midflight.

▲ **Snorkelers' treasure** The guesthouse tree on the previous page was decorated with a multitude of tropical fauna ornaments; this one is inspired by the Moorish Idol reef fish. The Hawaiian name for the fish is *kihi kihi*, meaning "angular," a reference to its shape—which offers a nice contrast to the round cocktail umbrellas.

▶ **Tropical tranquility** This limited-edition collectible, titled "Paradise," depicts a white ship floating through an idyllic ocean sunset. What makes it unique are the raised flowers and leafy palm-tree fronds circling the ornament.

◀ **Island sunset** A Hawaiian-shirt ornament is handpainted with a rippling sea, swaying palms, and a distant volcano that hint at warm breezes and romantic nights.

▶ **Ribbons of light** Here, we used electric ribbon as an alternative to traditional Christmas tree lights— it is weather-resistant and safe for outdoor use. The tropical colors make it perfect for a poolside party. The potted flowers below serve two purposes: to secure the tree and to provide a decorative tree-stand cover.

ALTERNATIVE STYLE

SANTA CLAUS, RUDOLPH, and red and green are left behind, as nontraditional colors and ornaments replace them in holiday decorating. Tired of your green tree? Substitute hot pink, purple, or black. Hang your tree off the ceiling, replace ornaments with designer photographs and bath accessories, or create a theme with anything—including the bathroom sink!

This style of decorating is for all the unconventional freethinkers out there, those people who want a change from Santa and Frosty. No Dasher, no Dancer, nor Prancer, nor Vixen here. This is the land of zebras and leopards and the Society of Red Hats. The Eiffel Tower, the Hollywood sign, and a double-decker bus from London stand in for toy-making elves and Santa's flying sleigh. So, find the rebel in you and do something wild!

▶ **Ornamental scrubbie** In keeping with the fun, whimsical atmosphere of this spectacularly decorated bathroom, pink bath scrubbies were turned into flowery "ornaments."

◀ **Reflecting pool** Party guests will delight in this festive use of the bathtub. Lit candles of many different sizes and shapes fill and surround a common bathtub and transform it into a reflective pool of light.

▲ **Fantasy vanity** Candies and crystals give this ordinary bathroom countertop a chance to sparkle. Pink candy canes hang from pink, white, and black feather trees. Miniature tea lights give the room a rosy glow.

FASHION COLORS

Hot pink, black, passion purple, teal, yellow, and white are not color choices normally associated with the typical, everyday Christmas tree. If you are looking to decorate "outside the box" in a fun and funky way, try a tree in a nontraditional color. These alternative colors work well when used to set a mood or create a specific atmosphere. They look best when displayed in contemporary settings, making use of unusual locations.

Are you throwing a wild party? Are you interested in creating a conversation piece that your guests will talk about for years to come? Try placing your colorful creation in an unexpected place—like in a shower stall, in the middle of a pool, or hanging upside-down over your dining-room table to stand in as a holiday chandelier. If you have a white living room, try a black tree hung with black-and-white photographs to lend an air of sophistication and elegance.

▲ **Crystal copycats** This clear acrylic snowflake and glass-beaded wire heart replicate the look of fine crystal. They act as brilliant jewels on this black tree.

▶ **Smoke and sparkle** We chose this ornament to match the black-and-white photographs prominently displayed on the tree. Silver leaves add glitter.

◀ **Wet and wild shower** The bathroom-party theme from the previous page culminates in a hot-pink tree with glass "soap bubbles," accented with bath accessories and lit candles. Use outdoor lights; keep all cords away from water.

▲ **Photo gallery** This tree is a perfect example of how you can use one or more images to create your very own photographic exhibit for Christmas.

◀ **Lily in black-and-white** An elegant print by Edie Baskin-Bronson, acclaimed for her *Saturday Night Live* portrait photography, serves as a simple, stylish statement piece.

▶ **Travel treasures** Large, lit buildings are heavy statement pieces and require strong branches for support, so we used an artificial tree.

TRAVELER'S TREE

Your Christmas tree can be a perfect setting for all those collectibles and souvenirs gathered on your travels. Instead of placing your lit-house collection either under the tree or on a nearby table, make the buildings focal points on your tree. Here, pieces such as the Empire State Building and Radio City Music Hall were carefully wired into the tree. We added faux snow to provide separation between pieces, enabling you to see everything on display. The ornaments were collected from around the world. What better way to showcase an Egyptian pharaoh, the Hollywood sign, and a Turkish slipper than on your own personalized Christmas tree? We enhanced the nearby window with star lights, a Santa nutcracker, colorful finials, and a glass tree-shaped plate.

▲ **Egg art** A handcrafted egg created by a local tribe in the hills of Mexico provides a burst of color as well as fond memories.

▲ **Experience New York** A city taxicab and a famous landmark come together here. Try grouping related collectibles in your design.

TOPSY-TURVY

There are several different reasons you might choose to use an upside-down tree. Many retailers use an upside-down tree because it shows off decorations better, since they hang out of the tree and aren't obscured by branches. It also creates an unusual, eye-catching floor display. Collectors like this tree because it shows off their valued treasures to best advantage.

Another great reason to use this particular tree is that it takes up a minimum of floor space while providing the same amount of display area as a regular Christmas tree. Best of all, it looks cool and there is a lot more room for presents!

This tree needs to be attached to the ceiling in multiple locations with monofilament (fishing line) that is either tied around beams or tied to screws that have been drilled into ceiling joists. It also should be anchored properly at its base, using sandbags or something similarly heavy.

▲ **Tradition with a twist** This nontraditional tree is adorned with traditional ornaments and red-velvet ribbon accented with jingle bells, and it's grounded with a traditional felt tree skirt.

▲ **Holiday express** When using a collectible set that tells a story, it is important to hang them together in logical display order—like this molded-glass train set, which we hung in a straight line.

▶ **Up, up, and away!** This brightly colored hot-air balloon looks like it is floating through the air when suspended from the branches of our inverted Christmas tree.

◀ **Covered in glitter** The Chicago artist who created these two pieces sculpted each design out of clay. The sculptures were then made into master molds and filled with molten glass. After cooling, the glass ornaments were removed from the molds and glittered. The final results —a cute bear in a cowboy boot and a merry gingerbread man. ▼

STORYTELLING

Themed trees are another way of telling a story. You can design Christmas trees around books, favorite films, memorable experiences, or holidays. If you are a collector of hats, showcase them! Grandma's wedding dress makes a great romantic statement in a tree. Or, if you are a lover of animals, have fun with a design depicting endangered species or favorite breeds of cats or dogs—or design a tree dedicated to your own pet using photos and pet treats.

The size of your "story" will dictate the size of your tree. If you are planning on telling the story of the birth of civilization, you will need a very large tree! Joking aside, start thinking about your design by laying out the pieces you want to spotlight; then determine how big a tree you need to display your chosen decorations. Decide whether you would like to use a traditional green tree or something snazzier. Look for other pieces that will complement or add to your story. This can be done with color, ribbon, fabric, and other objects or ornaments. A decorative tree skirt makes a perfect ending for your story. The main goal is to have fun, be creative, and enjoy your collectibles.

▶ **The Red Hat Society**
There is an international society of ladies who get together, wear red hats and purple dresses, do wild and crazy things, and just flat-out enjoy themselves. The only catch is that you have to be of a certain age to join. This tree is fondly dedicated to all those wild women. It captures their carefree spirit, sense of fun, and red-hat style.

◀ **Haunted holiday**
Since people collect ornaments for various holidays, a great way to show them off is to create a small tabletop display dedicated to holiday themes. Then the decorations can be changed from holiday to holiday. Orange, purple, and green satin provide a colorful base for this spooky tribute to Halloween. The Victorian tree stand adds to the moodiness.

▲ **Wildlife treasures**
A hot-pink tree serves as the palette for these sophisticated, collectible animal heads in shades of black-and-white. Faux-leopard ribbon gives the tree added texture and dimension, while silver stars provide glitter. This tree was dramatic enough on its own, so we didn't use lights.

◀ **Bridal memories** A vintage wedding gown is this tree's statement piece. It is the perfect tree for a Christmas wedding, if the bride wants to include her mother's —or grandmother's —beautiful gown in the ceremony. The tree is hung with pearl garlands and gold and white ornaments, and finished with a regal embroidered-satin tree skirt.

DEBI'S CELEBRITY ORNAMENTS

Since moving to Hollywood, I've had numerous opportunities to collect celebrity autographs. I "stole" Bob's idea of having ornaments signed, but I tried to select ornaments that I felt suited each individual signer's personality. As you can see, this has made for quite an eclectic ornament collection.

1. Michael York / Mindy Sterling
2. Tracey Ullman 3. Jay Leno
4. Tai Babilonia 5. Majel Barrett
6. Jack Lemmon 7. Smokey Robinson 8. Whoopi Goldberg
9. Mickey Rooney 10. Julie Andrews / Blake Edwards 11. Wesley Snipes
12. Cindy Williams 13. Jon Cryer
14. Billy Crystal 15. Jack Paar
16. Steve Allen 17. RuPaul
18. Jillian Barberie 19. Peri Gilpin / Christian Vincent 20. Victor Alfieri / Peter Reckell / Kristian Alfonso / Joe Mascolo (Days of Our Lives)
21. Christopher Radko 22. Tom Leykis 23. Tim Conway / Harvey Korman / Carol Burnett (Carol Burnett Show) 24. Louie Anderson
25. Betty Garrett 26. Phyllis George
27. Jason Alexander 28. Bronson Pinchot 29. Yvonne Craig
30. Don Adams 31. Jerry Maren
32. Peter Tomarken 33. Michael Ansara 34. Dave Prowse
35. Stephen Collins 36. Walter Koenig 37. Jerry Springer
38. Connie Stevens 39. LeVar Burton
40. Dr. Joyce Brothers 41. Martin Mull 42. Vikki Carr 43. Michael Cimino 44. Johnny Brown
45. Tom Bergeron 46. Frank Gorshin 47. Valerie Perrine
48. Bruce Jenner 49. Richard Grieco 50. Jane Withers
51. Sam Rubin 52. Jackie Collins
53. Teri Garr 54. George Clooney
55. Tammy Faye 56. Ken Osmond
57. Lisa Loring / Ken Weatherwax (The Addams Family) 58. Bret Saberhagen 59. Markie Post
60. Joey Heatherton 61. Rita Rudner
62. Adam West 63. Rod Taylor
64. Al Michaels 65. Deidre Hall
66. Dorothy Lucey 67. Robin Williams 68. Bobcat Goldthwait
69. Marta Kristen / Angela Cartwright / June Lockhart / Bill Mumy / Bob May (Lost in Space)
70. Candy Clark 71. David Selby

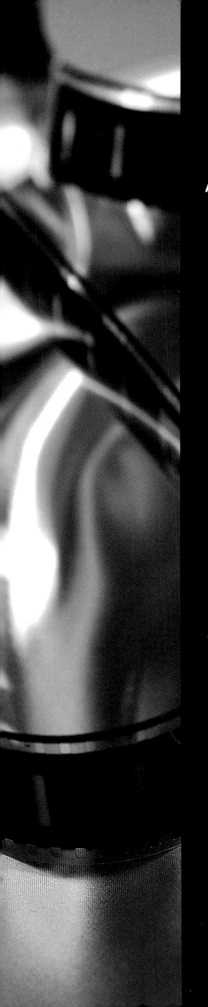

2

THE 12 DAMES OF CHRISTMAS

I've always loved the expression "What a dame," especially when it was uttered by some he-man type in those fabulous old movies I used to watch as a kid. I understood that the men never meant the word *dame* as an insult, but as a sign of respect. They recognized dames as strong women who were unwilling to be pushed into the background. I also loved that you always knew when a dame entered the room, and you also knew when she left.

But why dedicate an entire section to the great dames of film and stage in a book about Christmas? I could answer that "The 12 Dames of Christmas" makes for a great play on words (you know it does). I could give you a long-winded designer-type speech about concepts and creative expression (blah, blah, blah). But I won't. The simple truth is that these women should be talked about and remembered. Yes, even at Christmas.

Also, how often is a designer privileged enough to work with authentic costumes and vintage movie props? I had this rare and happy opportunity thanks to The Hollywood History Museum in the Historic Max Factor Building, the Alex Theatre, and History for Hire, all in Los Angeles.

This is just another way of looking at Christmas-tree design. While you probably wouldn't recreate any of the trees shown here, what you could do is feature your own private favorite celebrity on a tree, using pictures, CDs, album covers, or any other relevant (or irreverent) ephemera.

All of the following women were chosen for their larger-than-life personas, the sense of "WOW" that they bring to the world, and most of all, their ability to survive it all. My only regret is that there wasn't enough space to include more of the ladies. In my defense, I can only say that if you enjoy looking at the Dames as much as I enjoyed recreating them, then there will be books including even more of your favorites in the future. Remember, in Hollywood, if it's a hit, there's gotta be a sequel!

ELIZABETH TAYLOR

—— Cinema's Queen of the Nile ——

SHE HAS BEEN CALLED "the last movie star" and the most beautiful woman in the world. Women have envied her, and men have sought her favors even if it meant personal ruin. So what better choice to portray Egypt's legendary Queen of the Nile in the 1963 movie *Cleopatra* than Elizabeth Taylor?

The role of Cleopatra was an obvious one for the actress, who at that time was at her cinematic peak. Cleopatra was considered by the ancients to be a woman of great power and beauty, a woman who almost toppled ancient Rome. The irony was not lost on Hollywood when the film became a financial disaster and nearly toppled 20th Century Fox.

But unlike the ill-fated Egyptian queen, Elizabeth Taylor survived and went on to play her greatest role: that of human-rights activist.

My goal as a designer was to find the perfect setting that would honor each woman's grand legacy. Under the cobalt-blue ceiling of the historic Alex Theatre in Glendale, California, I found it.

Egyptian splendor The tree is a tribute to Hollywood's version of ancient Egypt: the grand epic *Cleopatra*. The glittering gold and cobalt-blue ornaments are informed by Egyptian imagery: pyramids, gods, pharaohs, and queens.

Beautiful rulers Queen Nefertiti, like Cleopatra, was a strong woman whose beauty was legendary, but she ruled as well as any man—with strength and cunning. This ornament was based on the famous bust on display at the Berlin Museum.

Floating down the Nile This royal Egyptian barge provides a different shape for the tree, as opposed to the standard, round Christmas ball. Unusual pieces like this support the tree theme in 3-D. The sail is painted with the Eye of Horus, a symbol for the Egyptian falcon-headed sun god.

JOAN CRAWFORD

— Hollywood's Cinderella —

NO ONE COULD DENY that Joan Crawford was a star of the first order. She was a strong-willed woman and a dedicated actress who crafted and guarded her public image as if it was her sole purpose for living. Throughout her career—which spanned over 50 years—Joan Crawford played many roles, but many considered her greatest role ever to be that of Joan Crawford, "star."

Since Joan loved being a star and knew the value of good publicity, I placed her tree in the glamorous Art Deco lobby of the Historic Max Factor building, located in the heart of Hollywood, California. It was here that makeup and hair stylist extraordinaire Max Factor helped transform the Texan chorus girl Lucille Fay LeSueur into Joan Crawford.

In fact, he performed such a startling transformation that forever after Joan was known as MGM's Cinderella. Women around the world followed her life, copied her style, and eagerly anticipated her next fashion move. Her face, vanity, and fashion sense helped to make her famous, but it was her artistry, technical proficiency, and ability to adapt to change that kept her a star and made her a legend.

◀ **From duckling to swan** The swan ornament irresistibly parallels the fabled story of an ugly duckling turned swan and the transformation of the unpolished Lucille Fay LeSueur into the elegant Joan Crawford.

▼ **Fairytale coach** What better symbol than this to represent Joan's new life as young Hollywood royalty? The sparkling white, pink, and gold coach adds a whimsical element to this Cinderella story.

◀ **Beauty shot** The tree was composed like one of Joan's glamorous Hollywood studio portraits of the '30s and '40s; it reposes slightly, draped in satin, with an upturned "face" illuminated by strong, dramatic light.

LANA TURNER
⸺ One Cool Beauty ⸺

MGM's sultry "Sweater Girl" Lana Turner frequently appeared in shadow in film noir pictures such as *The Postman Always Rings Twice*, and she often portrayed women with shady pasts.

I designed this tree with an emphasis on black-and-white because that's how I always pictured her. She was a creature I never associated with color.

The tree was shot in Max Factor's blue "For Blondes Only" room, where he did hair and makeup for Hollywood's blond leading ladies. Blue represents the flashing neon signs and cold shadows in the backwater bars that Lana's characters often inhabited. Blue also stands for her icy beauty.

Matching sets Lana's tree is as glamorous as she was. Everything is coordinated—from her dress, purse, and hatboxes to the ornaments and tree fabric. Lana Turner's bad girls always had killer style.

Compact style A tool in any femme fatale's arsenal, her compact kept Lana looking her best. It also allowed her to look over her shoulder!

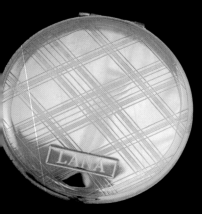

MARILYN MONROE

— Sweet Confection —

MARILYN MONROE is perhaps the most famous woman of the 20th century. Because of the myths surrounding her, I could never get a good sense of who she was. In fact, nobody ever seemed to get to know the real Marilyn.

She was always just out of reach to me, and in order to create this tree I knew I needed an inspiration, some kind of connection to her. That connection came to me at a county fair. I watched an older gentleman take ordinary sugar and red food dye and pour it into a large machine. The machine began to spin these common elements into something light, beautiful, and tastier than it was before. Then I thought, "This is what the Hollywood machine did to Norma Jean Baker. It made her into a cotton-candy confection called Marilyn Monroe."

◄ **Light as air** Celebrity photographer Milton H. Greene forever immortalized Marilyn Monroe in his 1955 photos of her wrapped in white fur. Here, Marilyn's glamorous fur wraps not only around her, but around the entire tree, in a room as airy as cotton candy.

▲ **Pretty in pink** In keeping with the theme of Marilyn's tree, this egg-shaped ornament appears to be delicately sprinkled with pink-tinted sugar crystals.

LUCILLE BALL

For Redheads Only

WHEN I THINK OF LUCILLE BALL, I see the movie star who was always glimmering just below her greatest creation, Lucy Ricardo. On those rare moments when the *I Love Lucy* scripts allowed her out of her 1950s housedresses, Lucille the movie star shone through. Many people confused Lucy Ricardo with Lucille Ball the actress. But long before *I Love Lucy,* there was a film career that introduced us to young Lucille's comedic ability and showed us that she was much more than just a beautiful redhead.

In fact, Lucille was born a brunette, arrived in Hollywood a blonde, and was transformed by Max Factor into the zany redhead we all know and love.

I placed Lucille's tree in Max Factor's "For Redheads Only" room, which was designed in complementary shades of green

with her specifically in mind. I chose to present her as Lucille the movie star at her dressing table, not Lucy the comedienne, to remind the world that Lucille had a film career both before and after *I Love Lucy.*

▶ **Green inspiration** This show-stopper—draped in green chiffon and sequined fabric—feels right at home within the light-green walls here in the "For Redheads Only" room, which Max Factor had specially designed for Lucille Ball to complement her fiery red hair.

▲ **Lucy's colors** The ginger and green ornaments shown here reinforce the tree themes: movie glamour and color. The different shapes hint at a showgirl's sexy curves.

▶ **Reflective beauty** A tube of lipstick and a hand mirror are two common elements in a star's makeup case, and Lucy was known for her bright red lipstick. A featured ornament gets its close-up.

JUDY GARLAND
—— The Girl from Oz ——

SO MUCH HAS BEEN WRITTEN about Judy Garland that she has become a part of our national consciousness. Her face looks out at us from CDs, birthday cards, book covers, calendars—and even Christmas ornaments—as well as from her many films and television appearances.

Judy Garland doesn't really need another *Wizard of Oz* tribute to be remembered. Yet as I designed her tree, I realized that this was unavoidable. No matter what Judy did throughout her career, she was always "returned to Oz" by her public. So I made ruby red the predominant color and focused on the Ruby Slippers, Dorothy's primary mode of transportation through the land of Oz.

I believe that Judy always felt trapped by the image of Dorothy, the tragic little girl looking for happiness over the rainbow. In truth, the people who were close to Judy knew her to be a brilliant performer with a wicked sense of humor who was passionate about life and full of love for her family. I chose to depict the grown-up Judy on a concert stage, mike in hand, ready to sing—with that yellow brick road never too far away.

◀ **The Ruby Slippers** In this case, although it's certainly not the largest piece here, this ornament is the main statement piece. The entire tree is designed around them, from the star on top to the red-sequined tree skirt.

▼ **The Rainbow** The multicolored ball introduces another element from *The Wizard of Oz*, the fabled rainbow that Dorothy sang about. How ironic that the song for which she is best remembered was initially cut from the movie!

◀ **Follow the Yellow Brick Road** Yellow satin represents the Yellow Brick Road, and on that road are an assortment of press photos, newspaper clippings, memorabilia, and *Wizard of Oz* ornaments—all leading Judy back to her beginning: a little girl from a theatrical family, literally born in a trunk.

BETTE DAVIS & KATHARINE HEPBURN

Hollywood Royalty

"TWO QUEENS, ONE THRONE." This could have been the head-line on any given day during the Golden Age of Hollywood. Epic battles were waged between actresses who sought to become "Queen of the Lot," and these wars were wickedly reported by the press.

Bette Davis and Katharine Hepburn each held this title during their careers, but they were queens in two separate kingdoms: Bette at Warner Brothers and Kate at MGM. This presented me with an intriguing idea. I did some research and, according to most historical references, Elizabeth Tudor, Queen of England, and her archrival for the throne, Mary Stuart, Queen of Scotland—although cousins—never met.

What if I brought these two Hollywood queens together to portray the two equally famous historical queens? Bette played Elizabeth twice in her career, and Kate played Mary, but never in the same picture. In fact, Bette and Kate never worked together onstage or onscreen. Since anything is possible in Hollywood, we can finally say that we have brought Bette and Kate together at last in the same "picture."

▼ **Mary's adornments** To recreate Mary's tightly curled hairstyle, textured copper-net ribbon was cut into strips, rolled into curls, and glued to the mannequin's head. A fabric headdress and pearl crown complete the illusion.

▲ **Elizabeth's ornamentals** Prominently featured are fabric ornaments—pearled and bejeweled—to mimic the famous red wigs Elizabeth wore throughout her reign.

◀ **Rivals** The two queens face off on a stairway to signify Mary Stuart's quest to ascend to the throne, which was firmly occupied by Elizabeth Tudor (at the top).

RITA HAYWORTH
—— Put the Blame on Mame ——

HE DEFINING MOMENT I chose for the Rita Hayworth tree was tually near the end of the carnival scene in the 1946 film *lda*. Surrounded by an audience of partygoers, Rita's aracter Gilda, having run out of options for escape, chose fiance as her revenge. Slinking across the screen in a black :in gown, she arrogantly tossed back her auburn hair and eled off her gloves to the musical strains of "Put the Blame Mame," and in that moment, Rita Hayworth went from ung Hollywood starlet to superstar.

Although the film is in black-and-white, while watching it, ould nevertheless imagine all of the colors that surrounded lda, from the blues and purples of the nightclub to the eens and yellows of the decorations. So I surrounded r here in jewel-toned ornamentation.

By keeping the area around the tree in shadow, I created intimate setting, which represented the darkened supper ub in which Gilda performed. As an interesting side note, e two oversized faces bathed in hot pink and lilac light, which pear to float behind the tree, are rumored to have appeared the outdoor carnival scene in the film. I just liked them cause they added drama.

▶ **Party girl** The ultimate party girl, Rita Hayworth as Gilda rises from the center of the tree, which represents the swirl of the carnival surrounding her as she performs. Black satin cuts through the tree and pools on the floor to create a slinky, ruffled tree skirt. Theatrical lighting transforms the satin into vivid shades of red, purple, and blue.

◀ **Musical accompaniment** When Gilda sings "Put the Blame on Mame" for the first time, she is playing the guitar. The way music enhances a movie, the guitar featured here serves to embellish the tree design.

▶ **Mexican hat dance** Sequined felt sombreros add party spirit to the tree. Reputedly, the margarita cocktail was amed for Rita when she danced under her real name—Margarita—in a Tijuana club.

MAE WEST
— When She Was Bad She Was Better —

DID YOU EVER WONDER what it would be like to go through Mae West's attic? Think about the treasures that you would find there—from what I hear, she never threw anything away!

I got such a chance when the Hollywood History Museum was loaned a large portion of her private collection for a special exhibit. What fun I had . . . so much to play with, so many design choices.

For Mae's tree, I chose to re-create the famous black-and-white dress (seen in the rear of the photograph) that she wore in her final movie, the 1977 film *Sextette*—sequined, furred, and feathered. I added purple and red ornaments to complement several other Mae gowns in the exhibit, which surround the decorated tree. These gowns were featured in her films and stage shows, and they really showed off not only her figure but also her zest for life and her colorful persona.

Mae was very fond of jewelry—she loved to sparkle—so I included many pieces from her own collection and added some diamond-shaped ornaments as well. It was eerie—after the feathered-headdress treetop was added, the tree actually felt and looked like Mae to me. I could almost hear her imploring me to come up sometime and see her.

▶ **Fabric, feathers, and fur** These three elements are the statement pieces in Mae's tree. Combined, they create a wardrobe to dress her from. Sparkling, glittery ornaments stand in for jewelry and become accessories.

▲ **This girl's best friend** Whether wearing diamonds or rhinestones, Mae was a walking jewelry store. These rhinestone pieces were some of her favorites.

▶ **Diamond Lil** Her hard-as-diamonds exterior hid her heart of gold from the movie-going public. This oversized "diamond" is a tribute to one of her most famous characters.

GLORIA SWANSON
—— I'm the Greatest Star ——

WHEN GLORIA SWANSON'S character, Norma Desmond, declared "We didn't need dialogue, we had faces then!" in the 1950 film classic *Sunset Boulevard*, she spoke for all the forgotten souls left behind in the wake created by the onset of talking pictures. However, Gloria was not one of them. Her exotic beauty captivated movie audiences for six decades, and eventually she became the sole survivor of an era the world will never see again.

I wanted her tree to reflect a time of excess, when gold, leopard skins, and peacock feathers decorated both fashion and furniture; when silent screen stars drank free-flowing champagne under enormous crystal chandeliers while orchestras played. In other words, I wanted this tree to have a feeling of grand decadence that would represent both Gloria and Norma.

As the dominant color, black provides the foundation for a path into the black-and-white world of Norma Desmond, where beautiful people walked along Sunset Boulevard watched by the audience—to whom Norma Desmond dedicated her final close-up: "those wonderful people out there in the dark."

Wardrobe This flapper-style dress in a leopard print, attached to its ornament hanger and nestled in gold satin, stands for the stylish young Hollywood starlet that Norma Desmond once was.

Costars Custom-made fabric-covered balls provide both color and texture. Black is the main through-line, or unifying, color; the leopard print adds dimension and repeats the main pattern. Pearls add luxury.

Ready for my close-up This tree's over-the-top elegance makes it the star of the show. The movie camera and other props play supporting roles without diverting the eye from the main focus.

CHER

Just Plain Goddess

WHAT MUST IT BE LIKE TO BE CHER? I must confess that Cher is an enigma to me. For as long as I've lived, there has always been Cher. She has conquered the fields of television, music, and film. My love affair with her began when I first saw her on *The Sonny and Cher Show* all those years ago.

I was with her through the Disco Era (as a fan) and was fortunate enough to meet her when I was a lowly intern for *Saturday Night Live* at NBC Studios in New York City when she was hosting the show. My love for her deepened when she "allowed" me to fetch her a bottle of water. Ahhh, the memories!

When designing her tree, I approached it through the eyes of a lifelong fan, someone willing and in fact eager to stand off to the side, lucky enough to be backstage at one of her concerts, watching the Goddess perform.

Cher's tree is topped with beads and a tangle of brunette curls. I covered her tree in sequined fabric, feathers, satin, baubles, and large colorful lights, attempting to emulate the outrageous costumes she's worn throughout her career. I hope I have done her justice.

▼ **Designer medallion** Cher is known for wearing expensive designer couture. This piece has a beautiful, elegant, upscale design. The color complements the tree and adds an element of sophistication.

▲ **Feathered ball** Cher has worn many shockingly wild feathered headdresses (by designer Bob Mackie). This inspired me to add feathery fun and use these kicky plumed balls. What better way to say "Cher"?

◀ **Stage show** Center stage at the Alex Theatre, the tree faces the audience. Seen here is the back of the "costume," outrageous as it is. Yet it never overpowers Cher herself.

BOB'S CELEBRITY ORNAMENTS

My collection of signed ornaments started as a fluke. I was working for Kathy Hilton at her store in West Hollywood. One day Audrey Meadows walked in, and since I was a big fan, I asked for an autograph. Typically, I had nothing for her to sign, so she graciously suggested an ornament—and the rest is history!

1. Patrick Duffy 2. Ed Begly, Jr.
3. Gloria Allred 4. Mariska
Hargitay 5. Maureen McCormick
6. John Tesh / Connie Sellecca
7. Lorna Luft 8. Leslie Nielsen
9. JM J. Bullock 10. Stefanie
Powers 11. Suzanne Pleshette
12. Zubin Mehta 13. Cheryl Tiegs
14. Jaclyn Smith 15. Erik Estrada
16. Jennifer Tilly 17. Mary Hart
18. Jo Anne Worley 19. Richard
Simmons 20. Donny Osmond
21. Constance Towers
22. Ashford & Simpson
23. Joanna Kern 24. Marion
Ross 25. Joan Van Ark
26. Delta Burke 27. Carol
Channing 28. Daryl Hannah
29. Audrey Meadows 30. Kate
Jackson 31. David Cassidy
32. Bernadette Peters 33. Rosie
O'Donnell 34. Helen Reddy
35. Mary Frann 36. Nancy
Reagan 37. Dolores Hope
38. Bob Hope 39. Shirley
MacLaine 40. Priscilla Presley
41. Ann Miller 42. Angela
Lansbury 43. Jack Lemmon
44. Lynn Redgrave 45. Joan
Collins 46. Ed Asner 47. Jane
Seymour 48. Vicki Lawrence
49. Robert Stack 50. Cyd
Charisse 51. Shelley Winters
52. Lauren Bacall 53. Candice
Bergen 54. Estelle Getty
55. Sally Kellerman 56. Valerie
Harper 57. Nell Carter
58. Leslie Uggams 59. Brenda
Russell 60. Garry Marshall
61. Leeza Gibbons 62. Dick Clark
63. Phyllis Diller

3

TREE STYLING & TRIMMINGS

*P*utting a tree together is like making a movie. The tree must be "scripted" as well as cast. In other words, choose a theme, then select your ornamental "actors." Decorations are like stars, costars and extras. You, as the designer, get to direct your own movie. The following pages will guide you on where to start, what is available, and how to end up with the perfectly produced feature.

TREE LOCATION

Finding the right spot to set up your Christmas tree seems like an easy thing to do. Most of us simply choose a spot in the living room and put the tree there. But the place you would like the tree to go is not always the best place for your tree.

SITING YOUR TREE

First, decide what your tree is going to be used for: Family and package opening on Christmas Day? Will you even be home on Christmas?

▲ **Family gatherings** This long hall leads to a tree in the drawing room, where family can gather to celebrate.

Will the tree be a centerpiece for parties? Do you want to make it a canvas to show off your children's art or collectibles? Answering these questions will help you decide on the best location.

▼ **Entrance maker** This tree, cradled in the front-hall stairwell, is meant to be a stunning showpiece to inspire guests as they enter the home.

Your tree may look beautiful in the front hall, but will it be comfortable to sit around it on a cold floor on Christmas morning? Or should you consider placing it in a room where your friends and family will be cozier?

Consider decorating more than one tree. One can be for show: to get your guests into the holiday spirit the minute they walk in the door. The other can be warm and inviting, and put in a place where you can spend quality time with your guests.

POWER, HEAT & LIGHT

There should be an electrical outlet in the location that you're considering. You can use extension cords, but the farther lights are from the outlet, the more likely they are to burn out. Also, shorter cords eliminate the possibility of someone tripping.

Also consider environmental factors. Live trees should be kept away from "hot spots." If you place a live tree near a working fireplace, in direct sunlight, or near heating vents, the tree will dry out quickly and could become a fire hazard. While sunlight may not adversely affect your artificial tree, it can fade all of your decorations: fabric, ribbon, ornaments, dolls, and tree skirts can all be irreparably damaged.

SPACE

Next, how much space can you allow for your tree? Measure a tree's width and height before buying it. It helps to move furniture around before dragging

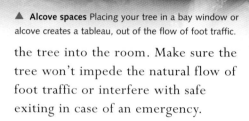

▲ **Alcove spaces** Placing your tree in a bay window or alcove creates a tableau, out of the flow of foot traffic.

the tree into the room. Make sure the tree won't impede the natural flow of foot traffic or interfere with safe exiting in case of an emergency.

PET SAFETY

Pet-proofing is not foolproof. However, there are a few things you can do to protect both your tree and your pet. Be sure to anchor your tree so that if it gets bumped (or your cat climbs up the branches), it won't come crashing down. And to limit access to the tree, either place it on a table if possible or build a barrier of boxes or even decorative fencing around it.

▲ **Elevated beauty** If you own pets, it may be safer to place a small tree on a table or other piece of furniture.

ARTIFICIAL VS LIVE TREES

Christmas trees represent a gathering place for family and friends, an emotional connection to the past, and an expression of creativity. Therefore, tree selection can be very personal, but there are practical factors to consider before you decide, such as the ones in the box below.

FACTORS	ARTIFICIAL TREES	LIVE TREES
PRICE	Cost is higher the first year—but since artificial trees are reusable, after the initial investment, you'll have a tree you can use for many years.	Prices vary depending on local availability, height, and style of tree. Generally, live trees are less expensive than artificial ones.
DISPLAY SPACE	They come in a wide variety of shapes and sizes—from slim-line to full-figured and from tabletop to mall-sized monsters—and are more versatile spacewise.	Many live trees are quite bushy. If space is limited, consider placing a shorter tree on a stable tree-riser, like a coffee table, side table, large wooden crate, or toy chest.
STORAGE SPACE	Storage is an issue if you buy an artificial tree. Ideally, the tree should be stored vertically, in its original package. Old sheets and tree-storage bags also work. Make sure you have clearance to get your tree to the storage space, which must be dry (and should be cool). Artificial trees may mildew in damp environments.	If you don't have room to store a tree, live is the way to go. Use it and lose it. Or, for the environmentally concerned, buy a potted tree and plant it outside if weather conditions permit.
STYLES	Artificial trees are symmetrical, and they can be shaped several ways to give different looks with just one tree. They come in a wide range of colors, including realistic-looking greens, retro silvers, and alternative pink, and "umbrella" hinges make assembly a snap. Sizes, shapes, and branch materials vary, so look around before making a purchase.	Pines, firs, and spruces are the most common trees used for decorating. Live trees are not perfect or symmetrical, so expect to search through unevenly spaced and missing branches, bent trunks, and imperfect tops. Flocking with artificial snow is available in many areas.
LIGHTS & DECORATIONS	Artificial trees need more lights to properly show off your decorations because of the density of branches. You can permanently light the tree, but it will take longer and you'll need more lights than for a live tree. However, many trees now come prelit. Set it up, plug it in, and decorate!	Live trees need fewer lights because of the shape and more spacious positioning of their branches. They are quicker to light and easy to unlight. They also need fewer decorations since they are bushier.
MAINTENANCE & FIRE SAFETY	Make sure to buy a flame-retardant tree: you can put it up whenever you want and wherever you want (as long as it's near an electrical outlet). Artificial trees will never dry out and become fire hazards, so you can put them up early and keep them up as late as you want. Valentine's Day and Easter trees, anyone?	The tree base should be freshly cut, so that your tree can "drink" water properly. Tree stands usually hold at least a gallon of water. Keep the tree watered throughout the holidays, and refill as needed. To keep your tree from drying out and becoming a fire hazard, keep it away from heat sources like fireplaces, heating vents, and direct sunlight, and keep the temperature down.
ACCIDENTS	Children and pets are attracted to both artificial and live trees. Minimize risks by elevating your tree, and/or building a barrier with packages, miniature villages, or fencing. Trees can be anchored to the wall with fishing line to prevent accidents.	Same as artificial trees, see left.
ALLERGIES	Dust accumulation over the years can cause allergic reactions. Dust your tree with a feather duster before storing, or use artificial-tree cleaning products to help prevent allergies.	Live trees can cause or exacerbate allergies, so if you or a family member suffers from hay fever, asthma, or any other respiratory ailment, an artificial tree is the better option.
INSECTS	Insects—and especially spiders—like to hide in stored artificial trees. Proper airtight storage and an annual dusting can prevent spider infestation.	Insects may be hiding in your tree. Shake the tree well before bringing it into your home.

ARTIFICIAL TREE SELECTION

In the artificial tree, the beauty of nature has been recreated with a few "plusses." The branches are evenly spaced, giving you a tree that can be decorated symmetrically. Trunks come unbent, and treetops are perfectly vertical so whatever you place on top stands straight. Artificial trees come in one or several pieces (depending on size); lit or unlit; in traditional or alternative shapes; and in a multitude of colors, widths, and heights. They are even available fully decorated.

▲ Spiky mountain pine   ▲ Rounded opalescent fir

▲ Light-colored blue spruce

▲ Frosted, with pinecones and berries

When selecting your tree, consider the size of your decorations. Here, the wide spaces between branches are excellent for highlighting your collectibles.

▶ **Full, dense branches** Most basic-shaped artificial trees have denser branches than live trees.

▲ **Needle types** A wide range of shapes, textures, lengths, and colors is available to the artificial-tree lover: long, short, round, blunt, soft, stiff, with pinecones and berries, frosted, and in every color under the sun.

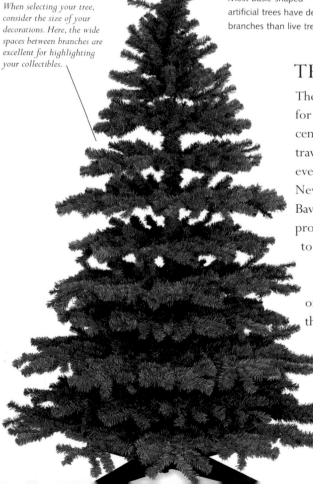

TRADITIONAL TREES

The custom of decorating fir trees for Christmas dates back to 16th-century Germany. The tradition traveled throughout Europe and eventually became popular in the New World. By the mid-1800s, Bavarian fir forests had dwindled, prompting German entrepreneurs to produce the first artificial Christmas trees.

The first faux trees were crafted of metal wires and covered with the decorative feathers of large birds like geese, ostriches, swans, and turkeys, usually dyed green. Feather trees

remained in vogue for many years, but they were limited in their ability to hold large or heavy decorations.

In the 1930s, the Addis Brush Company in the United States crafted the first artificial tree out of the same animal bristles they used to make toilet brushes (but dyed green), and "bottlebrush" trees hit the market. These trees were larger and sturdier than feather trees, and they could support heavier ornaments. Today, you can find artificial trees that are incredible reproductions of live trees, in a variety of styles almost as limitless as in nature.

◀ **Tiered construction** This novelty tree comes with widely separated branches that provide you with layers or tiers. It is a great showcase tree for train tracks, lit villages, or other collectibles.

TREE WIDTH & HEIGHT

If you're having space issues, there are a number of ways in which to compensate. One way to create the illusion of a much larger tree—and save money—is to place a small or medium-sized tree on a low, sturdy table. Elevating the tree also leaves more room for wrapped presents, train sets, Christmas villages, and nativity scenes. Another possibility is to try a trio-grouping with narrow slim-line or pencil trees bunched closely together: either use three different-sized trees, or use three of the same size, but placed at different height levels to create a natural, staggered look.

HEIGHT COUNTS

The taller an artificial tree is, the more expensive it is, so here are two money-saving tips for added height: tree stands may add an inch or two; and a tall treetop decoration can extend a tree's height by a foot or more.

◄ Thick, bushy branches
This medium-sized tree is accented with opalescent needles, giving it a shimmery quality.

▲ Pencil trees With their narrow construction and light, wispy, downswept branches, these trees provide petite splashes of greenery and need minimal decoration.

TIME & SPACE SAVERS

For people with extremely limited time and/or tight space, enterprising inventors have created roll-up and coiling trees—usually predecorated—that can literally be installed in seconds. Wall half-trees are available and especially helpful in dorm rooms, small apartments, and offices. And you can even buy a tree lit with both clear and several colors of lights. Plug in this gimmicky tree and choose one of several light colors in one of several patterns. You can change the light colors of your tree as easily as unplugging one stack of plugs and plugging in another. Then, with a remote control, change the light pattern and colors as often as you like.

◄ Roll it away This clever prelit, predecorated wall half-tree rolls up into about one cubic foot. It's perfect for small rooms and offices.

▶ Decorated spiral Another entry in the "instant decoration" category is this spiraling tree. The center support pole is removable. After the season, the tree flattens into a box the size of a jumbo pizza.

▶ Five-color light changer This tree offers the versatility of lights in red, green, blue, gold, and clear, or any combination of lights you might like—as well as several pattern options.

Clear miniature light bulb

Multicolored miniature light bulb

C-7 light cover

NONTRADITIONAL TREES

The silver and white trees popular in the 1950s and '60s have had several comebacks over the years. Now, these "retro" trees are made with newer, safer materials, and you can make quite a fashion statement by choosing from a wide range of colors, including black, gold, red, pastels—even custom-blends of several colors. The trees come in sizes ranging from miniature tabletop to full-sized. If you choose to light your medium-to-large fashion-color tree, buy white cord light sets for lighter-colored trees, and green for darker tones; gold cords, for gold trees, are available as well. For miniature trees featured as lit-tabletop decorations, use battery-run lights.

If you're looking for something nontraditional, consider trees made of poinsettias, berries, or metal wire, or even alternative trees such as light-rope palm trees or upside-down trees. Newer fiber-optic trees don't provide much light, but they look quite dramatic in a dark room. Every year, innovative trees appear on the market with some new twist on lighting or music—like a tree attached to a box that makes your lights "dance" to music. So keep your options open—there are trees out there for everyone.

▲ **Fashion colors** These colorful trees in pink, silver, black, white, and gold are a small sampling of the array of colors available for trees in today's marketplace.

◀ **Color wheel** The revolving, tinted color wheel—a hold-out from the 1960s—is meant to be shined on a silver tree to create changing color effects.

▲ **Fiber-optic flair** To avoid blocking the tips of fiber-optic light, don't use large bows or wide ribbon. The tree center is unlit, so keep ornaments near branch tips.

▲ **Fiber-optic poinsettia** For indoor use only, this novelty tree makes a good decoration for a hall entryway. No ornaments or lights are needed, so just plug it in and fluff it.

▲ **Decorative wire** This display piece can hold several of your favorite ornaments, and it makes a good unlit tabletop decoration.

▲ **Lit palms** Looking for the most unusual display piece for the holidays? These prelit tropical trees fit the bill.

LIVE TREE SELECTION

There are many types of live trees available to use for Christmas. Although live trees are imperfect and often have bent trunks, missing branches, or asymmetrical tops, none of this matters to the live-tree purist. Problems can be hidden with creative decorating, like strategic placement of statement pieces or bows. Sometimes a lopsided tree can be doctored: if branches are missing, you can bore holes into the trunk and replace them. (This has even been done on New York's Rockefeller Center tree.)

TREE CHOICES

Live-tree choice will be influenced by availability in your area. The chart below provides some insight into the pros and cons of each tree type. Knowledge of needle retention is especially key. Trees that drop needles quickly should be bought just two weeks before Christmas to stay fresh indoors. Some trees, like the blue spruce, are so beautiful and ornamental that they are becoming popular as potted "living" Christmas trees that can be planted outside after the holiday season. Prices for live trees depend on the number of years it takes a tree to mature, growing conditions, and demand for each particular tree. However, most people still choose a tree simply based on its appearance.

TREE	COLORADO BLUE SPRUCE	NORWAY SPRUCE	NOBLE FIR	DOUGLAS FIR	SCOTCH PINE	EASTERN WHITE PINE	AUSTRIAN PINE
NEEDLE COLOR	Bluish gray-green	Medium green	Gray-green to bright blue-gray	Dark green	Bright to blue to dark green	Blue-green to silver-green	Dark green
NEEDLE TYPE	Short, stiff	Short (on longer branches), soft	Short and twisted upward, soft	Very short, soft	Short to long depending on cultivar, stiff	Long, soft	Very long, stiff but flexible
AREA	Western to northwestern US	Northeastern US, southeastern Canada, Europe	Pacific west coast; Danish noble firs available in Europe	Western Canada to California; exported to Hawaii, Guam & Asian markets	Northeastern, central & Pacific US; Canada, Europe & Asia	Most of continental US, excluding Gulf & West Coasts	Northeastern, central US; southern Canada, south & central Europe
NEEDLE RETENTION	2 to 3 weeks	1 to 2 weeks	6 weeks to 3 months	6 weeks to 3 months	4 to 6 weeks	4 to 5 weeks	4 to 5 weeks

TREE SETUP

Before setting up your tree, protect yourself—wear long sleeves and gloves to prevent cuts, and use something soft to kneel on (especially for artificial-tree setup, which takes a bit of time) to save you from aches and pains later. Both artificial and live trees shed needles, so after setup, vacuum or sweep before decorating to prevent the static-prone needles from adhering to everything in sight.

POTTED LIVE TREES

When purchasing a live, potted tree for Christmas, ask the nursery or tree lot how to care for the tree both during and after the holidays. Each species requires unique care. If you live in a cold climate, you may not be able to replant it outdoors until spring thaw. Be prepared to care for your potted tree indoors until then.

TREE STANDS

Tree stands weren't needed for the very first Christmas trees in Germany, during the Middle Ages, because people cut off the treetops and nailed the trees to the ceiling upside-down. When trees were finally set upright, a simple "X" of two boards was nailed to the tree bottom to serve as a stand. Next, trees were potted in baskets, pots, or urns and steadied with dirt and rocks. The first commercial stands appeared in the late 1800s with the advent of larger trees. Cast iron was popular for its weight and for how well it supported trees. Later designs, like the three-legged tripod, allowed for lightweight plastic construction.

ARTIFICIAL TREE STANDS

▲ Metal cross "X" stand

LIVE TREE STANDS

▲ Decorative metal stand

▲ Round plastic with on/off switch

▲ Round tiered plastic

Artificial tree setup

After finding the perfect spot for your artificial tree, make sure to protect your floor. Whether you have wood, tile, or another type of floor, and especially if you have carpeting, prevent damage by following a few easy steps. Move furniture out of the way, if necessary, before bringing your tree in. Place a piece of cardboard on the floor where the tree stand will go, to help you move the tree before and after decorating. It makes vacuuming, sweeping, or dusting easier because you can pull the tree around by the cardboard. Before assembly, lay out the pieces of your tree. The number of pieces will vary, depending on the tree size and style. Most new trees have umbrella- or hinge-assembly and come in three pieces. Follow the manufacturer's instructions provided.

BRANCHES

Bungeeing the branches while assembling your tree, and letting them down row by row, makes shaping quick and safe by preventing scratches.

PRELIT TREES

If your artificial tree is prelit, continue on to steps 4–6 on the next page to finish setting up your tree. If you'll be attaching lighting to your artificial tree, you should light each branch immediately after you shape it— continue from here on to page 140–41, and follow the directions for Lighting an Artificial Tree.

1 Assemble the tree stand according to directions and set on the center of the cardboard. Place the bottom of the tree into the stand. Check to make sure the stand doesn't wobble; adjust if needed.

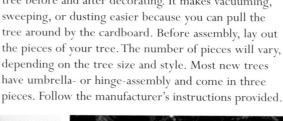

2 Wrap up all branches with bungee cords, except for the bottom row. Keep in mind that you don't have to shape the tree perfectly—you want it to look as natural as possible.

3 Starting at the trunk, grab the first two "greens" and pull them in opposing directions at an angle. Move out to the next two; angle perpendicularly to the first set. Continue along the branch, alternating angles. Pull the end green out and angle it slightly up.

LIVE TREE SETUP

It is as important to protect your floor when installing a live tree as when installing an artificial one—maybe even more so. First, move furniture and place cardboard down on the floor where the tree will go. Take the extra step of placing plastic sheeting or a tree bag on top of the cardboard to prevent water damage to your floor.

If you buy your tree at a lot, you can ask the salesperson to secure a wood stand to the base of the tree. Or, if your tree does not come with an attached

DROOPY BRANCH TIP

To raise up low-hanging branches on your live tree, and to make more room for trains, villages, or presents, try attaching a piece of floral wire to the middle of the low-hanging branch. Pull the branch just a little higher than you want it, and then attach the other end of the wire to a higher branch.

stand, then assemble your own tree stand first and place it at the center of the plastic-covered cardboard.

Shake your tree to get rid of loose needles and insects, and bring it inside. Water the tree immediately to extend its life. Make adjustments if your tree is not standing perfectly straight.

Since live tree branches will droop within a day or two of setup and can cover gifts or other under-tree items, you may want to prune back any that are too low, or tie them up with floral wire (see *Droopy Branch Tip*, left). It also helps to cut away a branch or two near the base to allow room to water your tree.

PET SAFETY

Do not permit your pets to dig in the potting soil in your Christmas tree stand; the soil and water may contain toxins that will irritate their digestive systems.

▲ Monofilament or fishing line
▲ Eye hooks

Anchor your tree so that it cannot be pulled over by a child or pet. Fishing line and eye hooks are a great way to insure safety for all. If your tree is near curtain rods or sturdy poles or pillars, you can attach fishing line to one, then run it to the top third of your tree and back to another attachment point. If these aren't available, place an eye hook or a nail in the wall. Attach a piece of fishing line to the eye hook or nail, then run the line to the top third of the tree and then to another eye hook or nail at a 90-degree angle from the first one.

Shape the treetop before putting it in place to give it a more natural look.

Pull outer branches out and up if they got bent during setup.

4 Move on to the next branch, and continue around the whole row until complete. Remove the bungee cord and let down the next row above. Continue shaping until you finish this part of the tree. Insert the next tree part and repeat from step 3.

5 The treetop requires slightly different shaping. Before placing it on the tree, grab each green, starting at the trunk, and pull it up and out. Then put your treetop in place and blend the branches between the middle tree section and the treetop.

6 The finished tree. Remember: the more time you spend fluffing the branches, the easier the tree will be to light and decorate, and the better it will look.

LIGHTING

Until the late 19th century, Christmas trees were lit with candles. Three years after Thomas Edison invented the electric light bulb in 1879, an associate of his, Edward Johnson, put the first electric lights on a Christmas tree—paving the way for the evolution of Christmas lights into the spectacular array of styles now available on the market.

LIGHTING AN ARTIFICIAL TREE

The tree lighting shown here will help you turn an unlit tree into a permanently lit tree that doesn't have to be relit every year. Although you can buy a prelit tree, you may choose to light your own because you already own a nice artificial tree, or because you'd like to custom design the lights. Make sure you have enough bulbs on hand to light the tree and to allow for replacement bulbs and strings in the future. Do not mix bulbs. Voltages and bulb housings may vary among manufacturers.

While sets of 100 bulbs are okay for live trees, use sets of 50 for permanently lighting an artificial tree. 100s are really two sets of 50 spliced together, and frequent handling of the cords may cause half the set to burn out. Look for lights with generous spacing between bulbs to give your lighting a cleaner look with less cord-crossover.

▶ Do not permanently wire C-7 or C-9 bulbs to an artificial tree; they are fragile and don't store well. Remove them at the end of the season.

Lighting method

Artificial-tree lighting varies from live-tree lighting. You must light each section of the tree separately if you want to store the tree in pieces. The artificial tree will be lit row by row, starting at the bottom. Before lighting, assemble and bungee your tree as shown in steps 1–3 in Artificial Tree Setup on page 138. Do not light it in vertical thirds, as demonstrated on the live tree, on page 142.

CORD COLORS

White cord lights were used here for demonstration purposes only to make it easier for you to follow the steps provided. Use green cords for green and any other dark-colored trees, white cords for white and pastel trees, and gold cords for gold trees.

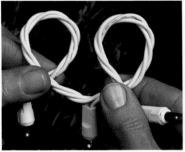

1 Plug in your lights. Make two loops with the cord spaced between the lights closest to the plug end.

2 Insert one loop into the other and pull that loop through tightly to make a noose.

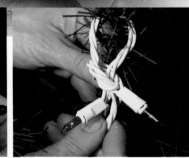

3 Start near the tree trunk on the bottom row. Slip the open loop over an inner green, slide it down, and pull tight.

6 Wrap lights around the next green near its tip, then wrap back to the branch. For moderate lighting, wrap every third green; for showcase lighting, wrap every green (see top of page 141).

7 Continue working back to the trunk. As you go, cross the cord over and around the branch occasionally to secure it. When you near the trunk, wrap the cord around the second-to-last green.

8 Move on to the next branch and keep adding lights. When you finish one row, move on to the next, remove the bungee cord, and continue lighting until you reach the end of each tree section.

Lighting intensity styles

Determine how brightly you want your tree to be lit. Trees in dark display areas need fewer lights. Denser trees need more lights to help show off your ornaments.

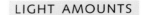

LIGHT AMOUNTS

For lighting a standard 7-foot tree, you need approximately 15 sets of 50s for subtle lighting; 25 sets of 50s for moderate lighting; and up to 60 sets of 50s for full, dramatic showcase lighting.

LIGHTS THAT LAST

You should use no more than 300 lights in a row before starting back at the power strip (or wall plug); otherwise, they are likely to short out. Power strips are recommended, due to the number of lights that will be in use.

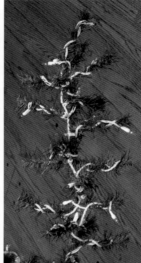

After lighting the tree, blend the branches wherever new tree sections start.

▲ **Fully lit branch with subtle lighting** This is an inexpensive option that works well for a sparse style. Simply stretch the cord back to the center after you complete step 5, below; then secure, and move on to the next branch.

▲ **Fully lit branch with moderate lighting** Here, every third green is wrapped. This style looks good on trees that have longer needles and an average number of branches. It also provides more light to show off ornaments if your tree is near a window or in a brightly lit area.

▲ **Fully lit branch with full showcase lighting** For the most intense, dramatic lighting, light every green. This is the most expensive and labor-intensive option, but it's well worth it: every one of your ornaments will sparkle and shine!

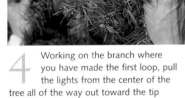

4 Working on the branch where you have made the first loop, pull the lights from the center of the tree all of the way out toward the tip of the branch.

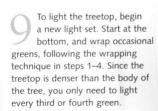

5 Wrap the light string around the outermost green twice. If you want subtle lighting, skip steps 6–8 and refer instead to the far left caption above; then proceed to step 9.

9 To light the treetop, begin a new light set. Start at the bottom, and wrap occasional greens, following the wrapping technique in steps 1–4. Since the treetop is denser than the body of the tree, you only need to light every third or fourth green.

10 Moderate lighting such as this is adequate for most tree styles. This tree is lit with miniature, multicolored bulbs—you can also try all clear, all one color, or a combination of any or all of these.

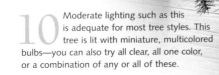

LIGHTING A LIVE TREE

Because you cannot permanently light live trees, they offer you the opportunity to play with color design like an artist with a blank canvas. The tree doesn't have to be lit with only clear, multicolor, or single-color lights. Try mixing several single-color light sets in colors that complement your decorations. Or you can create irregular blocks of color by stringing three cords of one color together and placing them on one section of the tree, then go on to plug in three more sets of another color and continue lighting the next tree section.

Many people walk around and around a live tree to light it, randomly wrapping the branches to keep the lights secure. The problem with this technique is that as the tree dries, the branches snag your cords and make unlighting the tree difficult at the end of the holidays. It is best not to wrap live branches at all; laying light sets on the branches offers better illumination for your special ornaments and makes light-set removal quick and easy.

The technique we use calls for lighting your tree in thirds: simply layer the lights on the tops of branches with minimal anchoring and light only one-third of the tree at a time. When it comes time to remove the lights after Christmas, you can stand in one place, pull on each light string, and strip the tree without any cord tangling. Of course, this only applies to miniature light sets. Clipped-on C-7s and C-9s should be carefully removed bulb by bulb.

▶ **Multicolor magic** A live tree lit with C-9s provides subtle light.

Lighting made easy

The lighting technique shown here is for trees with relatively flat branches. For bushier trees like the Douglas fir, apply the same principles—but since there is no natural branch spacing, weave lights in and out starting at the bottom row, then move up about 1 foot and repeat. This technique assures virtually no visible light cords.

SIMPLE REMOVAL

When you lay lights on branches instead of wrapping them, light removal at the end of the season is quick, easy, and less messy!

CORD COLORS

Use green cords—white-cord lights were used for demonstration purposes only to make it easier to follow the steps provided.

1 Plug your lights into a power strip. Starting near the trunk of the tree, at the bottom, place lights on a branch nearest the trunk and stretch them out toward that branch's tip.

2 Using a "ribbon-candy" pattern, begin to cover the branch with lights. Once the branch is uniformly covered, pull the light set back toward the tree trunk.

3 Lightly secure the lights to an inner green by separating the light cords and poking about an inch of green through the hole. This will prevent the lights from slipping.

4 Move on to the next branch and repeat this process on the third of the tree facing you. Move up from branch row to branch row as needed until you reach the top.

TROUBLESHOOTING: IF SOME OR ALL OF THE TREE WON'T LIGHT

ONE-SET QUICK FIX

1. First, check that all light sets are plugged into an outlet or power strip, and that the power strip is turned on. Also check light-set plugs; if one has burned out, replace the whole string.

2. If your light sets have fuses, check that they are not burned. If you find a blackened, burned-out fuse, replace it.

3. Make sure circuit breakers were not tripped. If using multiple light sets, you may need to divide them between two different outlets, each on a separate breaker, using extension cords. Use a power strip for each outlet, and plug only one extension cord into each strip.

4. Check for missing or burned-out bulbs. At the same time, you should "run the string"—push

on every bulb to check for loose ones. There are several types of light sets. Some go out entirely if a bulb burns out. Another type stays lit if a bulb burns out, but goes out if a bulb pops out. The newest sets will stay lit even if one or more bulbs pop out of their sockets, but these sets are only available regionally and are pricier than traditional sets. If a bulb is black, just replace that bulb. Burned-out bulbs should be immediately replaced. Leaving them in causes the entire set to burn out more quickly.

▶ Burned-out bulb

5. If pushing on the bulbs doesn't work, try removing each bulb. There are two wires that must make a connection to the

sides of the socket in order for the bulb to light. Make sure that each is straight and long enough to touch the socket. Straighten the wires and place the bulb back in its socket.

6. If a wire is missing or too short to make contact, replace the bulb. However, this approach takes time if you have to replace multiple lights. If, after replacing one bulb, the set still won't light, just replace the whole set.

▶ Bulb with one shorter wire

7. As a last resort, unplug the dead set, remove it (cutting it in a few places speeds up the process), and replace it. Do NOT cut plugged-in or still-functioning cords!

A quick fix for one dead set—especially if your tree is already decorated—is to plug in a new set and simply lay the lights into the "dead area." Place lights carefully, making sure to work them deep into the tree.

For artificial trees that you wish to light permanently, this is only a temporary fix: before you store your tree for the year, remember to remove the temporary light set, then remove the dead set and replace it with working lights.

Never permanently affix new, working light sets over nonworking ones. Layering set upon set causes the greenery to flatten and will leave you with an unbushy branch of light cords. Remember: For easy unlighting, use sets of 50s on artificial trees.

5 After one-third of the tree is lit, as shown above, move onto the next third. Start at the bottom and repeat steps 1–4.

6 When you're done, the tree will be uniformly lit. If you have extra lights left over when you reach the top of the tree, work back toward the bottom.

7 Large bulbs (C-9s or C-7s) clip onto tree branches, and they should be spaced as far apart as the cords will allow. Remember to light the inner tree branches as well so that your ornaments have sufficient illumination.

KEEP YOUR BULBS STRAIGHT

Position C-7s and C-9s to point straight up. If the tree droops in a day or two, readjust them.

LIGHTING STYLES

The sheer variety of lights to choose from is as dazzling as the lights themselves. Here is a description of the different bulb types—from minatures to medium-sized to large novelty bulbs—to help you sort through the maze:

Miniatures, or "mini" lights, are standard incandescent bulbs ranging from 2.5–5 volts.

LED stands for "light emitting diode," and these lights are relatively new to the Christmas arena. They are energy efficient, long-lasting, and they burn cooler.

C-7s and C-9s are large, incandescent lights in the 5–7 volt range, with glass or ceramic bulbs.

Novelty/alternative lights come in a variety of shapes and sizes; this category includes rice lights, which are popular in floral design; fiber optics; bubble lights; and even licensed figures and shapes.

Light-cover attachment

Light covers and caps are decorative accessories that slide directly over mini lights and add color, texture, and style. They come in an endless assortment of shapes, are generally made of plastic and metal, and are easy to install.

1 Slip a miniature light bulb into the bottom of the light cover. Press hard to make sure it is secure.

2 Position the cover so that it won't fall off. If it has a cord, secure the cord to a green.

Pigtail attachment

Pigtails are specialty lights that attach to sets of mini lights. Pigtail plugs fit into most standard miniature light sets. They may light, spin, or both. Bend branches out of the way for spinners so they can rotate freely.

1 Remove the light bulb from its housing, and store it so you can replace it when storing your tree.

2 Plug the pigtail into the empty socket. Wrap excess cord around a branch or green.

LIGHT GALLERY

Note: see pages 187–89
for supplier information

MINI LIGHTS

1 Bouquet of fashion colors
   from seven strands
2 Bouquet of clear lights
   on green, white, and
   gold cords

LED LIGHTS

3 Multicolor LED stars
4 New rounded-tip type

C-7s, C-9s & C-50s

5 Round globe opaque
   multicolor set of C-50s
   (these fit into C-7 sockets)
6 Multicolored C-7s on
   green cord
7 Pink C-7s on white cord

NOVELTY LIGHTING

8 Silicone spiky bulb on
   decorative lamp base
9 White Father Christmas
   bulb on decorative
   lamp base
10 Multicolored berry lights
11 Silver and gold berry lights
12 Multicolor diamond
   pattern (precapped
   on mini lights)
13 Specialty preattached
   aluminum star-shaped
   reflectors on multicolored
   C-7s
14 Fiber-optic lights
15 Rice lights
16 Tool set: hammer,
   screwdriver, pliers,
   and saw
17 Candle-flame-shaped
   frosted-glass lights
18 Chili peppers
19 Purple light sphere
20 Red rope lights
21 Red electric-ribbon lights
22 Silicone spiky lights
23 Flicker flames
24 Clear glitter-bubble light
25 Multicolored bubble light
26 Church and Christmas tree
   bubble lights

LIGHT CAPS & COVERS

27 Multicolored PVC
   (polyvinyl chloride)
   bulb caps
28 Clear acrylic 3-D star
29 Fabric Santa-hat
   light cover
30 Jewel-tone, glittered
   shatterproof globes
31 Tear-shaped, sculpted
   glass light covers
32 Clear acrylic church

PIGTAILS

33 Glass candle with
   miniature mirror
34 Ornament spinner:
   glittered snowman with
   hanging   strawberry
   ornament
35 Glittered gold lamp
36 Faux-beaded acrylic
   golden apple
37 Red lantern-sconce

SNOW

Snow is breathtaking when it blankets the branches of evergreen trees and glistens in the sun, so it was natural for tree designers to come up with ways to recreate that dazzling look indoors. Artificial snow gives your tree a homey feel, conjuring up images of cool winter mornings in a mountain lodge. Retro-design trees are particularly suited to "faux snow" because of the contrast between the stark snow and the large, colorful lights and ornaments.

FLUFF OR SPRAY?

Artificial spray snow is recommended for live trees only, since the dried spray snow will clump and rub off your artificial tree when you take it down. If you want a frosty look on an artificial tree, buy a preflocked or prefrosted tree. You can create a unique look by snowing an artificial tree yourself using cotton and sprinkle snow, following the below method. (This is not a good technique for live trees, since their branches droop and the unanchored snow falls off.) You should light your tree before snowing it, but take care to keep all types of snow away from light sockets.

▲ **Presnowed artificial tree**
This tree appears lightly dusted with snow.

Snowing an artificial tree

To create the illusion of snow on an artificial tree, it's best to start with fire-retardant, soft-cotton batting. You also need artificial bagged snow. There are several kinds on the market—the most realistic-looking is the fluffy Styrofoam type. The look is finished off with pastel-tint opalescent glitter. Off-white, vintage mica snow is best for use with old decorations; white snow makes aged pieces look dirty. Look for faux snow in your local craft or holiday stores.

MATERIALS NEEDED

▲ Cotton batting

▲ Styrofoam-type artificial snow

▲ Antique "mica" snow

▲ Opalescent snow

1 Tear off a small piece of cotton batting. Place it into the tree on a branch and smooth it down. Pull the end toward the branch tip. Shape the snow mound into a natural shape. As with spray snow, don't cover every branch, every third or fourth one is fine. Otherwise, the snow will overpower the other decorations.

SNOWING A LIVE TREE

Spray snowing is ideal for live trees. When applying, don't spray every single branch tip or it will look unnatural. When snow falls on trees naturally, it creates random patches; this is the look you are trying to recreate. Practice on a piece of paper first, or better still, outside. Also avoid spraying snow directly onto ornaments, bows, or ribbon, as it will permanently stain.

◄ **Tree-lot flocking** If you don't want to spray your tree yourself, many tree lots will cover them for you right at the lot with a huge flocking machine, giving you a very snowy effect.

▲ **Flocked branches** Flocking comes in many different colors: blue, yellow, green, pink, even black.

SPRAY-SNOW SAFETY

Be careful not to spray directly into light sockets to avoid shorting out your lights. Also keep pets and small children away from flocking; it can be toxic if ingested in large quantities.

▲ **Spray-snow technique** Use a light, sweeping motion to avoid unnatural clumps. Spray branch tips only, and vary the amount of snow you use from branch to branch to make it look like the snow fell naturally.

LIGHT & HEAT

Hair spray is flammable and must be kept away from heat sources like fireplaces, heating vents, and larger Christmas light bulbs. Also, do not use spray glue in place of hair spray—it will yellow the cotton. Take special care to check that light bulbs do not touch the snow.

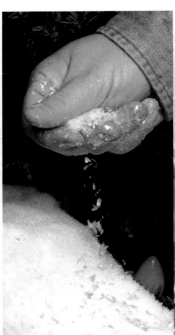

2 To make cleanup easier, lay plastic on the floor under the tree to catch the excess sprinkled snow. Lightly cover each cotton patch with artificial bagged snow to give it texture.

3 Lightly dust each cotton patch once again, this time with opalescent glitter, which simulates sunlight on new-fallen snow. Cover the entire patch, but don't overdo it.

4 Lightly mist each snowy patch with hair spray to set it. Be careful not to aim the spray directly into light sockets. Don't saturate the cotton—a light spray is sufficient. The finished tree is now ready to decorate.

STATEMENT PIECES

A STATEMENT PIECE is anything you choose to feature in or near your tree as a focal point or specialty decoration. Some statement pieces can stand alone as tabletop decorations, but may also work well in trees, wreaths, or garlands. You can have a grouping of related pieces, like a collection of carnival masks—just make sure that your statement pieces are bright, colorful, or eye-catching. Leave enough space around each piece so it won't be hidden behind branches, ornaments, or trimmings.

▲ **Jeweled party mask**
Costume pieces like this are stylish and create a fun mood.

ENDLESS VARIETY

Statement pieces can be the jumping-off point for "theming" your tree. For example, on a kids' tree, showcase large stuffed animals surrounded by smaller action figures; a pet tree might feature ornaments shaped like your favorite breed, with dog bones or cat toys as supporting elements. If you're an art lover, create an art-gallery tree with family drawings and photographs, framed or mounted on foamboard. Gardeners can experiment with floral pieces (best for special occasions, unless you're using artificial flowers). And Christmas-themed figurines or plates make quite an impact when showcased in a tree or window. Try placing lit tabletop decorations on mantels or in the center of your tree: use your imagination and experiment!

Securing pieces

Place pieces deep enough into the tree so that they'll be fully supported and won't fall. Avoid placing very large or heavy pieces at or near the top of the tree, especially on artificial trees, which won't be able to support the weight. Light, tall, and narrow pieces may be set, albeit sparingly, on the top third of the tree. If you're featuring several pieces, place the smaller ones near the top and the larger pieces near the bottom. Try to avoid placing anything on the bottommost branches, or the tree will look unbalanced. Small pieces may be hung with ornament hooks. Large pieces should be firmly attached with floral wire or fishing line (monofilament) or placed on several flattened branches that can serve as a foundation (both techniques shown at right).

LIVE-TREE TIP

Live tree branches will naturally droop a little after a day or two. To compensate, either place your statement pieces higher in the tree, or watch and see if you need to adjust the height by repositioning your pieces after the tree "settles."

HANGING WITH WIRE OR MONOFILAMENT

1 Tie the floral wire or monofilament around your piece. Then make a loop with the other end of the wire or monofilament. Loop this end around a green.

2 The statement piece should be worked into the tree, not placed at branch tips, so that the branches can support the weight. It also looks better this way.

PLACING PIECES ON A FOUNDATION

1 Flatten three or four branches to create a base, then lift others up to make space. Place a piece of cardboard on the base for support and cover with cotton batting.

2 This collectible house is nestled in a snowy landscape behind a candy-cane fence. To prevent slippage, attach the house to an inner branch using floral wire.

STATEMENT PIECES GALLERY

Note: see pages 187–89 for supplier information

COLLECTIBLES

1 Collectible lit houses can be displayed in the tree as well as under it, allowing more room for Christmas presents.

FAMILY MEMORIES

2 Take a beloved personal photograph and place it in a frame that complements the theme or style of your tree.

FLOWERS & FRUIT

3 Fill a pine-cone sleigh with brightly colored fruits and flowers to create a vivid focal point for your room or tree.

4 Adding fresh-cut flowers to a tree provides interesting shapes and enticing aromas. Look for unusual vases to enhance the look.

SEASONAL ITEMS

5 Recreate a theme from a favorite story, like *The Nutcracker,* or build a miniature Christmas scene on a red-velvet stage.

6 This two-sided wooden Santa plaque is a perfect decorative accent for a country stairway or window.

7 Retro tabletop decorations like this kitschy felt-covered reindeer look cute when placed on tree branches or wreaths.

8 Flattened branches make room for tabletop pieces. This snowman fits well with frosty tree themes.

9 A novel way to display a collectible Christmas dish is to cradle it in tree branches and arrange extra lights behind it for illumination.

10 This lovely angel with movable arms can be posed to fly, pray, or even lend a hand stringing garlands. Just attach the garland's end to her hand!

11 Use an incredibly intricate wood carving like this to light up a garlanded mantelpiece, dark window, or tabletop display.

RIBBONS & BOWS

RIBBONS AND BOWS ARE VERSATILE ACCESSORIES that add depth and texture. We consider them "through-line" decorations, meaning they can tie the whole look of your tree together and, when used throughout one or more rooms, unify entire themes or color schemes. We highly recommend wired ribbon, which lets bows and ribbon patterns keep their shape. If you are using both bows and ribbon in your design, start with the overall ribboning pattern, and finish with bows.

RIBBONING STYLES

Consider your personal "fashion sense" as well as the style of the tree and its decorations when choosing ribbon. Ribbon comes in an almost limitless selection of colors and fabrics, compatible with any type of tree design—plain and multicolored, patterned and textured, even reversible. While wired ribbon is more expensive than unwired, it's well worth the price because it's much more versatile and holds its shape longer than unwired ribbon. It can twist, turn, lie flat, or make full 360-degree spirals. Wired ribbon is widely available, comes in many styles, and allows anyone to make professional-looking designs.

▲ **Green and red** Choose contrasting colors when using two ribbons to really create a standout ribbon statement. Both ribbons should complement ornament tones.

Vertical line pattern

Lines cascading down the tree give a very symmetrical look to your design. This helps tie a look together if you have many different kinds of ornaments and want to help them look coordinated. You might look for a ribbon with an image or pattern echoed on your ornaments.

ATTACHING RIBBON

Attach the ribbon loops to your tree by bending the branch around the ribbons (on an artificial tree), or with floral wire (if your tree is live).

RIBBON AMOUNT

For standard-size trees, each style (except Picture Frame, p. 152) uses about 25 yards of ribbon. Buy three 10-yard rolls or one 25-yard roll.

1 Fold the end of the ribbon over into a loop and pinch it together. Anchor the loop to the tree with floral wire or by bending a green around the bottom of the loop.

2 Make a half-loop shape with the ribbon, and anchor it to a green about a foot below the first anchor. Don't attach it at the branch tip; go in about three inches.

3 Making sure the loops are nicely rounded, continue creating loops down the length of the tree, slightly increasing the loop size as you go downward.

Finishing ends

Complete the end of each ribbon with a decorative touch. This gives your design a pretty and professional look. Using wire snips makes cutting wired ribbon a snap!

Starting slightly below the treetop leaves you room to add bows or another type of treetop decoration.

Start with clean, sharp cutting tools to prevent ragged ribbon edges.

1 Leave enough ribbon at the bottom to create a tail. Fold the end of the ribbon in half, and cut it at an angle to create an inverted "V."

2 The "V" gives the ribbon pattern a sharp, finished look, which works well on contemporary designs.

3 Alternatively, you can curl the ribbon under and let it hang. This finish looks best on Victorian designs or trees with a soft, feminine look.

4 Make three to five vertical ribbon lines around the tree, repeating steps 1–3 each time, and making sure to space evenly between lines.

Picture frame

Framing is an excellent way to draw the eye to statement pieces that you wish to showcase in your tree. You can make and use one or more frames—in many assorted shapes, including triangular (shown here), square, diamond, and rectangular—depending on how many special items you wish to highlight. However, with this pattern, less is definitely more. Leave enough room for your piece to fit inside the "ribbon frame" without looking too cramped; leave at least several inches of space between the item and the ribbon. Once you have the spacing, measure out enough ribbon to make the frame. The amount of ribbon depends on the size of the item you're showcasing and what shape frame you want to use.

This snowman fits his frame well. He is placed so that the space between him and the ribbon is fairly equal all the way around.

1 Start a roll of ribbon near the treetop and attach it to a green. Then, using the looping technique shown for the Vertical Line Pattern (pages 150–51), create the first diagonal line of the triangle. Next, make the bottom, horizontal portion of the triangle. Then continue the same piece of ribbon back up to meet the green where you began your pattern. Cut the ribbon and secure.

2 Place your statement piece in the ribbon frame (if you haven't done so already) using the attachment methods outlined in Statement Pieces (pages 148–49). Repeat the Picture Frame ribbon treatment around the tree if you're using more than one statement piece.

Apply this ribbon style after your tree has been fully decorated, so you can place strips wherever you see a "hole."

Use bows in contrasting colors or picks (branch-tip accessories), especially at corners, to accent your frame.

Freeform

Freeforming is a great way to save money—you can use one or more types of complementary ribbons and make use of scraps you may have left over from package wrapping. By cutting ribbon into different lengths and randomly placing the strips about your tree in half-loop patterns, you create the illusion of having swirled ribbons on your tree—at a fraction of the cost.

1 Cut the ribbon into strips long enough to create half-loops, or gather together leftover scraps of sufficient length. Place each loop deep enough into the tree to stay in place, and hide the ends.

2 Continue randomly around the tree, using small, medium, and large loops. Using smaller pieces near the top helps keep your tree proportions balanced.

3 Loop placement is freeform, and depends on where you want to fill a space.

Wraparound

Wraparound ribboning that spirals diagonally down and around gives more of a sweeping feel to your tree, and if you add bows, it mimics the look of a ball gown. This style is slightly more formal in appearance than the Vertical-Line ribboning pattern. You can also accent this pattern with an ascending or descending parade of ornaments. Display a set of collectible train pieces "chugging" up the tree, or a series of sled ornaments "sliding" down.

Whenever you use two different ribbons, make sure they are the same width and that the materials are of similar weight. Then choose any complementary colors, patterns, or textures.

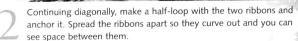

1 Lay the two different ribbons one on top of the other. Fold the doubled ends over to create a loop. Attach the doubled loop to the treetop by bending a green over it, then pull it slightly apart.

2 Continuing diagonally, make a half-loop with the two ribbons and anchor it. Spread the ribbons apart so they curve out and you can see space between them.

3 Keep spiraling down and around the tree and attaching the ribbons with tree greens. The loops may very gradually increase in size as you progress down and around the tree.

4 Finish the tail off by cutting inverted "Vs" into each ribbon end, as shown at right. Above, the fully ribboned tree is now complete and ready to be decorated with ornaments.

BOW STYLES

Bows add bright, decorative bursts of color and texture to your tree. The 3-D quality of bow loops gives the eye "stopping points" as it travels around the tree.

Use four-loop bows made of lightweight materials as accents at points of attachment along ribboning patterns. Pom-pom bows look great on a tree with ribboning, or by themselves on a tree, green garland, or wreath.

Bob's easy pom-pom bow

Bob never had much patience for following step-by-step directions, so he developed his own short-cut method for making pom-pom bows.

We don't recommend this technique for thicker ribbons like brocades or velvets, but it works well for lightweight and pliable ribbons made from fabrics such as satin and silk.

ADDED DECORATION

Try adding a "pick" (stemmed decoration) to the center of your bow for extra pizzazz and color.

RIBBON AMOUNTS

You need about 3 yards for both Bob's Easy Pom-Pom Bow and Debi's Full Pom-Pom Bow.

1 Make a loop and hold it between your thumb and index finger. Leave enough ribbon to create a tail.

2 Continue to make loops until you have enough to create a full bow; between 11 and 19 is best.

3 Pinch the bases of the ribbon loops tight, then wrap snugly several times with medium-gauge floral wire (or a pipe cleaner).

4 Twist the floral wire or pipe cleaner to secure. Leave enough floral wire untwisted to allow you to attach the bow to your greenery.

5 You may want to add a pick to your bow. Insert the pick end into the center of your unfluffed bow. Be sure it is secure within the floral-wire wrap.

6 To fluff the bow, round each loop and twist it at the bottom of the loop. Move loops around so they aren't all angled in the same direction.

7 Attach your bow to the tree with floral wire. Make any necessary adjustments to the picks, loops, and tails so the loops are rounded and the tails hang freely.

Debi's full pom-pom bow

This bow incorporates the "half-twist-between-every-loop" technique. The advantage to this method is that the neck area in the center of the bow is quite narrow; thus when you secure it with floral wire, you're assured that the loops won't slip and the bow will keep its shape. This is especially helpful if your ribbon is slippery or heavy.

1 Reversible or double-sided ribbon is ideal for this bow. Allow about 1–2 feet of ribbon for a tail, and give the ribbon a half-twist.

2 Make the first loop, and then give the ribbon another half-twist. Make a second loop and give the ribbon yet another half-twist.

3 Continue making loops, being sure to make half-twists between every loop. Make enough loops to create a full-looking bow, about 15–21 altogether. Wrap the bow with floral wire, then twist it to secure.

4 Fluff the bow, then attach it to your tree with the floral wire. Once the bow is in place, fluff all the loops so they are fully rounded. Position the tail to hang freely.

Two-ribbon pom-pom bow

Using two ribbons to make a bow is tricky and may take some practice, but it does enable you to create a full swirl of color, form, and texture. Two-ribbon bows add panache to a tree and should be prominently featured; they look best on taller, fuller trees. For beginners, sheer, lightweight ribbon is easier to shape. Use three to five yards of each of the two ribbons for this bow.

RIBBON WEIGHT

Bows made out of heavier ribbon should be placed deeper in the tree for support, and so they're better "anchored."

1 Select two identical-width ribbons of similar-weight material and in complementary colors and/or patterns. Leave about two feet on both ends for long tails.

2 Lay the ribbons one on top of the other. Holding tightly, give both ribbons a half-twist to make the first loop. Follow steps 1–4 in full pom-pom bow demo above.

3 When fluffing this bow, pull the inner loop out and twist slightly to fill any spaces. Take turns pulling the inner loops to the left and right of the outer loop, so that colors alternate.

4 Finish all tails with an inverted-"V" cut, and attach the bow to your tree with floral wire. Make a half-loop on each long ribbon end, angle it diagonally, and attach it with a green. This is an ideal bow for filling empty spaces on a tree.

Four-loop bow

These clean-looking bows provide light, gentle touches of color to a tree, and they work especially well on smaller trees. Scaled-down versions of the bows make great decorations for tabletop-sized trees without overpowering them. This style is best suited for light and narrow ribbons. If you're making small bows, use very narrow ribbon.

To make a four-loop bow with a long, trailing tail, you need less than two yards of ribbon. With such a simple bow, it is important that the ribbon looks evenly spaced. A simple trick for making similar-sized loops is to use the spacing between your index finger and thumb as a makeshift measuring tool!

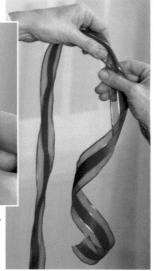

1 Leaving enough ribbon for a tail, grasp the ribbon and give it a half-twist to start your first loop. Pinch either side of the twist tightly between your thumb and index finger.

2 Create your first loop, holding the ribbon between your index and middle fingers. Don't crimp it!

3 With your other hand, give the ribbon another half-twist. Now pinch the entire loop between your thumb and index finger.

4 Make a second loop. Give the ribbon another half-twist. Grasp it firmly between your thumb and index finger.

5 Make the third and fourth loops, then secure the bow at the center with floral wire. Leave enough wire untwisted to attach the bow to the tree.

6 Make a smaller fifth loop and wrap with the wire. Pull the wire back, out of the way of the loops and the tail. Fluff the bow.

7 Attach the bow to your tree with the floral wire. Fluff again if necessary.

CREATIVE USE OF RIBBONS & BOWS

Because contemporary ribbons are of much better quality than the old paper ribbons of the past, they can be used more creatively as decorative design elements. Use four-loop bows to accent interesting architectural features in your home. Use short lengths of ribbon as tiebacks for draperies. Make pom-pom bows and attach them to gifts that won't be wrapped—large children's toys like bicycles and scooters. We've even seen oversized ribbons that were used to "wrap" automobiles! Give someone the gift of flowers, and add a bow you've made for them. And outdoor ribbon-and-bow treatments can enhance doors, trees, lampposts, gates, and fences.

▶ **Lamp bow** In warm, dry climates, even rich velvet ribbons can be used to decorate outdoor light fixtures.

▲ **Electric ribbon** Lit ribbon allows you to both light and decorate. Drape it on your tree and tie it into a top bow.

OUTDOOR RIBBON

For outdoor decorating, use ribbons specially made to withstand the elements. Plastics, lamés, and even leathers, endure better than velours and delicate fabrics.

▲ **Alcove accent** Beribboned garlands aren't just for stairways and windows. Draw attention to small, decorative areas like this alcove by framing them with lit garland accented with bows.

◀ **Gold cascade** For a loose, freeform design, combine bows and draped fabric to complement ornaments and statement pieces.

GIFTWRAP

Instead of always wrapping presents in Christmas paper, try placing your gift in fabric. Gather the ends together and tie it up with some wired ribbon.

◀ **Spiral design** Swirl ribbon around and around draped green garland for an exciting, lavish look.

RIBBONS

Ribbons and bows were not a part of early Christmas decoration in Germany, where the first Christmas trees were designed. Until the 19th century, silk and velvet ribbon was reserved for the clothing of nobility; ribbon was so popular that it festooned the hairstyles, hats, dresses, jackets, and shoes of the European aristocracy. In the Victorian era, people began to attach ribbons and bows to their Christmas trees as well. Velvet, considered especially luxurious, was a popular trimming material in Victorian England, and later in America.

We still decorate our Christmas trees with ribbons and bows, as well as our Christmas presents! Now bows are made from a wide variety of fabrics, in many different colors and styles, and with the introduction of plastics, leathers and metals, many ribbons are able to endure harsh outdoor-weather conditions.

Silk, satin & nylon

Silks and satins are lightweight, and they have a light, ethereal look as well. They can be textured, like silk dupiones, or shiny and sleek like polished satins. Use these when you want to create a crisp, sharp ribbon statement. Nylon ribbons are also light. They cost less than silks and satins, but they don't provide quite the same richness. All three materials work well with most bow and ribboning styles.

Velvet & velveteen

Velvets have long been associated with nobility, and they still lend a regal air to Christmas greenery. These ribbons are plush in appearance and add a rich, upscale quality to decorations. Silk velvet is among the most expensive of all ribbons on the market, but the sophisticated look it provides is well worth the cost. Velvet ribbons made from cotton or rayon are almost as rich as silk and slightly less expensive. Cotton velveteen is the most inexpensive velvet, but it can make a fine substitute. Burgundy and green velvets look spectacular in Victorian settings.

Novelty

Novelty ribbons are made of unusual fabrics or materials designed with a unique twist. These ribbons are great for creating a theme or setting a tone. Stretch-terrycloth ribbons, which are reminiscent of beach towels, can be used with electric ribbon to create a beach-themed design. Faux-fur ribbons and animal ornaments make excellent pet or wildlife trees. And there's even something for motorcycle enthusiasts: black leather ribbon, with or without zippers!

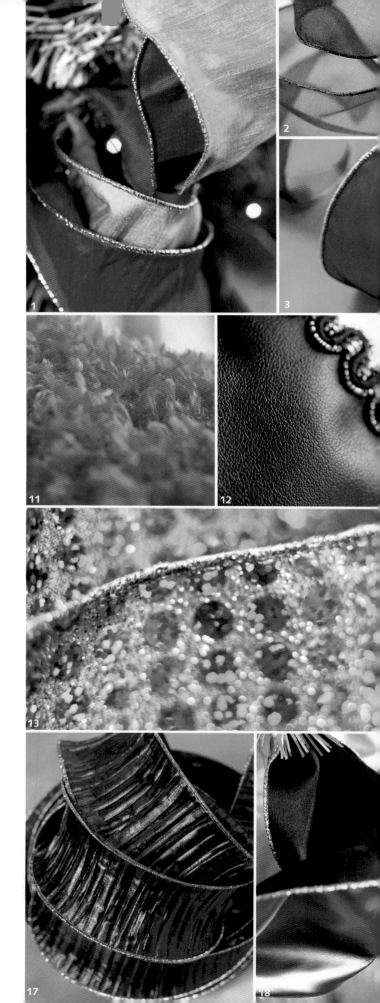

RIBBON & BOW GALLERY

Note: see pages 187–89 for supplier information.

SILK, SATIN & NYLON

1 Red and chartreuse silk dupione with gold edging

2 Satiny sheer, pastel blue with gold edging

3 Satiny, translucent fuchsia with gold edging

VELVET & VELVETEEN

4 Black burnout velvet with leaves edged in gold

5 Teal lamé with black burnout velvet and gold glitter

6 Maroon velvet with gold-beaded edging

7 Jewel-tone velvet harlequin

8 Two-sided maroon velveteen with gold, hot-drop metal

9 Green velvet ribbon with embroidered gold crests

10 Black velveteen with sequined diamond shapes and gold piping on edges

NOVELTY

11 Hot-pink stretch terry-cloth

12 Black faux leather with gold rickrack

13 Gold-on-gold faux sequins

14 Reptile-patterned gray latex

15 Gold wire mesh

16 Tan leather with gold, hot-drop metal, and black stitching

17 Crimped red lamé with gold edging

18 Two-sided black polyblend and gold lamé

19 Faux snow leopard with black leather edging

20 Hot-pink leather with black stitching

21 Indoor/outdoor teal vinyl

22 Red velvet with metal jingle-bell accents

FABRIC

LIKE RIBBON, FABRIC CAN BE USED as an element
to tie together the colors in the room with the
colors you choose for your tree trimmings. Since
fabric is fuller than ribbon, it looks best on trees
that aren't too bushy. It also works well to fill
space if you don't have many ornaments
or decorations for your tree.

SUITABLE MATERIALS

It's best to use brightly colored fabric, as dark colors tend
to get lost in the green of the tree. Use lightweight
materials like satin, tulle, lamé, or moiré. Although thick,
heavy fabrics can help create a spectacular display, they
don't drape well and can cause tree branches to droop,
so use them sparingly. If you do use a heavy fabric like
faux fur, as we did on the Mae West tree (opposite
page, inset), let it hang straight down.

Fabric flowerette

Instead of adding ribbon bows to a tree draped in fabric,
you could create one or more flowers from the draping fabric.
They can be used at the treetop as the starting point for your
drape, or placed throughout the tree.

FABRIC ALLOWANCE

Use two yards of fabric per
foot of tree. Allow up to 10
more for a draped tree skirt.

▲ **Couture** Here, two different fabrics were
overlapped and styled to create the impression that
the tree is actually "dressed."

1 Choose a fabric that complements the color of your
tree decorations. Fold over about one foot of
fabric—by doubling the material, you can create
soft, rounded "rose petals." Start a rosette by curling the
doubled material around into a spiral.

2 Tighten the spiral on the rosette. Firmly grasp
the finished "flowerette" about six to eight
inches from the top. You may want to wrap it
with floral wire to prevent the fabric from shifting; this
is especially helpful with slippery fabrics like satin.

3 Attach the flowerette to the treetop by bending
several greens around it. Once it has been secured,
open the "petals" of the flowerette by shaping the
fabric. If you're just creating flowerettes for the tree, cut
the fabric. If you're continuing with loops, go on to step 4.

FABRIC GALLERY

1 Synthetic metallic gold
2 Sheer red tulle with blue sequins
3 White silk dupione
4 Gold and saffron chiffon
5 Faux leopard-spotted acetate
6 Sequined silver nylon
7 Turquoise satin
8 Hand-stitched ivory sequins on sheer fabric
9 White faux fur
10 Red velvet

LARGE-BULB FABRIC SAFETY

If you use this technique on a tree lit with large C-7 or C-9 bulbs, keep fabric away from the warm bulbs. If the fabric needs to be attached near a bulb to accomodate your design, cheat! Unscrew the bulb until it is no longer lit.

Notice that the rose is angled up. Don't let it droop and weigh down your design.

▲ **Mae West homage tree**
Since this tree was an ode to excess, we bunched heavy faux fur to frame the tree and allowed it to flow to the floor.

4 Create "loops" on the tree, in much the same way as shown in the Vertical Line Pattern ribbon demonstration on pages 150–51. Anchor the loops by bending greens around the fabric. Make sure the fabric loops are full and billowy by fluffing them out when all of the fabric is attached.

5 Let the fabric drape down to the floor, and create your tree skirt by surrounding the tree stand with fabric. Finish by folding under all unfinished ends to give the skirt a soft, rounded look.

GARLANDS

GARLANDS, LIKE MOST OTHER TREE DECORATIONS, come in a variety of styles. They can be made of plastic, paper, glass, metal, ceramic, and even food. Many ornament manufacturers even make matching or complementary garlands to go with their ornaments.

HANGING PATTERNS

There are several different ways to hang bead, pearl, and novelty garlands. Note that if you choose a symmetrical garland pattern for your tree, you should hang them before adding ornaments so the garlands will hang as evenly as possible. It's easier to hang ornaments around garlands than to look for an available branch after you've hung an ornament on every single tree branch. For those of you with pets—especially cats—you may want to rethink using garland at all. One good swat and it's goodbye garland. (And your pet probably won't be too thrilled if the tree topples its way.)

Metallic or tinsel garlands have been used over the years to decorate trees, stairways, windows, lampposts, mailboxes, and even work cubicles. Invariably, tinsel garland used to be attached with cellophane tape, but now, a variety of attachment devices are available, including plastic hooks with two-sided tape, floral wire and even Velcro.

Tuck pattern

Tinsel garlands work well on both live and artificial trees because they are lightweight. Instead of looping this garland in the "Wedding Cake" pattern (see next page), try tucking it a little deeper into the tree. This gives the design more depth, and the light reflected off the shimmery garland actually bounces more light off your ornaments and makes them brighter. Don't hang ornaments off decorative garland since it is so light that the ornaments might pull the garland off the tree! The only exception is our sturdy Charm Bracelet garland (see page 164). For a seven-foot-tall tree, use eight to ten strands of six-foot-long-tinsel garland.

▲ **Candy glass** A few well-placed glass garlands make attractive accents without taxing your budget.

If your tinsel garland is vintage and made of actual metal, keep it away from the sockets of larger bulbs to avoid electrical shorts.

1 Start at the bottom of the tree. Lay garland along the branch, "tucking" it into the tree and creating "U" shapes. At the end of one garland, start another.

2 After finishing the first row of branches, move up to the next row. The completed tree should look like it's covered in soft ruffles. Decrease loop size slightly as you move up.

Wedding cake pattern

One of the most familiar patterns—where garlands are strung symmetrically in tiers—"Wedding Cake" works well with almost any type of bead garland. The spacing must be done evenly to look right. It is more difficult to drape on a live tree since the branches are random shapes and lengths. Since garlands should be hung near branch tips, use lightweight garlands on live trees or your branches will droop. If the garlands slip when they're draped over branches, you may want to attach them with floral wire or ornament hooks. For a seven-foot-tall tree, use between eight and ten strands of bead-chain garland. These usually come in lengths of nine feet.

For shorter rows, you can tuck the garland into the tree or tie it into a knot if you don't want to cut it short.

Use garland of a single color and bead size or any combination of colors and bead sizes.

You can "cheat" by using ornament hooks or floral wire to make the garlands hang exactly where you want them.

1 Start at the bottom of the tree. Attach the first garland to an artificial green (by bending it around the garland), or to a live branch (with floral wire).

2 A more decorative way to start and end each garland is by tying the beads around the green and making a knot.

3 Drape the garland horizontally over branches, creating a loose loop pattern. When you finish looping one garland, attach another. After completing one row, move up to the next.

4 Decrease loop width slightly as you move up the tree. Here, every row was garlanded. You may also choose to hang beads only on every other row.

Charm bracelet

Are you worried that your garlands are too thin and insignificant? Try our "Charm Bracelet" solution. You can create a flashy charm bracelet for your tree by twisting several garlands together and attaching small ornaments every few inches with ornament hooks, or try the special technique demonstrated below. The Charm Bracelet garland looks best hung symmetrically, with a mix of beads in different sizes and colors.

1 Make a knot with three to five garlands, twist them together, and hang the knotted end off of a high green. Drape the garland around the tree using Wedding Cake or Random Swag method.

2 Once the garland is hung, begin adding the "charm" ornaments. First, pop the metal legs out of the crown of the ornament and slip the metal piece over a bead strand.

3 Position the ornament under the legs, replace the crown, and insert the legs back into the ornament. Add an ornament about every eight to ten inches. Use a few different styles and shapes.

Random swag

Another option is a random pattern, which involves many strands of garlands and careful, patient work. Although it's called random, the garlands must be placed carefully so they aren't too tightly or loosely draped. Drape garlands diagonally from branch row to branch row, many times, crossing strands over one another. This pattern will give your tree a drippy, ornate look.

Leave the top of the tree unbeaded to save room for your treetop design.

Random patterns looks best with small glass-bead garlands.

1 Make an irregular loop with one type of bead garland and drape it over a high branch. Continue looping over branches at random heights. Don't make the loops too tight.

2 Repeat with a separate color or style of bead garland, crisscrossing them and varying the shape of the loops.

3 Create visual diversity by varying how many branches you skip to form loops. Avoid making a symmetrical pattern.

4 The final tree is covered with garlands crisscrossing every which way.

DECORATING WITH GARLANDS

Garlands can be used inside or outside, to embellish fireplaces, to frame windows and doorways, to dress up a buffet table, or to wrap a mailbox or lamppost. Bead chains can be hung alone on the wall or added to a tree, wreath, or green garland. Floral garlands look great when laid on top of green garlands and accented with ornaments. Make a table-centerpiece garland by cutting a piece of green garland, tying the ends together, and placing a decorative piece in the center. Fluff any bushy garlands well before adding lights or decorations.

▲ **Dressing up**
Adding an upscale bead chain to a green garland dresses it up considerably.

◄ **Bridge the gap**
Unite a tree with its environs by hanging matching garland along the windows.

▼ **Stone fireplace**
This commanding feature required decorations that were large and substantial.

▲ **Draped glamour**
Multiple layers of bead chain look dramatic on a wall. Metal architectural elements make natural hooks for this elegant garland.

▶ **Limited space**
Frame a window in your kitchen to tie in with decorations in the rest of the house.

▼ **Suede greens**
A piece of greenery and a few ornaments on your table dress up place settings. This suede garland looks live, but doesn't leave needles or sap.

GARLAND STYLES

Garlands have been used as celebratory embellishments since Roman times, when they were used to deck doors and walls during festivals. The tradition continued into the Middle Ages, when Germans hung wooden hoops decorated with boughs as symbols of good luck at Christmastime. The Germans were also the first to trim their Christmas trees with glass-bead garlands, in the 17th century, and with silver tinsel garland in the late 1800s. The Victorians strung their trees with glass beads, berries, and paper. Garlands have evolved in contemporary times; today you can find contemporary fluffy tinsel in a rainbow of colors, and strung garlands made of everything from popcorn to plastic to fine crystal.

Plastic

Plastic garlands can be safely used either indoors or out. They are inexpensive and have greater durability than their more expensive and fragile glass counterparts, and they come in an even broader range of shapes, from simple beads to freeform acrylic to the most fanciful forms imaginable.

Craft / Natural

Beads made of colored wood and fabric have a country feel, and they work well on floral-themed trees. Everyone remembers making rings out of colored aluminum ribbon or construction paper; this retro look is fun and easy to make at home (although preassembled metallic rings are available in stores). Classic popcorn and berry garlands are also do-it-yourself nostalgic looks. You can buy garlands made of twigs and pinecones to add texture and a nice rustic accent. Green garland will never go out of style, and you can choose from a myriad of live or artificial needles.

Glass

The variety of glass garland is limitless—there are styles and colors to suit any type of tree or theme. You can find classic round beads, abstract shapes, novelty shapes, and luxurious crystal.

Tinsel / Fashion

In 19th-century Germany, tinsel garland was made from real silver—contemporary versions are made from new flame- and tarnish-proof materials and come in a wide variety of bright, shiny colors. "Fashion" garlands are artificial branch-style garlands made of PVC (polyvinyl chloride) in colors other than green, such as white, black, pastels, and many color combinations.

GARLAND GALLERY

Note: see pages 187–89 for supplier information.

PLASTIC & STYROFOAM

1 Miniature mirrored-acrylic "disco" balls linked by tiny silver beads

2 Purple hearts and clear, blue, fuchsia, gold, and red shatter-proof multishaped beads

3 Red, white, and pearl triple bead strands

4 Acrylic "ice" chips on silver wire

5 Round and faceted beads in gold, copper, and burgundy

6 Gold-tone metal bells on red-and-crystal bead chain

7 Vintage white plastic lanterns with holly accents on white chain

8 Frosted Styrofoam berries on a branch

CRAFT / NATURAL

9 Retro metallic-ribbon chain links

10 Twig garland with pinecones

11 Felt bead chain in shades of blue, gray, and beige

12 Wooden C-9 light bulbs on corkscrew wire

GLASS

13 Upscale beads and candy chain

14 Matte-finish jewel-tone beads

15 Lemon-and-lime chain with semi-matte finish

16 Small, shiny faceted and round beads in jewel tones

17 Upscale retro ornamental beads

18 Sunflowers with varied bead shapes and colors

ORNAMENTS

THE EARLIEST CHRISTMAS-TREE ORNAMENTS were paper flowers, fruit, and sweets. The 16th-century Germans decorated their fir trees with these elements to symbolize the Tree of Knowledge in the Garden of Eden. Soon after, German markets began to offer painted or gilded wax ornaments, usually shaped into angels, during Christmas fairs. Victorian trees were decorated with foodstuffs, including sugared nuts, sweets, and local fruit; and ornaments ranging from intricately cut paper or crocheted snowflakes, to handmade wood and tin figures, to glass ornaments imported from Germany.

BLOWN GLASS

Europeans are still practicing the ancient art of glass-blowing, a technique discovered in the 1st century BC by the Phoenicians. The first glass-blown Christmas ornaments appeared in the 17th century in Bohemia (now the Czech Republic) and Germany; they were created as an afterwork pastime by glassblowers.

Queen Victoria first imported glass ornaments from Germany in the 1850s, making them fashionable throughout England. In 1880, F. W. Woolworth began to import glass ornaments to the United States to sell in his numerous stores. By 1890, he was importing more than 200,000 ornaments annually.

The ornament starts its life as a hot, molten globe of glass. The molten glass is mouth-blown by a craftsperson or machine-blown in a factory. After an ornament is blown and shaped, it is left clear or "silvered," which involves pouring silver nitrate into the interior of the piece and swirling it to coat and strengthen it. The ornament is then handpainted, dipped in paint, or sprayed, making every ornament unique. Finally, glitter can be added.

OTHER GLASS TECHNIQUES

There are other techniques that produce exceptional styles and shapes of glass Christmas decorations, too. Stained-glass pieces create a beautiful glow when they are hung and lit properly, and exquisite handcut Austrian crystal pieces lend a touch of glittering class to a tree.

BLOWN-GLASS GALLERY

Note: see pages 187–89 for supplier information.

1 Lime-green ball with handpainted red poinsettias

2 Red-and-green-striped handpainted ball

3 Frosty pink egg with pink floral-glitter design

4 Long, tapering copper drop with paint-and-glitter highlights

5 Etched Egyptian glass with 18-carat-gold highlights

6 Etched Egyptian glass with 18-carat-gold highlights and burgundy-tinted bands

7 Clear bell with white snow-scape and 18-carat-gold accents

8 Red balls handpainted with paisley motif

9 Gold drop with handpainted Three Wise Men

10 White frosty ball with handpainted pussywillows

11 Blue-tinted etched Egyptian glass with 18-carat-gold highlights and oblong drop

12 Red ball with handpainted white lilies

13 Pale peach ball with handpainted contemporary floral pattern

14 Clear ball with handpainted red-orange tulips

15 Red egg with handpainted golden pears

16 White ball with pink glitter roses and pink rose-ball drop

17 Blue-tinted etched Egyptian glass with 18-carat-gold highlights and crystal drop

18 Pointed frosted teardrop with tinted translucent floral design and gold glitter

19 Zebra-patterned ball with gold flecks

20 Ruby-red traditional ball with shiny leaf pattern and ball-drop accent

21 Clear ball with 18-carat-gold swirl stripes

22 Bronze ball with ornate floral-motif glittered paint

23 Green ball with gold mottling and green feather accent

OTHER GLASS TECHNIQUES

24 Flat fusion-glass ball ornament with stars and stripes

25 Silver-wire heart with clear faceted beads and ribbon tie

26 Silver spiky diamond shape with stained-glass look

27 Medium-sized stained-glass Santa window decoration

MOLDED GLASS

The practice of creating molded-glass objects dates back to ancient Egypt. Contemporary developments in glass-molding techniques allow artists to create complicated and highly sculptural designs. First, the glass artist creates a drawing of his vision. Then a sculptor creates a 3-D clay mold of the design, so that glass can be poured in and take on the same form. When the glass cools, the mold, which is made of two halves, is opened and removed, and what remains is clear glass in the shape of the original design. Silvering, painting, and glittering complete the process. Illustrated here are just a few of the molded-glass ornaments created by modern artists and companies.

Ornament hangers

Ornament style dictates ornament-hanger type: some ornaments come with their own ribbons or cords. Retro designs should hang from classic metal hooks, while designer glass and crystal pieces demand upscale hangers. For heavy and collectible pieces, two hooks are safer.

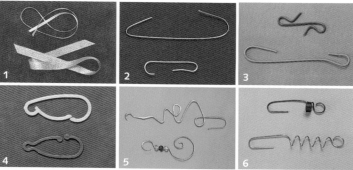

1. Ribbons and braided cords are old-style ornament hangers.
2. Simple metal hooks work, but they can scratch ornaments.
3. Coated metal hooks cause less damage to fine glass pieces.
4. Plastic hooks are great: they're safe to store on fine collectibles.
5. Designer hooks may include clear or tinted crystals.
6. Springy, expandable hangers help with ornament placement.

Securing ornament crowns

Make sure that crowns on collectibles or pricey ornaments are secure before hanging them. Loose crowns can be secured with a drop or two of glue. An alternative fix is demonstrated below (protect your hands by applying hand lotion before using a glue gun). Serious collectors may not want to do either, since altering the ornament will lessen its value.

1 Carefully remove the crown from the neck of the ornament. Spread the legs of the insertion wires apart.

2 Gently insert the legs halfway back in. Add a dab or two of hot glue to the rim of the open ornament.

3 Gently push the crown down until it's firmly in place. If any glue seeps out, remove it with a toothpick. Let dry.

MOLDED-GLASS GALLERY

Note: see pages 187–89 for supplier information.

1 Two-piece red bikini molded onto miniature gold wire hangers

2 Red reindeer with gold glittered antlers and feet

3 White teapot with delicate pink-rose pattern

4 Gold angel in flight with horn and banner

5 Red London-style telephone booth with silvered-glass panels

6 Spiky, glittered glass icicle twist in bright jewel tones

7 Cheery yellow duck pull-toy on wagon with button wheels

8 Four-piece blue train set with glitter "steam" and details

9 Bright-red cardinal seated on a leafy branch

10 Tropical island sunset hand-painted on a Hawaiian shirt

11 Gold-and-white cross with faux-jewel accents

12 Handpainted egg with ocean scene and raised palm fronds

13 Deep blue Star of David with gold-glitter edging

14 Delicately molded green leaf with gold-glitter veins and stem

15 Handpainted, glittered clip-on hummingbird in midflight

16 Gold camel with purple saddle and yellow rope reins

17 Maple leaf "cookie" with orange frosting and white glitter

18 White-glittered heart with red AIDS-Awareness ribbon

19 Green-clad boy, with scarf and hat, making a snow angel

20 Spiky-bottomed jewel-tone drop with glittery patterns

21 Vintage-looking glittery gold Father Christmas with tiny tree

22 Reproduction of a sock monkey doll, holding a banana

23 Festive heart-shaped sweet with waffle pattern

24 Retro-style pink-and-blue striped ball with sunburst cutout

25 Blue, white, and gold Star of David and dreidel

26 Frosted red heart with a shiny indent edged in gold glitter

27 Sexy leopard-print dress molded onto a gold hanger

28 Pink patchwork quilted tree for Breast Cancer Awareness

29 Roly-poly snowman outfitted for snow removal

30 Three nested bells with candy-cane motif

31 Glittered gingerbread man with mittens, earmuffs, and wreath

32 Blue-and-gold miniature replica of the Eiffel Tower

33 Bright gold lion with faux-ruby eyes

34 Exotic fish in brilliant tropical colors

35 Multifaceted silver star with glittered edging

36 "Christmas pickle," a German family tradition

37 Red glittered fire engine with gold ladder

PORCELAIN

Porcelain ornaments are finely crafted ceramic pieces with a translucent quality. The handpainted and white drop-shaped ones that we used throughout this book project a delicate femininity that's perfect for Victorian or all-white design themes.

RESIN

Solid ornaments of resin are substantially more durable than lightweight hollow plastic and delicate glass baubles. They are produced by pouring resin into carved molds and are then painted and glazed.

METAL

Silver, gold, copper, brass, and tin are all used in ornament design. Metal ornaments range from whimsical miniature tin sculptures, to flat metal-beaded shapes, to exquisitely crafted upscale sterling-silver or gold sculptural pieces.

WOOD

Carved wooden pieces lean toward the whimsical side of the ornament spectrum. Whether plain, lacquered, or painted, wooden ornaments look best on country- and children's-themed trees.

PLASTIC

With innovations in manufacturing, some plastic ornaments now look as expensive and pretty as glass ones. Their advantages are lower price, lighter weight, and durability.

FABRIC

Fabric ornaments are lightweight and durable. Handcrafted dolls, toy-inspired characters, and felt decorations are appropriate for retro or children's trees, while elegant Styrofoam balls covered in fabric and decorated with piping, ribbon, and beads complement upscale trees, whether Victorian, Traditional, or Jewel-Tone.

FOOD

Home-baked cookies, store-bought candies, and even citrus peels crafted into figurines lend a warm, homey feeling to your tree. Your food ornaments can be reused from year to year—simply store them in an airtight container.

PAPER

Photographs and drawings, origami shapes, and cutout snowflakes are perennial favorites. Pictures of family and friends make great party conversation pieces. Keep paper ornaments away from larger bulbs.

GALLERY OF OTHER MATERIALS

Note: see pages 187–89 for supplier information.

PORCELAIN
1 White porcelain pointed drop with raised white pattern
2 White porcelain ball with white raised poinsettia and holly

RESIN
3 Vintage sleigh with girl in red
4 Brightly colored hot-air balloon
5 Antique toy spinner with Santa in center
6 Gold leaf on gold resin harp
7 Beaded circle with quatrefoil design in the center
8 Pie-shaped potpourri-holder ornament

METAL
9 Flat, hand-beaded, decorative pewter Christmas tree
10 Distressed-tin antique toy boat
11 Red tin heart with arrow and flame
12 Art-deco sterling-silver reindeer

WOOD
13 Ribbon-wrapped straw wreath with wooden bears
14 Felt-covered Styrofoam snowman with wood-stick arms

PLASTIC
15 Purple, shatterproof, glittery pears with stems and leaves
16 Acrylic, pastel-blue snowflake
17 Lightly frosted red-berry ball with cord hanger
18 Acrylic gold crown with ruby-red-beaded drop
19 Retro kitchen appliances: iron, fan, mixer, and toaster
20 Handbeaded Mexican heart
21 Plastic red-and-gold eight-pointed star
22 Shatterproof clip-on butterfly in shades of blue
23 Acrylic red pomegranate with red crystal seeds

FABRIC
24 Gold ball with pearl-and-sequin pins and red tassel
25 Black-and-leopard ball with pearl beading and bow
26 Beige fabric ball with gold piping in Medieval pattern
27 Red brocade ball with white fur trim
28 Chartreuse felt bag with red stitching and candy-cane appliqué
29 Wood nutcracker head and torso with tassel bottom

FOOD
30 Homemade gingerbread man with icing accents
31 Red-and-white-striped candy canes
32 Orange-peel-and-rope angel with wood-ball head

PAPER
33 Paper cocktail umbrellas, shown with glass pineapple
34 Paper-fabric gold and silver leaves on inverted teardrop
35 Beige-and-cream cardboard stars with textured paint

COLLECTIBLE ORNAMENTS

ONCE PURCHASED, A COLLECTIBLE ornament continues to increase in value every year, due to limited supply, attrition due to breakage, and the frailty of ornaments in general—making the collectible-ornament business a booming industry. Ornaments in many different media have found favor with collectors. Government mints have issued gold-plated 3-D filigree pieces, retail chains release continuing series from year to year, and individual manufacturers produce ornaments in porcelain, metal, wood, resin, and of course blown and molded glass.

LIMITLESS APPEAL

There seem to be collectibles that appeal to just about everyone. Whether you are a lover of glass balls, tin trains, cut and etched crystal, carved wood, or lit and animated ornaments, there's something somewhere for you. The Internet has made access to small companies easier, and fine craftspeople capable of limited production have found a larger audience than in the past because of improved online searching and purchasing technologies.

So how do you know what is collectible? Simply put, the most important way to start a collection is by collecting ornaments that you like, without worrying about investment potential. Collecting pieces you don't like and have no interest in, simply to wait for them to appreciate in value, is no fun. Instead, look for a style, shape, or theme that you feel a real fondness for. That way you'll not only build a strong, solid collection; you'll also enjoy each and every piece along the way.

There are a few criteria that will affect collectibility: Limited editions, where a finite quantity of pieces is produced, are more valuable; the edition number should be marked on the ornament or on an accompanying certificate of authenticity. If a piece is retired from a collection and you already own it, it becomes instantly more collectible. A craftsperson's signature on an ornament provides additional value.

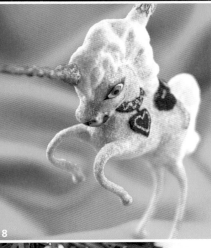

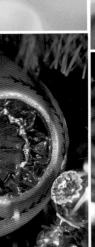

COLLECTIBLES GALLERY

Note: see pages 187–89 for vendor information.

1 This glass "Flower Power" van by Department 56 was a hit with lovers of automobiles from the 1970s.

2 Egyptian glass by De Elena is tinted, decoratively cut, and accented with fine gold paint.

3 An exquisite Swarovski crystal by J.P. Brown reflects the light beautifully. Accompanying crystal and metal hangers add to the upscale quality.

4 This collector-series piece from Ornaments to Remember is numbered and depicts the erupting Kilauea volcano.

5 Joy to the World, creator of this "Big Apple," donates a portion of the profits from each ornament to a charity, and each piece is championed by a celebrity spokesperson.

6 This retired piece by Polonaise was popular due its unique construction. Each glass wing was carefully attached to the dragonfly's body.

7 Series ornaments like these "12 Days of Christmas" glass balls by Abigail's Collections make a great tree theme.

8 The creator of this line, Larry Fraga Designs, is known for the whimsy of his pieces. Also, glitter plays a large part in the decorative process.

9 Each piece by Mary Margaret Cannon's Sacred Season has a spiritual significance, and some have been limited and numbered.

10 This gold reflector ball by Christopher Radko is a hand-painted reproduction of a classic Polish design.

11 Small sterling-silver ornaments, like this reindeer from Hand & Hammer Silversmiths, can also serve as jewelry or gift-box adornments.

12 This pink quilted tree by Joy to the World is dedicated to Breast Cancer Awareness.

13 This medallion by Austrian Christmas Tree, inspired by a couture-clothing designer, was chosen to grace the cover of a Barbra Streisand Christmas CD.

14 Mattarusky artist Matt Litavasky first carved this snowman ornament out of clay. It was then made into a mold, and the final piece was handpainted and glittered.

15 Each of these blown-glass wonders by Ne'Qwa is painted on the inside through the tiny opening on top.

16 A translucent piece of art by Mark Klaus; his work is highly valued for the attention to detail and intricate design of each ornament mold.

FINISHING TOUCHES

YOU CAN COMPLETE YOUR TREE by dressing it with decorative branch-tip accessories (called "picks") and glass or tinsel icicles. Picks are decorations attached to pointy stems that you simply stick into tree branches. They make colorful and textural space-fillers. Glass icicles are replicas of ice formations that hang like ornaments. In medieval times, tinsel icicles were made of hammered silver strips and draped individually onto greens; now they are made of aluminum paper. Icicles add sparkle and vertical elements to your design.

PICK & ICICLE STYLES

Icicles—both the tinsel and glass types—were a Christmas staple in the 1950s, but it seems to us that people are not quite sure what to do with picks, so here are some tips for both. Picks come in a wide variety of styles, shapes, and colors, and can be made of glass, metal, or plastic, or found in nature. Both artificial and natural shapes include everything from berries, flowers, and pinecones to birds and feathers. There are two attachment methods, depending on the pick: inserting directly, and wiring. Picks with long stems usually stay in place. Heavy picks with short stems may need to be attached with floral wire. Our unique method for attaching icicles and tinsel is demonstrated on the next page.

Inserting picks

The key to natural-looking picks is in their shaping and placement. Place picks near branch tips, on every second or third branch. Use enough picks to make an impact.

▶ **Correct placement** Insert the pick point about eight inches back on the branch, and bend it around the branch or wrap a green around the pick stem. Reshape if needed; the berries and branches should be spread out, not crushed.

NATURAL-LOOKING PICKS

Things found in nature usually look best when placed naturally—Mother Nature knows best. Place flowers in your tree so that they appear to be facing the sun, and carefully shape flower petals so they appear natural. Birds should not be hung upside down! Spend time attaching each bird securely, because the wires on their feet are prone to slide. Shape the bird's feet before wiring, so it looks like the bird is perched on a branch.

▶ **Picks alone** Bunches of artificial cherries placed in a small tabletop tree create a simple, clean design.

Wiring picks

You can make your own picks by wiring a wide variety of items. Fruits and pinecones can be attached to trees, wreaths, or garlands. Avoid using fresh fruits in very warm climates, or if you have children or pets.

WIRING PINECONES

1 Attach floral wire to the pinecone by wrapping it tightly around its wider end and twisting to secure.

2 Wire the pinecone about three to four inches from the branch tip of your tree, wreath, or garland.

WIRING FRUIT

1 Take a strong piece of floral wire and push it all the way through whatever fruit you choose to use.

2 If hanging the fruit, twist the wire above the top of the fruit. If placing it in a branch, twist at the bottom.

Glass & tinsel icicles

Icicles add long, lean lines that are nice contrasts to round ornaments and give the eye "jumping-off" points when viewing the tree's design.

GLASS ICICLES

1 Loop the icicle's string or plastic loop around a green. Then wrap several times around the green so the icicle, not the string, is featured.

2 After wrapping the string, you may need to move a green or two to allow the icicle to hang straight.

TINSEL ICICLES

▲ **Tinsel icicles** Use tinsel sparingly for a clean look. Don't throw clumps of them onto your tree. Separate the strands and place a few at a time on branches to give your tree a nice shimmery quality. You should be able to see your tree through the tinsel.

TOXIC TINSEL

Keep cats, dogs, and babies away from aluminum tinsel. It can be toxic if ingested.

FINISHING TOUCHES GALLERY

Note: see pages 187–89 for vendor information.

ARTIFICIAL PICKS

1 Silk, long-stemmed, pale gold poinsettia

2 Lightly snow-frosted plastic berries, leaves, and pinecones

3 Plastic, clear-frosted, red-berry bunch

4 Plastic bunch of gold pears and white berries with green-fabric leaves

5 Plastic bunch of gold pinecones, colored berries, and leaves

6 Molded-glass sunflowers with long, delicate stems

7 Plastic, gold-glittered quill feather with bendable wire center

NATURAL PICKS

8 Tip of a jewel-toned peacock feather

9 Pastel pink roses and lilac waxflowers

10 Flowering-kale and orange half

11 Fresh green apple pick

ICICLES

12 Molded-glass spiral-shaped icicle and purple transparent-glass icicle

TREETOPS

TREETOPS, LIKE TREE SKIRTS, help to balance your Christmas tree. The treetop is the crowning touch, but it should make a statement without overpowering your tree. If you have "themed" your tree, you should use one of the theme elements on top. Traditionalists simply place their electric angel at the top of the tree, plug her in, and are done. Crafty people might whip something together using ribbon, fabric, feathers, picks, and whatever else they have lying around. The rest of us go to the store and hunt. Luckily, you can find many things to put on top of your tree.

▲ Tree tops can be used anywhere on a tree. This beaded star is featured as a statement piece near the treetop.

TREETOP STYLES

Electrical decorations include angels, stars, and any other small pieces that would match the style of your tree. Make sure to hide the cord so the focus is the treetop, not a tangle of wire. Nonelectrical decorations include bows, picks, sprays, angels, dolls, toys, feathers, garland, fabric, picture frames, tabletop decorations, glass spires, and live and artificial flowers. You can even create special looks by removing the treetop entirely and replacing it with one large specialty piece or prop.

Multiple-element themed top

Illustrate the story of your tree theme in one eye-catching display by creating a visually interesting treetop. Try combining several elements: surround an angel with bows, group an odd number of finials, or cluster several ornaments used in your tree. Here, we mixed a gnarly tree branch with a red-berry garland and three teddy bears for a cute country look.

▲ **Multibow treetop** Instead of using only one bow on your treetop, create a superbow to add drama and form to your treetop. Attach two or three medium-sized bows around the top row of branches on your treetop, and then shape them to create the illusion of one bow. Let the tiptop green stand out above the bows.

1 Stick a bare branch into the tree. Make sure it's deep enough so that its weight is supported. Then use several pieces of floral wire to attach the branch.

2 Add berry picks or garlands to the branch. They provide bright contrasting color and match the colors in the bears' outfits.

3 Finally, position the bears along the branches. These colors and decorations should be carried down into the rest of the tree design.

Electrical treetops

Many electrical tabletop decorations make fine treetops alone or combined with other items.

1 Plug in your lit piece or pieces, hide the cords within the tree, and position into place. These lampposts were secured using the tree's greens.

2 To add a large piece such as this doll, you may have to flatten a few branches first. Then attach the doll in two places with floral wire so it will stay in place.

SIZE MATTERS

If you have a very tall or full tree, use a large treetop. Thinner, slighter trees can make do with smaller treetops. Don't use anything too heavy at the top, or your tree will look unbalanced. Whatever you choose to use, you should use floral wire to help secure the treetop to avoid any mishaps.

TREETOP GALLERY

Note: see pages 187–89 for vendor information.

1 A bouquet of fruits, berries, and sprigs of rosemary burst forth from the treetop, accented with pine-cones of various sizes.

2 Angels have been treasured treetops since Victorian times. Here, three angels surround a silver starburst.

3 Using several glass-spire treetops clustered at the top of the tree makes a much more interesting design than a single spire placed alone on the top green.

4 Cover the entire treetop with wide loops of wired ribbon. Make sure the loops are twisted around to ensure there are no large gaps in the design.

5 For a spectacular headdress to cap off a tree inspired by Mae West, we placed large, fluffy ostrich feathers in red, white, and black into the treetop.

6 This large, lit treetop star was used on the front of the tree near the very top, but not attached to the topmost green. Display heavy pieces slightly lower than the top of the tree to avoid top-heaviness.

7 Electric ribbon, which is actually a light set enclosed in clear ribbon made from PVC and tinted in bright colors, can be tied into a bow and used alone as a lit treetop.

8 Three different treetop stars were attached in a vertical line, and a wired ribbon bow was attached behind them to serve as a decorative background.

9 This collectible doll was used in place of the green treetop. The dress holds her in place, and at its base we placed ribbon rolled into tight loops to create the illusion of a ruffled crinoline.

10 We draped the neck of this mannequin head in fabric to create the top of a dress and then used a pearl garland as an elegant necklace. We placed glittering stars around her head at different levels to complete the fashion statement.

TREE SKIRTS

THERE ARE MANY VARIETIES of tree skirt on the market, from traditional 1950s felt cutouts, to waterproof plastic rounds, to elegant and upscale satins, silks, and brocades.

You should place something around the bottom of your tree for several reasons. The most practical reason is to hide your tree stand. From a fashion standpoint, the tree skirt "grounds" your Christmas tree. It finishes off the look of the tree the way accessories in fashion complement an outfit. It also balances your tree. Most trees are so covered in decorations that they can look top-heavy without a skirt. Finally, if your carpet or flooring is not of a complementary color to your tree, the fabric between it and the tree serves as a color buffer zone and blends everything together. Remember—your tree's not fully dressed without a skirt.

▲ **Decorative motifs** Patterned tree skirts can help continue your design theme to the tree's base. Here, the snowy theme was boldy emblazoned on the skirt with festive snowflakes that brighten up the shadowy areas under the tree.

◀ **Good coverage** Make sure that your tree skirt is wide enough to extend beyond the longest lower branches, so that it can be seen. Otherwise, by the time you finish decorating your tree and adding houses, nativities, a train, and packages, the skirt will be completely covered.

▲ **Choosing colors** Tree skirts should contain one or more of the colors used on your tree, or complement the tree's colors by providing a nice contrast. The skirt should not overpower the tree: here, the vivid jewel-toned ornaments are able to stand up to the fuchsia skirt, which would be too overwhelmingly bright for softer-toned themes. Generally, avoid dark-colored fabrics, since the tree casts a shadow.

SKIRTS FOR LIVE TREES

Live tree trunks have larger diameters than the metal poles of artificial trees, so make sure the tree-skirt opening is large enough. Keep the skirt out of the tree stand to avoid water damage (or use a water-resistant fabric). Launder your skirt before storage.

Fabric tree skirts

Fabric may be substituted for tree skirts. Whether or not you use fabric on the tree, you can buy several yards of fabric and loosely pool it under the tree. Nonstiff fabrics like satins and moirés work best. If you launder and press the fabric annually, it will look fresh every Christmas.

FABRIC AMOUNT

Use about 7 to 9 yards of fabric for a standard 7½-foot tree; when pooled on the floor, the fabric should extend beyond the longest branches.

1 Lay the fabric in a circle around the tree. Starting at the back, lift a piece of fabric and hang it over a bent green on a low branch. Choose a green halfway between the branch tip and trunk.

2 Continue this technique on every few branches until you go all the way around the tree, as seen on the finished tree above. Finish the look by loosely tucking the edges under, creating a soft, round appearance. For live trees, you should leave an opening in the back of the tree for watering.

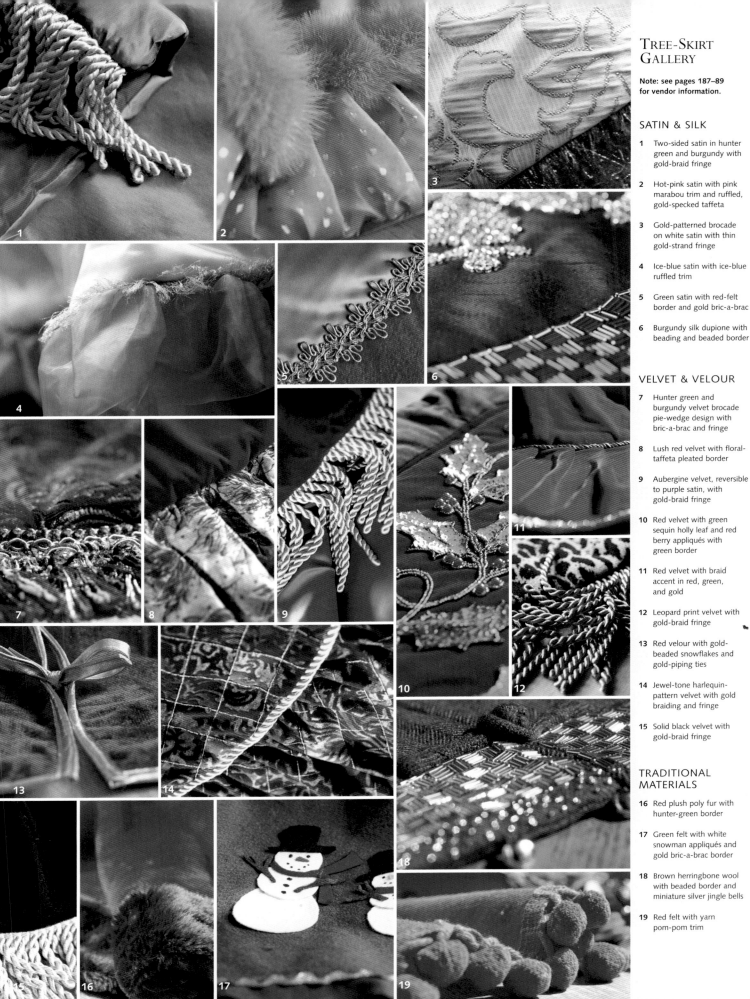

TREE-SKIRT GALLERY

Note: see pages 187–89 for vendor information.

SATIN & SILK

1 Two-sided satin in hunter green and burgundy with gold-braid fringe

2 Hot-pink satin with pink marabou trim and ruffled, gold-specked taffeta

3 Gold-patterned brocade on white satin with thin gold-strand fringe

4 Ice-blue satin with ice-blue ruffled trim

5 Green satin with red-felt border and gold bric-a-brac

6 Burgundy silk dupione with beading and beaded border

VELVET & VELOUR

7 Hunter green and burgundy velvet brocade pie-wedge design with bric-a-brac and fringe

8 Lush red velvet with floral-taffeta pleated border

9 Aubergine velvet, reversible to purple satin, with gold-braid fringe

10 Red velvet with green sequin holly leaf and red berry appliqués with green border

11 Red velvet with braid accent in red, green, and gold

12 Leopard print velvet with gold-braid fringe

13 Red velour with gold-beaded snowflakes and gold-piping ties

14 Jewel-tone harlequin-pattern velvet with gold braiding and fringe

15 Solid black velvet with gold-braid fringe

TRADITIONAL MATERIALS

16 Red plush poly fur with hunter-green border

17 Green felt with white snowman appliqués and gold bric-a-brac border

18 Brown herringbone wool with beaded border and miniature silver jingle bells

19 Red felt with yarn pom-pom trim

TAKE-DOWN & STORAGE

"Striking the set"—also known as putting away the decorations—should be a breeze if you've prepared everything in advance. First, get out the trash bags, storage boxes, and/or totes. The way to "undecorate" is in reverse order of how you decorated. Strip your tree in this order: tree skirts, icicles, bows, beads and garlands, picks, ornaments, ribbon and fabric, statement pieces, treetops, and lastly, lights (for live trees and specialty light sets only). Ideally, you should store all Christmas items in a cool, dry place. Attic storage is the reason so many heirloom ornaments fade and mildew. Extremes in heat and humidity will damage every type of decoration.

▲ A laundered, neatly folded tree skirt

TREE SKIRT
The skirt is the last item placed on (or actually under) your tree, and it should be the first item removed, so you won't step on it, soil it, or tear it. A skirt under a live tree can get damaged by water or sap: launder or dry clean it before packing it away for the year, so stains will not set permanently. Store your tree skirts in a cool, dry place, or try vacuum-sealed storage bags.

ICICLES
Tinsel icicles look best if they are fresh—you can try to pack them away carefully, but they crinkle easily, so it is best to buy new packs every year. Besides, they're inexpensive

and readily available. Plastic icicles don't need special care, but glass ones should be rolled in tissue paper before storage.

BOWS
Bows need special attention to look fresh for multiple-year use. Take single sheets of white tissue paper and gently crumple each sheet into a ball. Avoid using tinted tissue, which may bleed when damp. Remove bows from your tree one at a time. Insert a paper ball into each loop. Then place the bows gently into either storage boxes or large trash bags.

Bow boxes should be kept on top of all other decorations, since they are the lightest and most fragile items. You can hang

▲ Tissues balls inserted into bow loops

bags in storage areas (attics, crawl spaces, garages, or lofts) on walls, from nails or hooks, or on racks. This can be a great space-saver. High temperatures damage fabric, so avoid attic storage in hot climates.

BEADS & GARLAND
Beads also need special care. Glass beads crush easily, and strands can tangle and become next year's nightmare. Carefully remove bead strands from the tree. Ideal storage is in the original manufacturer's box. Otherwise, wrap beads around a piece of cardboard or a plastic lighting-storage rack. Another inexpensive option is to wrap each bead strand

▼ Garland in its original cardboard box

around a paper-towel tube. This is not as effective for preventing tangling, but it's definitely better than piling all of your beads into one huge lump. Once they're wrapped, place the beads in a storage box.

We do not suggest plastic bags for bead storage, as the beads may be painted with a food-based paint, like many ornaments. If they are exposed to any humidity, the paint may bubble and peel off. Store light metallic garlands on top of other decorations. Artificial branch garlands should be loosely coiled and stored separately in cardboard boxes.

PICKS
Most picks don't require special attention. They shouldn't be placed at the bottom of a box of heavy decorations, but piling them into the corner of a storage box usually keeps them fresh-looking. If the picks are long and look like they might tangle, wrap them in paper towels. Glass picks should be packed carefully in tissue, like ornaments. Live fruit or flower picks should be thrown away, unless you want to dry them.

TAKE-DOWN & STORAGE

ORNAMENTS

Ornaments need the greatest care. They're your most valuable Christmas items and should be well protected. Remove metal ornament hooks before storing ornaments to avoid scratching. Newer plastic hooks are safer and can be left on, which will save you time next year.

▲ Protective ornament storage box

The safest storage is in boxes or tubs made specifically for ornaments. They usually come with cardboard inserts and keep ornaments individually protected. Even though some totes are made of plastic, they are still safe for long-term storage. The cardboard inserts absorb moisture in the air, and they aren't tightly sealed, which allows the ornaments to breathe, so they won't mildew.

If you live in an earthquake-prone area or will be moving the totes often, try using crushed white tissue paper under each ornament to provide an additional layer of protection.

If your space or budget is limited, wrap each ornament in plain paper, then carefully place them all in big cardboard boxes.

We use plain paper so that colors don't transfer. (Never use plastic or waxed paper. They both retain moisture and are harmful to all Christmas items.) This is also a safe way to care for less fragile ornaments, but even paper, clay, resin, Styrofoam, and plastic can crack under pressure.

Want to make your life easier? Use brightly colored permanent magic markers (red is a festive and appropriate color) to identify what you've packed. Write the word "Fragile" as well as a list of the contents on all of your Christmas-storage boxes, not just the ornament boxes; it will save you from having to keep opening the boxes throughout the year because you're wondering what's inside. And write this on all sides of the boxes, so that no matter how the box is stacked, you will be able to read the labels. Of course, those of you who are computer-savvy can always print up a stack of "Fragile: Christmas (fill in the blank)" signs, and tape them to every box.

RIBBON & FABRIC

Ribbon should be removed piece-by-piece and rerolled. Reroll the ribbon onto its original cardboard spool to keep it fresh from year to year. Start by attaching the end of the ribbon to the spool with cellophane tape. If it is "slippery" or doesn't stay rolled, secure each roll with a straight pin, a rubber band, or even baggie ties. However, don't roll it too tightly or it will crinkle. Fabric should also be removed at the same time. Launder it before storing.

STATEMENT PIECES & TREETOPS

To protect statement pieces and treetop decorations, try to store similar items together. Use several smaller boxes rather than one large one, to prevent pieces from being crushed or broken in the box. Layer the bottom of each box with lightly crushed balls of tissue paper—they will act as shock absorbers if the box gets jostled or dropped.

▼ Ribbon rerolled onto a spool

Gently wrap the head in tissue. If the hair is fibrous, take extra care so it won't get mussed in storage.

Wrap angels' hands in tissue to avoid chipping or peeling.

▲ A fragile angel

If you used wire to attach your pieces, remove it now so nothing will be scratched; fishing line is safe and can be left in place. Pictures and frames should be wrapped in layers of tissue or separated with sturdy corrugated cardboard, stood on end, and placed against one of the sides of the box. Wrap the hands and heads of dolls and angels in white tissue paper to prevent damage. Fragile angels should be the last items packed in the box.

Carefully wrap the electrical cords of any lit or animated piece. Collectibles like ceramic houses should definitely be packed back into their original boxes, not just for protection but also because keeping the original box adds to the value of the collectible.

LIGHTS

Lights need to be removed from live trees. To make it easier, plug them in and work in the reverse order of the way you added them to the tree.

Starting at the top, begin to pull lights off from the end that is not plugged in. Remove one string at a time, unplugging when you get to the plug end of each set of lights.

There are several simple and inexpensive storage techniques for lights that will prevent cord tangling. The easiest is self-wrapping in a ball, oblong, or cylinder. For the ball method, start at the end without the plug. Wrap the lights around your fingers a few times. Then continue to wrap the lights into a ball shape. When you reach the plug, tuck it under a wire and place the ball gently into a storage box.

The oblong method is similar; instead of making a ball, fold the lights to create a bunch with bulbs at each end (shown below, at right) and wrap them with their own cord. This is a great method for large bulbs like C-7s.

▼ Cylinder (below), ball (below left), and oblong (below right) light-storing methods

▲ Light spools in a storage bag

For the cylinder method, wrap the lights around an old paint roller or empty cardboard paper-towel tube. You can wrap lights around a flat piece of cardboard as well.

There are also a number of lightweight and inexpensive plastic frames on the market that make wrapping and storing lights quite easy, and they hold many light sets. You can wrap them as fully as you like: the idea is just to keep the cords from tangling.

For optimum storage, try storing your lights in plastic spools that come with their own storage bag. Lights are easily wrapped, and they are protected in breathable, durable bags—they unspool just as easily when it comes time to decorate your tree the following season.

Whether they are used on artificial or live trees, you should also remove specialty light sets. Bubble lights, flicker flames, and novelty lights can all become damaged if stored on an artificial tree. Remove the sets and wrap them in tissue if necessary.

TREES

Trees are "struck," or taken down, last. If you have a live tree, drain the tree stand with a suction pump or turkey baster. Then dry the inside of the bowl with a paper towel or rag to prevent dripping. If you placed a tree bag under the tree, pull it up, tie it at the top, and remove the tree. If not, be prepared to vacuum a trail of needles to the front door.

If you own an artificial tree, store it in its original box to keep it safe and free from dust and bugs. Don't pile anything heavy on top, especially if the tree is prelit. If the box will be stood on end, ensure that the treetop is in the top part of the box. Carefully position tree stands so they won't break under the weight of the tree.

▲ Bungeed artificial tree in original box

A prelit tree may no longer fit into its original box. Don't cram it in; instead, wrap one of the pieces separately and place in a smaller box or a tree bag.

To prepare your prelit tree for storage, first unplug the lights. Remove the treetop and lightly flatten it. Use bungee cords to help you fit your tree back into its box. Start at the top and tightly bungee rows one at a time. Be careful— bungee cords can hurt you if they snap loose. After one entire section is tightly bungeed, place it gently in the box.

▲ Set-up and rolled wall half-tree

Repeat for each section. Place extension cords and power strips in the box so they will be handy next year. You can also use bungees to seal the box.

Wall half-trees and collapsible spiral trees are easy to store: simply roll up the first and flatten the latter, and place them in a box.

The ornaments and ribbons are preattached to the tree

▲ Partially and fully collapsed spiral tree

SUPPLIERS

PARTS I & II

HERE IS IS A LIST OF ITEMS SEEN IN THE ROOM SETTINGS IN PART 1, AND IN THE DAMES' SETS IN PART 2. REFER TO PAGES 188–189 FOR DETAILED SUPPLIER CONTACT INFORMATION.

6–17 Majestic Statement

AMERICAN RIBBONZ LTD: Wired ribbon • ARCADIA HOME: Bead and ornament garlands • BARTHELMESS USA: Tree • CHRISTOPHER RADKO, INC: Silver bell with leaf pattern • DE ELENA COLLECTIONS: Clear Egyptian glass with 18-carat gold • GKI/ BETHLEHEM LIGHTS: Lights • MY CHRISTMAS WISH: Tree skirt • ORNA MENTZ: Small balls with pinned beads • POTTERY BARN: Wire heart with red beads • THE RHYN-RIVÉT COLLECTION, INC: Porcelain drops with poinsettia designs

18–19 Stunning Spiral

ARCADIA HOME: Beige beaded-fabric ornaments and beaded-silver star treetop

20–21 Victorian Influence

BETHANY LOWE DESIGNS, INC: Paper cone • DEPARTMENT 56: Lit village • ORNA MENTZ: Balls with fabric and pinned pearls • THE RHYN-RIVÉT COLLECTION, INC: Porcelain drops

22–23 Regal Banquet

CHERRY DESIGNS, INC: Heart with flower design • CHRISTOPHER RADKO, INC: Tree ornament with pastel decorations • FITZ AND FLOYD: Santa pitcher • MY CHRISTMAS WISH: Fabric-covered ball with tassel • ORNA MENTZ: Balls with fabric and pinned pearls • THE RHYN-RIVÉT COLLECTION, INC: Porcelains

24–25 Victorian Innocence

CHRISTINA'S WORLD: Father Christmas, blown-glass balls • MY CHRISTMAS WISH: Red fabric balls with white-fur trim • NEW EXPRESSIONS: Dolls and red hats • ORNA MENTZ: Balls with fabric and pinned pearls • TANNENBAUM TREASURES: Lit carved wood pieces • WALNUT RIDGE: Angel

26–27 Angelic Tableau

BROOKDALE COLLECTION: Angel • CHRISTINA'S WORLD: Mouth-blown-glass balls • MY CHRISTMAS WISH: Fabric covered balls with tassels and tree skirt • ORNA MENTZ: Balls with fabric and pinned pearls

30–31 Combined Traditions

J.P. BROWN: Bavarian and Swarovski crystal ornaments • THE RHYN-RIVÉT COLLECTION, INC: Porcelain drops

32–33 Elegant Ice

MY CHRISTMAS WISH: White ball with silver piping and tassel • THE RHYN-RIVÉT COLLECTION, INC: Porcelain drops

34–35 Christmas

BROOKDALE COLLECTION: Angels • MY CHRISTMAS WISH: Purple-velvet balls • ORNA MENTZ: Balls with fabric and pinned pearls • POLONAISE COLLECTION: Gold cross and trumpeting angel • SACRED SEASON: Handpainted mouth-blown-glass balls "Hosanna!" • VARSOVIA EASTERN EUROPE IMPORTS, INC: Camel, Magi ornament, and green swirly balls

36–37 Hanukkah

BARTHELMESS USA: Clear-and-blue shatterproof balls • DE ELENA COLLECTIONS: Blue-and-purple Egyptian glass with 18-carat gold • DEPARTMENT 56: Lit synagogue • EURO VUE: Blue Star of David • GROOVY HOLIDAYS: Felt bags • MITZVAHLAND: Crystal dreidel • SACRED SEASON: Handpainted blown-glass balls and eggs, and Star of Peace (charity) • TANNENBAUM TREASURES: Hanging eggs • WAXBERRY: Oil candles

38–39 Kwanzaa

ORNAMENTALS, INC: Handpainted blown-glass balls • TANNENBAUM TREASURES: Glass vegetables • ZAMBEZI BAZAAR: Kwanzaa items

42–43 Golden Opulence

BARTHELMESS USA: White tree and garlands • MY CHRISTMAS WISH: Fabric ornaments, sleigh, and tree skirts • ORNAMENTALS, INC: Hand-painted blown glass balls • ORNA MENTZ: Balls with fabric and pinned pearls • SACRED SEASON: Handpainted mouth-blown glass balls, white with gold "Hosanna!" • TANNENBAUM TREASURES: White angel with fur collar ornament •

VARSOVIA EASTERN EUROPE IMPORTS, INC: Long gold-and-silver ornaments and gold lion

44–45 Decadent Design

EURO VUE: Red heart • J.P. BROWN: Clear Bavarian and Swarovski crystal ornaments and pearl garlands • THE MICHAEL WEEMS COLLECTION, LLC: Etched glass candleholders • MY CHRISTMAS WISH: Velvet balls in black-and-leopard print and leopard sleigh • VARSOVIA EASTERN EUROPE IMPORTS, INC: Glass ornaments

46–47 Royal Velvet

AMERICAN RIBBONZ LTD: Wired ribbons • AUSTRIAN CHRISTMAS TREE: Clear glass balls with 18-carat gold • MY CHRISTMAS WISH: Velvet-covered balls with rope piping

48–49 Jewel-Tone Glamour

THE MICHAEL WEEMS COLLECTION, LLC: Etched martini glasses • VARSOVIA EASTERN EUROPE IMPORTS, INC: Glass ornaments

50–51 Crown Jewel

GOLDEN MOR INTERNATIONAL, INC: Suede table garland • THE MICHAEL WEEMS COLLECTION, LLC: Etched mini cocktail glasses • MY CHRISTMAS WISH: Pink tree skirt • ORNAMENTALS, INC: Painted glass balls • VARSOVIA EASTERN EUROPE IMPORTS, INC: Jewel-tone colored-glass ornaments

52–53 Dining Fantasy

AUSTRIAN CHRISTMAS TREE: Designer-inspired medallions and various-shaped ornaments • CHERRY DESIGNS, INC: Feather trees • DE ELENA COLLECTIONS: Tinted Egyptian glass with 18-carat gold • GOLDEN MOR INTERNATIONAL, INC: Jewel-tone candelabras • MY CHRISTMAS WISH: Gold silverware cozies and velvet-covered balls with rope piping • TANNENBAUM TREASURES: Eggs, glass-bead garlands

54–55 A Feast of Colors

AUSTRIAN CHRISTMAS TREE: Designer-inspired handpainted-glass medallions, hearts, and balls • CHERRY DESIGNS, INC: Feather

trees • CHRISTOPHER RADKO, INC: Gold finial holder • DE ELENA COLLECTIONS: Tinted Egyptian-glass with 18-carat gold • THE MICHAEL WEEMS COLLECTION, LLC: Etched glasses and red glass candles • MY CHRISTMAS WISH: Gold silverware cozies • TANNENBAUM TREASURES: Finial

58–59 Country Warmth

BETHANY LOWE DESIGNS, INC: Beige paper stars • BOARDWALK STUDIOS: Wood Santa and snowmen • CHERRY DESIGNS, INC: Glass cookies, candies, gingerbread men, and Santa • CHRISTIAN ULBRICHT: Nutcracker • GKI/BETHLEHEM LIGHTS: Lit holly bush • GROOVY HOLIDAYS: Decorative felt bags • INSPIRIO: Stuffed bears • MY CHRISTMAS WISH: Felt stockings • ORNAMENTALS, INC: Painted glass balls

60–61 Country Craftsmanship

BETHANY LOWE DESIGNS, INC: Standing snowman and beige-paper stars • CHERRY DESIGNS, INC: Glass candies, donuts, frosted cookies, gingerbread men, red reindeer, and white heart • GROOVY HOLIDAYS: Felt ornaments • MY CHRISTMAS WISH: Red felt stocking • ORNAMENTALS, INC: Painted glass balls • SACRED SEASON: Pears on red egg • TANNENBAUM TREASURES: Candle on a clip and pickle

62–63 European Country Buffet

BETHANY LOWE DESIGNS, INC: Wood Santa and seesaw • CHERRY DESIGNS, INC: Glass candy-and-cookie ornaments and gingerbread men • CHRISTIAN ULBRICHT: Nutcrackers • PARTYLITE: Gingerbread house with votive candle • PEGGY KARR GLASS: Dishes • SACRED SEASON: White egg with "The Holly and the Ivy" • TANNENBAUM TREASURES: Glass vegetables and wood pyramid

64–65 Holiday Hearth

AUSTRIAN CHRISTMAS TREE: Painted glass bell with 18-carat gold • BETHANY LOWE DESIGNS, INC: Moon and Santa decorations • CHERRY DESIGNS, INC: glass frosted leaves and stick candies •

120–21 Rita Hayworth
HISTORY FOR HIRE: Oversized prop heads • ORNAMENTS TO REMEMBER: Gold-wire-wrapped turquoise and fuchsia hearts • VARSOVIA EASTERN EUROPE IMPORTS, INC: Glass rainbow balls and miniature guitars

122–23 Mae West
HOLLYWOOD HISTORY MUSEUM: Mae's costumes and jewelry • VARSOVIA EASTERN EUROPE IMPORTS, INC: Silver-glass ornaments

124–25 Gloria Swanson
AMERICAN RIBBONZ LTD: Faux-fur ribbon • HISTORY FOR HIRE: Vintage camera • J.P. BROWN: Bavarian and Swarovski crystal ornaments and pearl garlands • MY CHRISTMAS WISH: Fabric balls, sleigh, and tree skirt • ORNAMENTS TO REMEMBER: Leopard dress glass ornament • VARSOVIA EASTERN EUROPE IMPORTS, INC: Large gold-and-silver glass ornaments

126–27 Cher
AUSTRIAN CHRISTMAS TREE: Hearts and medallions and • CHRISTINA'S WORLD: Feathered balls • GKI/BETHLEHEM LIGHTS: Round novelty-light sets • VARSOVIA EASTERN EUROPE IMPORTS, INC: Cher's headdress and jewel-tone ornaments

PART III
THIS IS A LIST OF ITEMS SEEN IN PART 3. THE VENDORS IN THE NUMBERED LISTS ARE KEYED TO THE NUMBERED LISTS IN THE GALLERIES ON PAGES 144–81. REFER TO PAGES 188–89 FOR DETAILED SUPPLIER CONTACT INFORMATION.

132 Tree Location
Artificial trees by BARTHELMESS USA

134–136; 138; 140–41 Artificial Tree Selection, Setup & Lighting
Artificial trees by BARTHELMESS USA; wall half-tree by KURT S. ADLER, INC.

144–45 Lighting
All lights by GKI/BETHLEHEM LIGHTS except for:
9 CHERRY DESIGNS, INC.
21 AMERICAN RIBBONZ LTD.
30 BARTHELMESS USA

146–47 Snow
Vintage mica snow by MICA SNOW; Styrofoam snow by DEPARTMENT 56

148–49 Statement Pieces
In demonstrations: moon by BETHANY LOWE DESIGNS, INC, house by DEPARTMENT 56

In Gallery:
1 DEPARTMENT 56
2 Authors' own
3 DONALD CLAY DESIGNS
4 DONALD CLAY DESIGNS
5 DR. CHRISTMAS RENTS
6 BETHANY LOWE DESIGNS, INC.
7 Authors' own
8 BETHANY LOWE DESIGNS, INC.
9 PEGGY KARR GLASS
10 BROOKDALE COLLECTION
11 TANNENBAUM TREASURES

150–59 Bows & Ribbons
All AMERICAN RIBBONZ LTD. except for 9 & 22 on p. 159, by ARCADIA HOME

166–67 Beads & Garlands
All authors' own except:
2 BARTHELMESS USA
11 ARCADIA HOME
12 BETHANY LOWE
13 CHRISTOPHER RADKO, INC.
14 TANNENBAUM TREASURES
16 TANNENBAUM TREASURES
17 CHRISTOPHER RADKO, INC.
18 CHRISTINA'S WORLD

168–69 Blown-Glass Ornaments
1 ORNAMENTALS, INC.
2 ORNAMENTALS, INC.
3 CHRISTINA'S WORLD
4 VARSOVIA EASTERN EUROPE IMPORTS, INC.
5 DE ELENA COLLECTIONS
6 DE ELENA COLLECTIONS
7 AUSTRIAN CHRISTMAS TREE
8 CHRISTINA'S WORLD
9 VARSOVIA EASTERN EUROPE IMPORTS, INC.
10 CHRISTINA'S WORLD
11 DE ELENA COLLECTIONS
12 SACRED SEASON
13 CHRISTINA'S WORLD
14 CHRISTINA'S WORLD
15 SACRED SEASON
16 CHRISTINA'S WORLD
17 DE ELENA COLLECTIONS
18 EURO VUE
19 ORNAMENTALS, INC.
20 CHRISTOPHER RADKO, INC.
21 AUSTRIAN CHRISTMAS TREE
22 CHRISTINA'S WORLD
23 CHRISTINA'S WORLD
24 PEGGY KARR GLASS
25 POTTERY BARN
26 Authors' own
27 A TOUCH OF GLASS

170–71 Molded-Glass Ornaments
1 ORNAMENTS TO REMEMBER
2 CHERRY DESIGNS, INC.
3 CHERRY DESIGNS, INC.
4 POLONAISE COLLECTION
5 POLONAISE COLLECTION
6 VARSOVIA EASTERN EUROPE IMPORTS, INC.

7 CHERRY DESIGNS, INC.
8 MATTARUSKY DESIGNS
9 VARSOVIA EASTERN EUROPE IMPORTS, INC.
10 ORNAMENTS TO REMEMBER
11 POLONAISE COLLECTION
12 ORNAMENTS TO REMEMBER
13 EURO VUE
14 AUSTRIAN CHRISTMAS TREE
15 TANNENBAUM TREASURES
16 VARSOVIA EASTERN EUROPE IMPORTS, INC.
17 CHERRY DESIGNS, INC.
18 EURO VUE
19 MATTARUSKY DESIGNS
20 VARSOVIA EASTERN EUROPE IMPORTS, INC.
21 CHRISTINA'S WORLD
22 CHERRY DESIGNS, INC.
23 CHERRY DESIGNS, INC.
24 CHRISTOPHER RADKO, INC.
25 POLONAISE COLLECTION
26 EURO VUE
27 ORNAMENTS TO REMEMBER
28 JOY TO THE WORLD
29 CHRISTOPHER RADKO, INC.
30 CHRISTOPHER RADKO, INC.
31 MATTARUSKY DESIGNS
32 POLONAISE COLLECTION
33 VARSOVIA EASTERN EUROPE IMPORTS, INC.
34 ORNAMENTS TO REMEMBER
35 EURO VUE
36 TANNENBAUM TREASURES
37 VARSOVIA EASTERN EUROPE IMPORTS, INC.

172–73 Gallery of Other Materials
1 THE RHYN-RIVÉT COLLECTION, INC.
2 THE RHYN-RIVÉT COLLECTION, INC.
3 BETHANY LOWE DESIGNS, INC.
4 HARBOUR LIGHTS
5 BETHANY LOWE DESIGNS, INC.
6 KURT S. ADLER, INC.
7 Authors' own
8 Authors' own
9 ARCADIA HOME
10 BETHANY LOWE DESIGNS, INC.
11 Authors' own
12 HAND & HAMMER SILVERSMITHS
13 KURT S. ADLER, INC.
14 KURT S. ADLER, INC.
15 BARTHELMESS USA
16 KMART
17 POTTERY BARN
18 Authors' own
19 KURT S. ADLER, INC.
20 Authors' own
21 Authors' own
22 BARTHELMESS USA
23 POTTERY BARN
24 ORNA MENTZ
25 MY CHRISTMAS WISH
26 Authors' own
27 MY CHRISTMAS WISH
28 GROOVY HOLIDAYS
29 PEKING HANDICRAFT, INC.
30 RICHARD ROCHA

31 Local grocery stores
32 Authors' own
33 Local party stores
34 Authors' own
35 BETHANY LOWE DESIGNS, INC.

174–75 Collectible Ornaments
1 DEPARTMENT 56
2 DE ELENA COLLECTIONS
3 J.P. BROWN
4 ORNAMENTS TO REMEMBER
5 JOY TO THE WORLD
6 POLONAISE COLLECTION
7 ABIGAIL'S COLLECTIONS
8 LARRY FRAGA DESIGNS
9 SACRED SEASON
10 CHRISTOPHER RADKO, INC.
11 HAND & HAMMER SILVERSMITHS
12 JOY TO THE WORLD
13 AUSTRIAN CHRISTMAS TREE
14 MATTARUSKY DESIGNS
15 NE'QWA ART
16 MARK KLAUS

176–77 Finishing Touches
1 KURT S. ADLER, INC.
2 KURT S. ADLER, INC.
3 KURT S. ADLER, INC.
4 KURT S. ADLER, INC.
5 KURT S. ADLER, INC.
6 TANNENBAUM TREASURES
7 Authors' own
8 Local craft stores
9 DONALD CLAY DESIGNS
10 DONALD CLAY DESIGNS
11 DONALD CLAY DESIGNS
12 Local holiday stores

178–79 Treetops
In demonstrations: Bears by INSPIRIO, lit treetops by DEPARTMENT 56, dolls by NEW EXPRESSIONS

In Gallery:
1 DONALD CLAY DESIGNS
2 BROOKDALE COLLECTION
3 KURT S. ADLER, INC.
4 AMERICAN RIBBONZ LTD.
5 HISTORY FOR HIRE
6 KURT S. ADLER, INC.
7 AMERICAN RIBBONZ LTD.
8 Wire star by POTTERY BARN, beaded stars by ARCADIA HOME
9 NEW EXPRESSIONS
10 HISTORY FOR HIRE

180–81 Tree Skirts
All by MY CHRISTMAS WISH, except 6 & 18, by ARCADIA HOME

182–84 Take-Down & Storage
KURT S. ADLER, INC: Potted tree • AMERICAN RIBBONZ LTD: Bow and ribbon • ARCADIA HOME: Tree skirt • BARTHELMESS USA: Boxed tree • BROOKDALE COLLECTION: Angel • CHRISTOPHER RADKO, INC: Boxed garland • GKI/BETHLEHEM LIGHTS: Lights

SUPPLIERS' ADDRESSES

ABIGAIL'S COLLECTIONS
c/o Tannenbaum Treasures
20 Research Parkway
Old Saybrook, CT 06475
T: 866-395-1801
F: 860-395-1802
email: jpfeffer01@snet.net
www.tannenbaumtreasures.com
**Ornaments: mouth-blown
glass; "12 Days of Christmas"
series balls**

ALEX THEATRE
216 North Brand Boulevard
Glendale,CA 91203
T: 818-243-2611
Landmark theater

AMERICAN RIBBONZ LTD.
2543 North Hancock
Philadelphia, PA 19133
T: 215-425-3273
F: 215-425-3481
email: yackma2@aol.com
**Ribbon: custom-designed,
wired ribbon**

ANGELA'S
Christopher Radko's
Starlight Store
2329 Michael Drive
Newbury Park, CA 91320
T: 800-617-2356
email: info@radko.net
www.radko.net
**Ornaments: blown glass,
Halloween; Table decorations**

ARCADIA HOME
New York, NY
T: 212-787-3282
F: 212-787-3281
info@arcadiahomeinc.com
www.arcadiahomeinc.com
**Ornaments: fabric; Ribbon
(beaded); Tree skirts and
runners (beaded)**

AUSTRIAN CHRISTMAS TREE
P.O. Box 5753
Manchester, NH 03104
T: 603-668-6377
F: 603-627-6783
austrianchristmas@comcast.net
www.austrianchristmastree.com
Ornaments: blown glass

BARTHELMESS USA
T: 800-227-2262
www.barthelmessusa.com
**Light covers; Shatterproof
ornaments; Trees: full-sized,
tabletop, "fashion firs,"
prelit, and unlit; Wreaths,
green garlands, and
"fashion garlands"**

BETHANY LOWE DESIGNS, INC.
16655 County Highway 16
Osco, IL 61274
T: 800-944-6213
F: 309-944-3205
www.bethanylowe.com
**Ornaments: paper, resin, tin,
and wood; Pillows; Table
decorations: vintage**

BOARDWALK STUDIOS
P. O. Box 358
Bristol, IN 46507
T: 574-848-4183
F: 574-848-7579
**Wooden decorations; Full-size
snowman and Santa plaques**

BROOKDALE COLLECTION
brookdale@enter.net
www.brookdalecollection.com
Angels

CHERRY DESIGNS, INC.
12319 F. M. 1960 East
Huffman, TX 77336
T: 800-918-9140
F: 281-324-2399
cherry@cherrydesignsinc.com
www.cherrydesignsinc.com
**Ornaments: molded glass,
Halloween-themed; Trees:
multicolored feather trees**

CHRISTINA'S WORLD
27 Woodcreek Ct.
Deer Park, NY 11729
T: 631-242-9664
F: 631-586-1918
www.christinasworld.com
Ornaments: blown glass

CHRISTIAN ULBRICHT
www.ulbricht.com
Nutcrackers

CHRISTOPHER RADKO, INC.
see ANGELA'S

DÉCOR DIMENSIONS
105 Skegby Rd.
Brampton, ON
L6V 2T8 Canada
T: 905-455-5904
**Ornament hooks: adjustable,
spiral hooks**

DE ELENA COLLECTIONS
P. O. Box 4239
Irvine, CA 92616
T: 949-786-3231
Ornaments: Egyptian glass

DEPARTMENT 56
T: 800-548-8696
www.d56.com
**Lit buildings: seasonal
accessories and collectibles;
Snow effects: artificial snow**

DONALD CLAY DESIGNS
P. O. Box 1391
Running Springs, CA 92382
T: 818-642-1523
Floral design

DR. CHRISTMAS RENTS, INC.
1209 West Isabel Street
Burbank, CA 91506
T: 818-840-0445
F: 818-848-5923
www.drchristmas.com
dr_Christmas@hotmail.com
Props

EURO VUE
2370 Rice Boulevard
Houston, TX 77005
T: 713-520-0224
www.europevillage.com
Ornaments: molded glass

GKI / BETHLEHEM LIGHTS
www.gkilights.com
Lights; Tree: rustic, snowy-style

**GOLDEN MOR
INTERNATIONAL, INC.**
T: 562-531-4800
F: 562-531-4848
www.goldenmor.com
**Table decorations: jeweled
candelabras**

GROOVY HOLIDAYS
T: 212-625-1301
F: 212-625-0146
www.groovychristmas.com
Fabric bags

HAND & HAMMER SILVERSMITHS
2610 Morse Lane
Woodbridge, VA 22192
T: 800-745-8379
www.hand-hammer.com
Ornaments: metals

HARBOUR LIGHTS
1000 North Johnson Avenue
El Cajon, CA 92020
T: 800-365-1219
www.harbourlights.com
Ornaments: hot-air balloons

HISTORY FOR HIRE
7149 Fair Avenue
North Hollywood, CA 91605
T: 818-765-7767
www.historyforhire.com
historyforhire@aol.com
Props

**HOLLYWOOD HISTORY MUSEUM
HISTORIC MAX FACTOR BUILDING**
1660 North Highland Avenue
Hollywood, CA 90028
T: 323-464-7776
www.hollywoodhistory
museum.org
Museum

INSPIRIO
5300 Patterson Avenue, S.E.
Grand Rapids, MI 49530
T: 866-231-8239
www.inspiriogifts.com
Teddy bears

JOY TO THE WORLD
T: 877-676-2636
jttwcoll@aol.com
www.joytotheworldonline.com
Ornaments: molded glass

J.P. BROWN
c/o Younger & Associates
1000 North Johnson Avenue
El Cajon, CA 92020
T: 800-365-1219
www.harbourlights.com
**Ornament hooks: decorative,
with crystals or pearls;
Ornaments: Bavarian &
Swarovski crystal**

JUST POTS
755 South Wall Street
2nd Floor
Los Angeles, CA 90014
T: 213-623-4344
theorchidman@hotmail.com
Floral containers: decorative florist pots

KURT S. ADLER, INC.
www.kurtadler.com
Ornaments: resin, tin, wood

LARRY FRAGA DESIGNS
140 Fulton Street
Fresno, CA 93721
T: 559-441-8000
larryfragadesign@aol.com
www.larryfragadesigns.com
Ornaments: blown and molded

MARK KLAUS
P.O. Box 470758
Broadview Heights, OH 44147
Clayman63@aol.com
Ornaments: resin

MATTARUSKY DESIGNS
Chicago, IL
T: 630-469-4125
F: 630-469-5017
mattarusky@msn.com
www.mattarusky.com
Ornaments: molded glass, Halloween

MEYDA TIFFANY
T: 800-222-4009
info@meyda.com
www.meyda.com
Lit sculptures

MICA SNOW
22921 Belquest Dr.
Lake Forest, CA 92630
T: 949-581-6422
F: 949-581-6442
cordie@micasnow.com
www.micasnow.com
Snow effects: vintage snow

THE MICHAEL WEEMS COLLECTION, LLC
1103 North Washington Street
1st Floor
Baltimore, MD 21213
T: 410-327-9500
F: 410-327-9600
www.michaelweems.com
Glassware: goblets, flutes, martinis, and hurricanes

MITZVAHLAND
16733 Ventura Boulevard
Encino, CA 91436
T: 818-705-7700
www.mitzvahland.com
Hanukkah: Judaica

MR. GREENTREES
310-276-9827
Live trees, wreaths, and garlands

MY CHRISTMAS WISH
Bartlett, TN
T: 901-373-2229
www.mychristmaswish.net
Ornaments: fabric; Tree skirts and runners

NE'QWA ART
545 N. Cowan, Bldg. J
Lewisville, TX 75057
T: 877-821-8635
F: 972-219-9850
custom@neqwa.com
www.neqwa.com
Ornaments: blown glass

NEW EXPRESSIONS
2004@yahoo.com
Dolls; Ornaments: red hats

ORNAMENTALS, INC.
Tuscaloosa, AL
T: 205-349-3915
ornament@dbtech.net
www.ornamentalsinc.com
Ornaments: blown glass and Halloween-themed

ORNAMENTS TO REMEMBER
T: 800-330-3382
info@ornaments2remember.com
www.ornamentstoremember.com
Ornaments: molded glass

ORNA MENTZ
308 Victoria Ave.
Wilmington, DE 19804
sales@ornamentz.com
www.christmasballs.com
Ornaments: fabric

PARTYLITE
c/o Valerie Hayden
T: 805-520-0522
Candles

PEGGY KARR GLASS
100 Washington Street
Randolph, NJ 07869
T: 800-754-8585, x23
F: 973-659-1220
tseitz@peggykarrglass.com
www.peggykarrglass.com
Glassware: plates, platters, and dishware; Ornaments: fused glass

PEKING HANDICRAFT, INC.
1388 San Mateo Avenue
So. San Francisco, CA 94080
T: 800-872-6888
www.pkhc.com
Pillows: needlepoint; Rugs

POLONAISE COLLECTION
polonaise@kurtadler.com
www.kurtadler.com
Ornaments: molded glass

POM WONDERFUL
11444 W. Olympic Boulevard
Los Angeles, CA 90064
T: 310-966-5800
F: 310-966-5801
www.pomwonderful.com
Pomegranates

POTTERY BARN
T: 888-779-5176
www.potterybarn.com
Ornaments: metals, plastic

THE RHYN-RIVÉT COLLECTION, INC.
Brooklyn, WI 53521
T: 866-835-7886
www.rhyn-rivet.com
Ornaments: porcelain

RICHARD ROCHA
T: 323-440-2433
kameakuke@sbcglobal.net
Gourmet pastry chef

SACRED SEASON
P.O. Box 1744
Tuckerton, NJ 08087
T: 866-872-6635
www.4GloriousGifts.com
Ornaments: blown glass

SEASONAL CONNECTION
2810 Upland Avenue
Lubbock, TX 79407
T: 806-792-2429
www.ezupfasttrax.com
Ornament hooks: green-plastic "Ultimate"

SLAVIC TREASURES
T: 877-752-8428
SlavicT@aol.com
www.slavictreasures.com
Ornaments: molded glass

TANNENBAUM TREASURES
20 Research Parkway
Old Saybrook, CT 06475
T: 866-395-1801
F: 860-395-1802
jpfeffer01@snet.net
www.tannenbaumtreasures.com
Garlands: glass; Ornaments: molded glass; Treetops: glass finials; Wood: carved arches, pyramids, and nutcrackers

A TOUCH OF GLASS
4342 Via Alegre
Yorba Linda, CA 92886
T: 714-701-0632
Ken@Touch-of-Glass.com
www.touch-of-glass.com
Stained-glass artwork: Santa "ornament"

VARSOVIA EASTERN EUROPE IMPORTS, INC.
8037 Churchill Avenue, #1
Niles, IL 60714
T: 847-966-9903
F: 847-966-9469
varsovia1@aol.com
www.varsovia-ornaments.com
Ornaments: blown and molded glass

WALNUT RIDGE
www.walnutridge.com
Table decorations

WAXBERRY
909 East Fox Farm Road, #7
Cheyenne, WY 82007
T: 888-824-4006
F: 307-772-9850
www.waxberry.com
Candles; Decorative oil jars

YESTERYEARS TREASURES
Kathi@YesteryearsTreasures2004.com
Ornaments: red hats

ZAMBEZI BAZAAR
4334 Degnan Boulevard
Los Angeles, CA 90008
T: 323-299-6383
F: 323-299-2574
www.jzambezik@aol.com
Kwanzaa: gifts

INDEX

PHOTOGRAPHY CREDITS

t=top; b=bottom; l=left; r=right; c=center
All photographs © David Mager/DK Picture Library except:

6tl: © Jeff Katz; 8c (photo inside frame): © RoseMary Staron; 8br: © Brad Fowler, Song of Myself Studio; 9tr: © Jim Stewart, luckyshotsphoto.com
137 (chart): Norway spruce & scotch pine © Dave King/DK Picture Library; Noble fir © Stephen Hayward/DK Picture Library;

Eastern white pine © Sue Oldfield/DK Picture Library; Austrian pine © Matthew Ward/DK Picture Library
139tr (monofilament): © Steve Gorton and Andy Crawford/DK Picture Library; 139tr (hooks): © Dave King/DK Picture Library; 161 (Fabric Gallery): 1 & 8 © Laura Knox/DK Picture Library; 4 © Mark Harwood/DK Picture Library; 5 © Sue Baker/ DK Picture Library

ACKNOWLEDGMENTS

AUTHORS' ACKNOWLEDGMENTS
Thanks to the following people who contributed in many varied ways throughout our pursuit of Christmas glory.

For no particular reason, other than the fact that both of *our* names start with letters nearer to the end of the alphabet than the beginning, our list appears in reverse alphabetical order:

Stars / Locations
Robert and Rosemary Stack, Debbie Reynolds, Steve Radosh, Steve Nycklemoe, John Murphy, Barry McComb, BeBe McCloud, Linda Marder, Tim Malachosky, Elizabeth Lamont, Deidre Hall, Merv Griffin, Faye Grant, Whoopi Goldberg, Peri Gilpin, Andy and Marivi Garcia, Jo Jo Dellit, Donelle Dadigan, Steven Collins, Casa de Flores, Tom Bergeron, Peter Barthelmess, Ann and Steve Arvin, Vincent Arcuri, Beth Anderson, Kirstie Alley, Kristian Alfonso

Family
Ted and RoseMary Staron, Robert and Betty Pranga, Maurice and Louise Pippenger, Nancy Flowers, Sally and Koti

Suppliers
Kris Wilson, Tina Van Oss, Kathie Underwood, Gertrude Theriault, Shirley Strzemieczny, Sarah Stanley, Michael Solomon, Tim's Snowmaker, Wendy Shick, Tim Seitz, Michael Salomon, Kurt & Barbara Salomon, Mike Robinson, Katherine Reinert, Christopher Radko, Chris Quintos, Chris Puleo, Ken Pollack, Tom Poddebski, Jim Pfeffer, T. J. Persia, Ellen McGuire, Barbara McClay, Ann and Matt Litavsky, Mark Klaus, Lisa Kelechava, Joi Jibotian, Ashleigh Hanninen, Caryl Hamilton, Ray Hamby, Roger Gruen, Larry Fraga, Pam Elyea, Paulie Drissi, Mandy Del Rosario, Susan Cotter, Susan Cherry, Diane Carnevale-Jones, Mary Margaret Cannon, Kent Brown, Christine Bertucci, Barbara Bartoloni

Press / Contacts
Ken and Janet Zitterer, Susan Turner, Mark Stuplin, Michelle Stranahan, Loren Ruch, Bob Rosenblatt, Avery Roberts, Brent Ries, Jonathan Renes, Mark Rafalowski, Sue Procko, Christopher Pica, Quinn Monahan, Craig Modderno, Janice Lucas, Christopher Lowell, John Kip, Brent Hopkins, Cynthia Hayes, Harutune Hamassian, Lisa Gleason, Mary Ford, Jeffrey Epstein, Gabriele Edgell, Barry Diller, Bob and Helen Collier, Brandon Castillo, Kelly Carter, Gary Bryan, Grace Bradberry, Mark Bozek, Judy Blye-Wilson, Carol Bidwell, Jim Beckmann

Hair & Makeup (miracle workers!)
Sherri Simmons, Valerie Riccardi, Joe Jadeski, Michael Haumesser

Friends
Ann Wilson, Lynn Underwood, Donna Sloane, Tony Rosato, Otilia Orellana, Chris Monte, Donna Miller, Matt Mgee, Fern McMillan, Charley McCarley, Charles May, Maria Loverde, Mark Lohmann, Vicki Larkin, Gayla Hope, Jim Haynes, Tom Godfrey, Rob Freud, Sandy Dvore, Brian Conn, Elizabeth Campbell, Suzanne Boothe

Elves
Eric Woodard, Scott West, Lisa Teitelman, Jeff Taylor, Mike Pingel, Tim Maculean, Molly Lewis, Donna Lackey, Dayna Jackson, Owen Eden, Nelson Davila, Michael Dashiell, John Dallas, Bill Clark, Frank Bonventre

DK Publishing
Cathy Melnicki, Sharon Lucas, Chuck Lang

Photographer David Mager

. . . and Santa, without whom none of this would have been possible!

PUBLISHERS' ACKNOWLEDGMENTS
DK Publishing would like to thank the following people for their invaluable help: Leeza Gibbons, for the wonderful foreword; David Mager, for his stunning photographs and for his patience and dedication both on set and off; and indefatigable photographer's assistants Monica Morant, Beth Coller, and Charchi Stinson. We are indebted to the gracious homeowners and business owners in Los Angeles who opened their doors to our crew. Special thanks go to Donald Clay, for his beautiful floral designs, and Richard Rocha, for his delicious culinary creations.

We are also grateful to Dr. Christmas "Elves" Garry Kubel, Jay Krich, Lynn Klein, Gail Jorden, Brent Braun, and Brent Bateman for their assistance on set; Jacqueline Olson, Insurance Claims Administrator, and Wendy Cornell, Risk and Insurance Manager, at Pearson for so kindly providing needed forms at a moment's notice; Stuart Calderwood, John Searcy, and Shira Bistricer for their editorial help; Tai Blanche, Melissa Chung, Susan St. Louis, Stephanie Sumulong, and Miesha Tate for assisting with the design; Josephine and Catherine Yam, Colourscan, for the spectacular reproductions; Nanette Cardon, IRIS, for the index; and Sterling Youngman and David Zellorford for their prop loan.